Balancing Acts
Textual Strategies of Peter Henisch

Studies in Austrian Literature, Culture and Thought

Balancing Acts
Textual Strategies of Peter Henisch

Edited and with an Introduction by
Craig Decker

ARIADNE PRESS
Riverside, California

Library of Congress Cataloging-in-Publication Data

Balancing acts : textual strategies of Peter Henisch / edited and with an introduction by Craig Decker
    p. cm. -- (Studies in Austrian literature, culture and thought)
Includes bibliographical references (p.) and index.
ISBN 1-57241-112-0
    1. Henisch, Peter, 1943--Criticism and interpretation.
I. Decker, Craig, 1956- II. Series.

PT2668.E475 Z57 2002
833'.914--dc21
                                        2002074581

Cover Design:
Art Director, Designer: George McGinnis

Copyright ©2002
by Ariadne Press
270 Goins Court
Riverside, CA 92507

All rights reserved.
No part of this publication may be reproduced or transmitted in any form or by any means without formal permission.
Printed in the United States of America.
ISBN 1-57241-112-0 (paperback original)

Table of Contents

Acknowledgments   iii

CRAIG DECKER
Reading Peter Henisch Balance:
An Introduction   1

JEFFREY SCHNEIDER
"Henisch, Father and Son": Masculinity, Art,
and the Narrative of (Austrian) Shame   7

KATHY BRZOVIĆ
Papa's Nazi Past and the Anxiety of Influence:
Peter Henisch's *Die kleine Figur meines Vaters*   40

FRIEDEMANN WEIDAUER
The Lizard-King Can Do Anything: Hybridity and the
Cultural Logic of Globalization in *Morrisons Versteck*   54

JENIFER K. WARD
"The Inner Movie Screen": Film in/and *Hoffmanns
Erzählungen* and *Morrisons Versteck*   74

BOHDAN BOCHAN
A Morphology of Fragments in *Hoffmanns Erzählungen* 101

KATHY BRZOVIĆ and CRAIG DECKER
The Ironic Case of Austro/Jewish Identity:
Psycho-Political Rhetoric in *Steins Paranoia* 131

HELGA SCHRECKENBERGER
The Collective Nature of Subjective Crisis:
Peter Henisch's *Der Mai ist vorbei* 146

ANTJE HARNISCH
Literary Dialogues and Dialogic Literature:
Peter Henisch's *Vom Wunsch, Indianer zu werden* 166

ARND BOHM
The Politics of Quotation in Henisch's Poetics 185

CRAIG DECKER
Intertextual Satire and the Affluent Society: Production,
Consumption, and *Kommt eh der Komet* 210

EVA SCHOBEL
Facts and Fiction: On the Process of
Development in and to *Schwarzer Peter* 228

JENNIFER E. MICHAELS
The Jambalaya Principle: Otherness and
Multiculturalism in *Schwarzer Peter* 242

ANNE CLOSE ULMER
"A Person Who Is Normal . . . Doesn't Write":
A Conversation with Peter Henisch 267

A Bibliography of Peter Henisch's Works 285

Contributors 289

Index 293

Acknowledgments

A volume of this sort underscores the collaborative nature of all scholarly undertakings, and I thank the contributors to this volume for collectively enlivening and extending the discussion of Peter Henisch's work. At Ariadne Press I wish to thank Donald G. Daviau for inviting me to bring such a volume into existence; the two anonymous readers for their close attention to the manuscript; and Jorun B. Johns for seeing the text through to completion. Along the way, I have benefited from various forms of institutional support from Bates College: a Professional Development Grant enabled me to travel to Austria in search of materials by and about Peter Henisch; a one-semester sabbatical leave allowed me to complete the final stages of editing this volume with greater concentration and energy that would have otherwise been possible; and a Publication Grant enabled the completed manuscript to see the light of published day. In Austria, I benefited from the extensive and accessible holdings at the Dokumentationsstelle für neuere österreichische Literatur in Vienna and the Innsbrucker Zeitungsarchiv in Innsbruck. May these institutions be able to survive the hostile cultural politics and economic policies of the current Austrian regime. Closer to home, I thank Georgette Dumais for the patient and unfailing magic she worked on all manner of diskettes, and Tammy Couturier for formatting the final text so meticulously and with such good cheer. As always, I extend my deepest gratitude to Susanne Fetherolf, the best editor any editor could hope to consult on a continuous basis.

Craig Decker

Reading Peter Henisch Balance: An Introduction

CRAIG DECKER

> As long as the balancing rod—which is naturally also a measure of your inner balance—as long as the balancing rod stays horizontal, everything is okay.
> —Peter Henisch[1]

This volume takes it title from a recurring motif in the works of Peter Henisch (born 1943). In Henisch's most recently published novel to date, *Schwarzer Peter* (2000, Black Peter), we read early in the text of how the young title character, the son of a Viennese streetcar conductor and an African-American soldier, explores and attempts to appropriate post-World War II Vienna for himself. On one such adventure, the protagonist expands his field of inquiry, transgressing the boundaries imposed by his mother and discovering a meadow, on the edge of which rises a tree trunk. "I climbed that trunk and balanced upon it," Peter remarks, "But perhaps

I was balancing on a trunk in a parallel universe."[2]

Schwarzer Peter presents a broad sweep of postwar Austrian history, from the ruins immediately following the end of World War II through the increasing affluence of Austria's Second Republic to the growing intolerance and xenophobia of the Waldheim and Haider eras. Twenty-two years prior to the publication of *Schwarzer Peter*, *Der Mai ist vorbei* (1978, May Is Over) appeared, a novel in which Henisch focuses on the events and aftermath of the Austrian student movement. Like *Schwarzer Peter*, *Der Mai ist vorbei* incorporates both autobiographical and fictional elements to examine various social constellations—including student organizations, communes, and bourgeois marriages—and their attempts to balance individual and collective interests and demands. The multiple social, economic, and emotional balancing acts depicted in *Der Mai ist vorbei* are given explicit expression in the first part of the text, when the mother of Paul Grünzweig's tutee (and potential lover) Julia congratulates him on significantly improving her daughter's academic performance: "'I don't know,' her mother said, . . . 'how you do it, but I'm extremely satisfied.' Paul knew how he was doing it, and it was clear to him that the balancing act he was now performing was dangerous. Not only Julia but also he himself could cause him to lose his equilibrium."[3]

The difficulties of maintaining one's balance and the dangers of losing one's equilibrium appear throughout Henisch's work, and they are present on both a formal and thematic level. In what is certainly Henisch's best-known text, *Die kleine Figur meines Vaters* (originally published in 1975, revised and republished in 1980 and again in 1987; translated in 1990 as *Negatives of My Father*), the image of a tightrope walker functions as a central metaphor, and references to literal and figurative balancing rods and high wires abound. Indeed, the publication history of the text alone attests to Henisch's ongoing attempts to balance the shifting contours of public and private concerns, individual and collective histories, personal and national narratives. Through numerous narrative strands and multiple narrative voices, *Die kleine Figur meines Vaters* constructs an (auto)biography of Walter

Henisch, Peter Henisch's father and a highly decorated Nazi war correspondent. By confronting the dying father with his past and his continuing pride in it, the son engages in an act of literary and psychological daring reminiscent of the father's many acts of physical and photographic daredevilry. Walter Henisch himself does not allow this similarity to pass unnoticed, as he comments to his son towards the beginning of the so-called novel: "You seem to have found the path you want to take. But you're a tightrope-walker [sic], just like me."[4]

Given the extent to which father and son engage in a risky confrontation with issues of life and death, the image of the tightrope walker suits both Walter and Peter Henisch. While father and son recurrently apply this image to themselves, it seems applicable not only to the two individuals and to the relationship between them, but also to the son's attempt to write about that relationship. In *Die kleine Figur meines Vaters*, Peter Henisch repeatedly tries to strike a precarious balance between Walter Henisch as a nurturing father and Walter Henisch as a Nazi war correspondent; between a father who instilled in his son a lively ideal of freedom and an Austrian citizen of Jewish descent who went along with the dictates of National Socialism.

The examples cited above constitute but a few of the numerous instances of thematic and formal balancing acts that can be found in Peter Henisch's literary texts. From his initial publications in the early 1970s right up to *Schwarzer Peter*, Henisch's fiction manifests a continual and evolving attempt to represent social and literary concerns that may be both competing and complementary. As the essays in this volume attest, these individual balancing acts assume a variety of forms and address a range of subjects. As a self-consciously Austrian author, Henisch writes both within and against the traditions of Austrian literature. He pays frequent homage to his (largely Romantic) literary forefathers, while simultaneously seeking forms and contents adequate to the demands and dynamics of postmodern literature and society. Shaped by the protest movements of the 1960s, Henisch strives to produce literary texts that are highly accessible and usable, but ones that also draw heavily, and frequently ironically, on a rich array of cultural references, both well-known and arcane. His literary career evinces an ongoing commitment to confronting the discomfiting realities of Austria's Nazi past in a post-World War II Austria that largely insists on avoiding confrontation and mythologizing the nation's history into the narrative of Austria as the "first victim" of Nazi aggression. From the outset, Henisch resolutely focuses on what he considers to be the periphery of Austrian society in order to dissect its center.[5]

In one of his very early essays, "marginalien zur produktion von texten" (1972, marginalia on the production of texts), Henisch writes of the need to produce a "literature of possibilities" ("möglichkeitsliteratur"). Such a literature, according to Henisch, must be textually open; be aware of its own fictionality; evidence its own process of production within the text; and eschew a false sense of closure.[6] Both individually and collectively, the essays in this volume present possible ways of reading Peter Henisch's "literature of possibilities." The first four essays establish important categories for analyzing all of Henisch's work: the legacy of Austria's Nazi past; socio-literary shifts attending the emergence of a globalized culture industry; and prominent aesthetic trends in postmodern literature. The subsequent three essays examine Henisch's thematic and structural representation of individual identity and psychological imbalance as indicative of collective social crises. The next three essays focus on the varied forms of Henisch's complex and seemingly endless intertextuality, concentrating on the notions of quotation, dialogue, and the activation of the reader. *Schwarzer Peter* is the subject of the final two essays, which explore the ways in which Henisch balances facts and fiction, minority and majority cultures in the novel. The volume concludes with an interview with Peter Henisch. Following so much discussion of his work, it seems only appropriate to allow the author himself to have a word as well.

* * * * *

In keeping with the practices of Ariadne Press, all citations from the German have been translated here into English. Unless otherwise noted, the author of each contribution has done his or her own translations. The titles of Peter Henisch's works appear in the original German, followed by the year of publication in parentheses. If the text has been translated into English, the English-language title, in italics, and date of publication follow—e.g., *Steins Paranoia* (1988; *Stone's Paranoia*, 2000). If no English translation has appeared, the publication date of the German-language text is given, followed by an English translation of the title in Roman type—for example, *Der Mai ist vorbei* (1978, May Is Over).

Notes

1. Peter Henisch, *Negatives of My Father*, trans. Anne Close Ulmer (Riverside, CA: Ariadne, 1990) 172.
2. Henisch, *Schwarzer Peter* (Salzburg and Vienna: Residenz, 2000) 23. Subsequent to this episode, Peter visits a construction site with his mother and her lover at the time, Mr. Grandegg: "An apartment house, for which Mr. Grandegg strangely enough possessed plans, was being built on the site. Of course, it was forbidden to enter the site, but that no longer applied to us once Mr. Grandegg slipped the foreman fifty schillings. On steps without a railing we climbed up to the second floor. There we balanced on boards lying upon a concrete floor, still damp, between walls still unplastered" (74-75).
3. Henisch, *Der Mai ist vorbei* (Frankfurt/M: Fischer, 1978) 41.
4. Henisch, *Negatives of My Father* 7.
5. Henisch's focus on the periphery stems from his conviction that the periphery constitutes the "area of opposi-

tions, of contradictions" (*Baronkarl: alte und neue Peripheriegeschichten* [Weitra: Bibliothek der Provinz, 1993] 12).

6. Henisch, "marginalien zur produktion von texten," *Wiener Kunsthefte* 2 (1972): 27.

"Henisch, Father and Son": Masculinity, Art, and the Narrative of (Austrian) Shame

JEFFREY SCHNEIDER

Just inside the back cover of Peter Henisch's (auto)biographical exploration of his father, *Die kleine Figur meines Vaters* (1987; *Negatives of My Father*, 1990), is a photograph of the two taken sometime during the Second World War.[1] Never mentioned in the text itself, the picture shows the father from the waist up in his Wehrmacht uniform, holding his two-year-old son, who is bundled in a white winter costume. At the most basic level, the otherwise unremarkable photo documents a moment of familial idyll in the chaos of the war. In the context of Henisch's book, however, the image also seems to foretell the adult relationship between the photographer-father and the writer-son. With his smiling gaze cast on his progeny, the father exhibits a clear sense of pride and joy in the moment. Though exhibitions of pride and joy are often contagious, any impulse we might have to share in the father's moment is cut short by the son's distinct unease. Looking out from his father's arms at the camera rather than returning the adoring man's gaze, the young Peter seems ready to frown, while his eyes forecast the onset of tears;

even his brow reveals furrows of consternation. Merely evidence of a child's momentary dissatisfaction with the situation in which he finds himself, the expression nonetheless comes to signify the future uneasiness of the adult child, who is perturbed by his father's activities as a photographer during the war, by the pride he exhibits in wearing his army uniform, and especially by his ability to remain so morally unaware of himself and his surroundings.

Located physically "after" the text yet originating chronologically "before" it, the photograph resonates strongly with the book's father-son narrative and its collaborative structure. Positioned above a brief description of the author, the photograph replaces the traditional picture of the author with a telling portrait of the author and his subject—most likely taken by the subject himself.[2] Considering the image's ability to express Peter Henisch's adult discomfort with his father, we might want to view the photograph as something more akin to a collaboration. The ambiguity in the picture's caption—"Henisch, Father and Son" ("Henisch, Vater und Sohn")—seems to invite such speculation. Though the phrase identifies the subject matter—it is a picture of the father and son—the single name "Henisch" also seems to mark the image's "authorship" in such as way as to include both father and son at the same time. Likewise, Peter Henisch's goal in writing *Die kleine Figur meines Vaters* was to produce not one (auto-)biography, but two. On the one hand, he provides his father with the space to tell his own story in his own words, albeit under the controlling hand of the writer-son, who selects, shapes, and contextualizes the father's story in ways the father often resists. On the other hand, Henisch is also motivated by a need to learn about himself through an examination of his father. Early on in the book, the writer is confronted by his own Freudian slip at the typewriter: "I've made the same typing error twice in a row. Twice I rolled a new sheet of paper into the typewriter on that account. I wrote: I'd like you to tell me *my* life story. I don't believe I was guilty of that particular slip when I was talking to my father that day. But later I admitted to him that I really want to know who *he* is so that I can understand who *I* am" (3). The dual agenda that Henisch announces towards the beginning ensures that the book will be shaped by a tension between the father's self-understanding of his life and the son's own working through of those meanings and their impact on his own identity. Repeatedly, the two clash about the meaning of the father's enthusiastic participation in World War II as a celebrated war correspondent for Goebbels's Ministry for Public Enlightenment and Propaganda and his failure to confront the political and moral implications of that willing involvement, either during the war or, especially, afterwards. Indeed, rather than expressing contrition or regret about his participation in the Nazi war and propaganda effort, the father's life story is "shamelessly" organized around a relentless narrative of his achievement against unbeatable odds. Inevitably, that shamelessness is the source of the son's unease; indeed, it is a source of shame for him.

In reading *Die kleine Figur meines Vaters*, I focus on the issue of shame because it offers a dynamic model for unpacking some of the socio-psychological forces underlying Walter Henisch's enthusiastic participation in National Socialism, in particular, the relationship between masculinity and fascism. As George Mosse has outlined, National Socialism sought to build its new society according to radical biological principles, including not only a racially based anti-Semitism but also an extreme version of manliness.[3] Of course, the connection between masculinity and fascism is inevitably multifaceted and dependent upon how fascism is being defined. In *Male Fantasies*, for instance, Klaus Theweleit posits a fear of the feminine at the core of the fascist male, which he equates with the Free Corps soldiers and writers of the early and late 1920s.[4] However, in contrast to Theweleit's subjects—many of whom never fully embraced National Socialism after 1933—Walter Henisch represents the phenomenon best designated by the term "Mitläufer" (literally, "fellow traveler"), that is, someone who accommodates to the regime and profits from an association with it, without ever fully internalizing its ideology.[5]

Rather than an irrational fear of the feminine, I want to suggest that at the core of Walter Henisch's willing participation in the National Socialist war and propaganda machine is a narrative of shame and shame avoidance. According to Silvan Tomkins, the eminent American psychologist who developed Affect Theory in part around a complex account of shame, shame is the emotional experience most constitutive of the self: "an experience of the self by the self."[6] A rich and varied phenomenon ranging from a child's temporary shyness in front of strangers to a debilitating "inner torment, a sickness of the soul" (133), shame does not have any explicit, predetermined content but is rather a painful dynamic that shapes the self and its relation to the world and whose causes and effects are highly individual as well as cultural and historical. As Tomkins notes, against the backdrop of historical circumstances and cultural, even familial, conventions, each individual develops his or her own "shame theory," which plays a role "in activating shame, in alerting the individual to the possibility or immanence of shame and in providing standardized strategies for minimizing shame" (165). In the case of Walter Henisch, his shame and strategies to avoid it undergird his participation in National Socialism as well as his inability to come to terms with it after the war: his shame about himself as a particularly small and unmanly individual, and his various strategies to make himself "shameless" through the compensation(s) of a military uniform, of membership in explicitly male social organizations, and of "heroic" acts of photographic daredevilry that could be spun into a narrative of masculine achievement—even after the Second World War had ended in Nazi Germany's defeat. Though the toxic nature of shame inevitably ignites an urgent desire to escape, deny, and dissolve the self, Walter Henisch's willing self-dissolution in the Nazi military machine is only part of his story. Peter Henisch is also concerned with the moral consequences of his father's aesthetic practice as a photographer during and after the war, a practice the older man terms "brutal curiosity" (67). As Peter Henisch recognizes, his father's practice as a photographer is intimately related to his involvement in National Socialism. In addition to offering the older Henisch a narrative of achievement against deadly odds, the father's position behind the camera mitigates and even disavows the pain of his situation and its threat to the self by dissolving that self in the moment of aesthetic production, whether in perilous combat during the war or in mundane newspaper assignments after the war.

A source of profound embarrassment and discomfort for the son, the father's shameless pride often provokes Peter Henisch to try to shame his father into rejecting his past behavior as morally reprehensible. During many of the interviews and discussions reproduced in the book, the younger Henisch aggressively reminds his father of the Nazi horrors that his narrative of self-achievement so easily elides. In the end, however, the son's book offers a more compelling response to the father's shameful self than do the son's hurtful and ineffective attempts to shame his father into contrition. Indeed, the moral force of *Die kleine Figur meines Vaters* resides not only in its attempt to grasp the complex circumstances of the father's willing involvement with National Socialism and his positive interpretation of that involvement until the end of his life, but also in its insistence on exploring the potential contamination of the son's postwar male identity and aesthetics. Thus, tracing the father's desire for a militarized masculinity back to his shameful sense of self in childhood occasions the son's memories of various tests of manliness and results in a struggle to acknowledge his own similarities to the father while remaining committed to an antifascist politics. The similarities between the two appear most strongly, however, in the son's aesthetic stance, particularly vis-à-vis his dying father, the very subject of this literary effort. In probing his father's photographic career, Peter Henisch keeps in tension his moral purpose in writing the book and the potential perversions his aesthetic practice might share with his father's. The narrative works through these tensions by constantly shifting between the father's biography and the son's emerging understanding of himself in terms of his father, alternately interweaving transcripts of the father's first-person stories, the author's own childhood memories, interviews with the father, and the son's reflections on his father's "present" illness during the writing of the book. Ultimately, the book strikes a hopeful tone by closing with two stories in which the father seems to "break out" of the shameful cycles of repetition that have marked his life story and photographic efforts. Since these two stories do not represent the chronological end of the book's narrative, they make it possible for Peter Henisch to stage his acceptance of his father as a never-ending process of reflection mixed with anxiety. As such, it serves as an important intervention into Austria's own fraught staging of its Nazi past, one that moves beyond shaming but not beyond shame.

SHAME, MASCULINITY, AND AESTHETIC PRACTICE

Peter Henisch's exploration of his father's activities during the war takes place against the official silence about the Nazi period in the postwar Austrian public sphere. That silence is reproduced in the book's opening narrative, an account of an official ceremony to honor the father's achievements as a photographer for the *Arbeiterzeitung* (Workers' Gazette) in Vienna. As is typical for such occasions, the speech by the Madam Vice-Mayor relates Walter Henisch's biography, beginning with his birth in Vienna on November 26, 1913 and continuing through his accomplishments as a photographer in the postwar period, i.e., the present of the book's narrative. As Henisch notes with a certain amount of surprise and consternation, the speech completely elides his father's wartime activities as a Nazi correspondent. However, in contrast to the public disavowal of history that marks the public discourse on National Socialism in Austria before the Waldheim Affair breaks in 1986,[7] Henisch's paternal grandmother provides the missing continuity in a private whisper to the author: "My grandmother whispers in my ear: I still have a suitcase in the closet with your father's old medals. This badge of honor will go well with the *Iron Crosses*" (2). While the Vice-Mayor emphasizes the present to the exclusion of the past, the grandmother reverses the teleology by making the father's accomplishments during the war—his iron crosses—the core to which new awards are then added. In addition to giving the lie to the public narrative of Austrian identity as the "first victim" of National Socialism, the inclusion of this private reversal locates the problem of continuity in postwar Austria not only at the level of public discourse but also at the level of identity and self, at least among those Austrians who experienced National Socialism as a positive force. The impact of National Socialism for Austrians like Walter Henisch goes deep into the private core of the self, marked by the grandmother as a treasured suitcase inside a closet, stored in a hidden place safe from public scrutiny and those who would take it away.

As a result, in probing the moral issues at stake in his father's past, *Die kleine Figur meines Vaters* focuses on Walter Henisch's self-understanding rather than merely indicting his propagandistic role in supporting the Nazi war effort. As the author announces in the first of a series of unsent letters to his father:

> The visored cap [*Schirmmütze*] with the German eagle, the visored cap with the swastika—that hat was one of the major reasons why for a long time I put so much space between myself and your story, and thus between us. Not *that* you wore that cap, but *how* you wore it: gladly, even proudly. You, of all people. And the armband with the inscription ARMED FORCES WAR CORRESPONDENT still hangs in your laboratory today, like some athletic trophy. I simply couldn't come to terms with that. (12)

Though wearing Nazi insignia is reprehensible enough, Henisch makes it clear that his problem with his father stems primarily from the older man's investment in the military uniform as an expression of his sense of self, an investment that persists to the present day in the form of uniform paraphernalia displayed proudly in his developing studio, itself an isolated dark room that structurally mirrors the grandmother's hidden suitcase. The father's amoral pride originally caused the son to distance himself from the older man as well as from his stories, since until this point in his life the two have been virtually indistinguishable. Thus, it is only by going through the father's narrative about himself that Peter Henisch can ever hope to come to terms with his father, or help the father morally come to terms with himself.

Although over the course of the book Peter Henisch allows his father to tell many of the stories that depict the older man as a proud and accomplished "hero," he also asks his father to tell new stories about himself, especially about his childhood. These new stories present a markedly different person whose core sense of himself is inflected by shame. For example, one of Walter Henisch's earliest childhood memories concerns a game called "Little Marie" ("Mariechen"), a group activity with repetitive choral verses about a girl named Little Marie who waits for her brother with the knowledge that he will stab her in the heart. Though he remembers crying inconsolably for an entire afternoon because of "the obvious inevitability of the whole occurrence" (9-10), his reaction to this and similar games reveals a sense of self constituted negatively through shame: "Circle games in general, I tell you, were a [big] problem for me for a long time. I always wanted to join the circle with the others, but at the same time I was afraid to. I was always the smallest and most insignificant, and surrounded [UNTER] by the others I really become aware of it [me]. So most of the time I didn't play with the other kids, but hid in a corner" (10). As Tomkins postulates, shame's primary function is to reduce or inhibit our interest in another object "which the individual cannot achieve and yet cannot renounce" (149). In this scenario, Walter Henisch's ardent and repeated wish to be a part of the group strikes at his sense of self because it makes him painfully aware of what to him seems his glaring inadequacy—his small size—vis-à-vis the other members of the group. That small size is so central to the father's self-identity that Peter Henisch made it the German title of the book, itself an acknowledgment of the fundamental but ambiguous role that size plays for the father and the shame it provokes in the son.[8]

While this moment of childhood shame is experienced here in terms of a general deficiency in the self, it becomes clear that over the course of his childhood Walter Henisch localizes the meaning of that shameful self in terms of gender, that is, his small size signifies for him an inadequate masculinity. Certainly, this interpretation was reinforced through his experiences in the cramped apartment of his weak and relatively loveless mother and her protofascist husband Albert Prinz, a frustrated postal bureaucrat, failed operetta singer, and disfigured war veteran. As Walter Henisch informs his son, the latter "had acquired a virtually insatiable appetite for compensation" (19) in the form of masculine privilege, either as a fervent wish for the reintroduction of the imperial postal uniform or the practice of brutalizing his wife and stepson as part of his rights as male head of the household. Though his abusive behavior often provoked his stepson's hate, Prinz nonetheless figures as an ideal for Walter Henisch, even long after the stepfather has died. In recalling the successful Nazi invasion of France during World War II, for instance, Henisch invokes his stepfather's presumed approval: "My stepfather would have been delighted with us [the German war effort]. Also, and particularly, with me as a war correspondent. You see, I could have told him then, you underestimated me for the better part of my life! For even, and especially, as a photographer I stood my ground, I fulfilled my duty like any other German soldier" (25). According to Walter Henisch, the German Army's ability to stick to its precise invasion plans—conquering specific cities at specific times—corresponded to his stepfather's fanatical love of precision. But the elder Henisch's fantasy of his stepfather's approval is directed even more personally at himself, since his participation in the war effort—which he equates with his photography—allows him to commune with his stepfather on equal footing.

The fantasy of gaining the approval of his stepfather through the war effort suggests that Walter Henisch's attraction to uniforms has very little to do with militaristic impulses. Indeed, their importance for him rests in their ability to mitigate his sense of shame about himself. Socially, uniforms have an important leveling effect for their wearers; distinctions and hierarchical differences between men of the same rank—such as class background, educational training, wealth, physical strength, and, in Walter Henisch's case, size—are made to disappear. Even the non-military uniforms of the "Arbeitsdienst" (Labor Service), which Walter Henisch joins during the economic depression after his application to the Austrian Army is rejected because of his small size, give him limited access to equalized social relations with other men:

> In our uniforms—gray right down to the underwear—we looked like shabby gasmen. But I wore even this uniform with a certain joy and a certain pride. Just for the sake of belonging to some kind of group, I probably would have been willing to slip into a uniform with blue polka dots. . . . In the Labor Service I was still only a simple *workman*. Above me were foremen, camp commanders, chief camp commanders, field commanders, and the devil only knows what else. But I was on the same level as the others. Through work, I had become their equal. (43-44)

Though the uniforms of the Labor Service are unattractive and lack the social prestige of the army's uniforms, they meet the elder Henisch's desperate need for a feeling of belonging to something that can replace his shame with pride. And while he is aware that he stands at the bottom of a long hierarchy, the uniforms, in combination with the work activity, nevertheless ensure a ground floor through which he cannot fall vis-à-vis the majority of men.

It would be a mistake, however, to view Walter Henisch's attraction to uniforms solely in terms of social compensation vis-à-vis others, for that would underestimate their psychological function in mitigating his own enormous sense of shame about himself. An outcast at school, Walter Henisch had only one boyhood friend, a tall and strong neighbor boy whose friendship offered him a temporary reprieve from his sense of worthlessness. It is thus not surprising when Henisch expresses the wish to join the same youth group as his friend, the Social Democratic "Pfadfinder" (Pathfinders). Yet more fundamental than the desire to be with his only friend is the desire to wear a uniform: "The uniform—the uniform played a tremendous role for me, you know. My dream was to be able to put on a uniform like a [magic cap] of invisibility [*Tarnkappe*], and thereby cease my existence as the Shrimp, which was all I had been up to that point" (37-38). The "magic cap" of the uniform promises not only to hide the shameful self from others, but also to allow for the phantasmatic destruction of that self and all that is shameful about it.

In his son's morally watchful eyes, the depth of Walter Henisch's desire to obliterate the self through membership in a group makes him dangerously apolitical and amoral, since the political objectives of the group are insignificant compared to its function of providing a shame-free masculine identity. Thus, in recalling when his nationalistic (and eventually National Socialist) stepfather enrolls him in the right-wing "Deutscher Turnerbund" (German Gymnasts' Association) rather than the left-wing Pathfinders, Walter Henisch confides to his son: "And even though I didn't realize it right away, since I had really only wanted to stay with my friend, the German Gymnasts' Association served the same purpose for me that the [Pathfinders] would have" (37). As Henisch's career testifies, the strength of his desire to be an equal member of a male group, and thus free from shame, means that the identity and nature of the group is unimportant to him. Indeed, he traverses unproblematically from serving with the Hitler Youth and the German Army before and during the war to working with the occupying Russian administration, the Social Democrats, and the *Arbeiterzeitung* after the war.[9] In terms of ideology, Henisch can say with all honesty to his son and others that he was not a Nazi.[10] But even more than erasing political and moral considerations at the time, the need to erase the shameful sense of self permits no reflection about the past, as when Peter Henisch demands that his father account for the moral consequences of his involvement with National Socialism: "How could it have happened, why did you go along with it, why didn't you do anything against it? I was simply in the middle of it all, you answer, but that's not an answer" (139). It is the very success of his self-evacuation and escape from his shameful self that prevents any self-critique of his actions, since the purpose of this militaristic group membership—being "in the middle of it all"—erases the self that would have to be aware of itself and its shame.

Rather than merely indicting his father's moral failings, Peter Henisch's narrative also questions its implications for himself, a male born in the Third Reich to please the "Führer" and raised by his father in postwar Austria.[11] Like many of the men of his generation, the younger Henisch is concerned about his own possible contamination, about the transmission of these masculine ways from his father to himself.[12] His self-examination takes several different forms over the course of the narrative. Certainly, like his father, the younger Henisch has had to negotiate his own masculinity and its social and psychological dimensions. Not an inherent characteristic of men, masculinity is instead performative, that is, something that always needs to be attained and demonstrated over and against others through particular acts.[13] In one of Peter Henisch's memories of childhood, for instance, he accepts a dare from Friedi, the apartment manager's daughter, to run naked from his house to a nearby bakery and back. The stakes of the challenge increase when Friedi taunts him by suggesting that another neighbor boy has the courage he might be lacking (160-61). Though Henisch goes through with the challenge, his naked performance shocks an elderly lady knitting outside her door, who screams at the sight of his flopping penis. The shocking visibility of the penis in this narrative calls attention to the purpose of following through on the challenge: to prove his masculinity. While the neighbor woman's scream pales in comparison to the moral consequences of his father's attempts to achieve masculinity in his own eyes and the eyes of the world, Peter Henisch's childhood recollection suggests an awareness of certain structural dimensions to being and to performing male identity—dimensions that cross generations and that can, under certain political conditions, such as National Socialism, lead to moral catastrophe.[14]

Moreover, the younger Henisch remembers sharing his father's enthusiasm for war and its concomitant masculinity when, in his childhood, he found himself entranced by many of his father's war photographs. On the one hand, his relationship to the pictures of "the victorious German, machine-gun at the ready, triumph in the curve of his lip" evinces an amoral attraction to the visual power of his father's pictorial abilities: "I had examined the faces under a magnifying glass, and never tired of their expressions" (62). On the other hand, these pictures offer identificatory possibilities, in which the younger Henisch "fell into the picture with the infantry tank" and became part of it: "I *was* the bespectacled German soldier. I saw the scene through his glasses" (62). Such recollections suggest that militaristic influences at the level of masculine identity might have persisted beneath an explicit policy of Austrian neutrality. At the very least, the ability of photographs to hold a moment in the past and reproduce it in full force at a later date provokes concern (ours and Henisch's own) about the extent to which his father's pictures transcended the end of the war and influenced the young Peter. As he turns thirty, Peter Henisch begins to question the easy confidence in generational differences claimed by the student movement of the late 1960s and finds the need to explore his relationship to his father as a source of his identity and manhood. Since the age of twenty, Peter Henisch has fought this basic identification at the level of familial resemblance by growing a beard (to hide the physical similarities to his father around the mouth and chin). Nevertheless, the repressed returns with a vengeance as he begins to fight with the same kind of bald spot he remembers his father hiding under his Pullman's cap. The tenfold age difference that Henisch perceived in his youth is gone: "Today, as I delve into your story, you are only about twice as old as I. When your time comes to a standstill, I can catch up with you. Whether I want it or not, I'm getting closer to you" (12). Through such simple mathematics, Peter Henisch wonders whether certain unattractive and morally corrupt similarities to his father may be simply inevitable over time.

But the most pressing of these concerns about undue influence stems from the affection he feels toward his "shameless" father, that is, the father's self-portrayal as a proud man full of achievement.[15] Though Peter Henisch remembers with particular joy the stories about his father's days in the war, which the older man told on his birthday, at Christmas, New Year's, and other special occasions, it is the sense of his father's newfound freedom in the early years of the Second Republic that connect him most strongly to the older man: "I remember how much I loved you back then, I loved being your son. You gave everything a new beginning, you were so agile, so original, so active. Yes, Papa, you really impressed me back then, I wore my woolen cap [*Pullmannkappe*] at precisely the same rakish angle as you did" (146). It is that attraction to the shameless father that leads the son to want to imitate him, especially at the level of masculinity, signified here by the seemingly independent way his father wears his hat. As with the father's wartime pictures, the son identifies with— even imitates—what he sees without understanding what lurks behind it. Yet what seems like a new beginning to a loving child appears to the adult child as a kind of repetition compulsion at the level of masculine performance. As Peter Henisch accusingly tells his father in another unsent letter, 1945 "was no beginning back then, not even a fresh start, especially not for you!" (146). The text suggests that though the war is over, Walter Henisch's postwar activities are merely the continuation of his flight from himself that led him to fight so enthusiastically and unrepentantly for the Nazis: he has simply exchanged the military helmet for the Pullman's cap, an evidently civilian version of the father's need for masculine "magical hats." Nevertheless, Peter Henisch cannot merely condemn his father but rather must also deal with the pleasure he took in that "shameless" father. Ultimately, Henisch's narrative seeks to give his father the new beginning—for himself and for his art—that he was incapable of realizing at the end of the war.

Walter Henisch's desire and need for self-dissolution underlie his aesthetic practice, which he terms "brutal curiosity." As he notes, this aesthetic mode takes the form of effecting a difference between himself as an artist and as a human being. In both the war and the postwar period, Walter Henisch uses this aesthetic mode to maintain his self-integrity as a man over and against emotions and even physical harm that threaten his sense of self. This defensive mode has two different functions. Most obviously, his success as a photographer continues his strategy of minimizing his shameful self through a narrative of achievement, which provides the same kind of public, masculine compensation that uniforms afford. By becoming one of the most successful war correspondents in Goebbels's service, he was able to feel that he achieved real masculinity against all odds in an otherwise deadly war. Thus, as long as he is a successful photographer, he can stave off and deny that he essentially feels like a "shrimp" ("Schrapp") (86) on the inside, a feeling that repeatedly lurks in the background even during the wartime successes.

At a psychologically deeper level, however, the act of photographing also serves to minimize Walter Henisch's self-awareness through a process of distancing and self-bifurcation that occurs when he is standing behind the camera: "An icy intoxication comes over you, wiping out any sympathy or empathy you might otherwise feel. You're right in the middle of it all, but you're somehow outside" (67). On the front lines, for instance, Walter Henisch is confronted with the suffering, pain, and death of others as well as real physical danger to himself. By witnessing events through the lens, Henisch can deny their reality to himself and find emotional distance from horrific events that might otherwise lead to psychological dissolution. Indeed, the power of the camera as a device of self-integrity becomes clear when Walter Henisch is punished by the Ministry of Propaganda for staging a fake reunion between two brothers on the Russian front, a real event that he missed and then recreated for his camera. As punishment, Henisch must give up his camera and take up a weapon like the others around him. As he tells his son, killing another human being, particularly in hand-to-hand combat, is horrifying. Without the camera, Henisch lacks the mediated confrontation with death and destruction that normally protects him from fully acknowledging that reality: "For a long time you can't forget [the] eyes [of the one you kill]" (79). But Walter Henisch admits that even the magical self-effacing powers of the camera are ultimately limited: "There were a lot of times when I would have given a good deal to be nothing more than a camera. But unfortunately you can't unwind the memory of your brain as easily as you can take the film out of a Leica" (72).

If Peter Henisch is aware of the power of his father's war photographs, he must also grapple with the disturbing similarity between his own and his father's aesthetic strategies. Henisch's own text repeatedly seeks to locate important distinctions between the different media of writing and photography, and Craig Decker has argued convincingly for attributing to those differences a fundamental gesture for creating the kind of narrative discontinuity that breaks the "father's instrumental consciousness," which is associated with the stasis of photographs.[16] Yet as Peter Henisch admits, the specific attention his own narrative gives to his father's "brutal curiosity" during the war represents an attempt to project his own concerns about his aesthetic stance onto his father: "By capturing this aspect of my character in you, I can act as though I were rid of it" (69). Ashamed of this potential character flaw, the younger Henisch wants to pin it exclusively to the father's personality. Nevertheless, Peter Henisch realizes only too well and with great seriousness that he is repeating the same methodology in his text about his dying father. In several sections of the narrative he uses the strategy of "brutal curiosity" to record with great distance images of his father in his hospital bed or hooked up to transfusion machines. Like his father's confrontation with death on the battlefield, the hospital visits and the oncoming death of his father confront Peter Henisch with emotionally disturbing and painful situations which strike at the integrity of his sense of self. As he writes in an unsent letter to his father, "Do you see, Papa, I make everything into material. First and foremost you, who transformed everything into material. And my criticism of you, for making everything into material. And my criticism of myself, for making even my criticism of you into material" (70). Only by finding a way to tie this "brutal curiosity" to broader moral convictions can any hope of a positive outcome arise—for the father as well as for the son.

Break Out Attempt: Overcoming Shame and Finding the Present

Richard Mitten has suggested that it was Kurt Waldheim's "personal fate to stand as the symbol of a postwar unwillingness or inability to adequately come to terms with the implications of the National Socialist abomination."[17] Though the problem of "Vergangenheitsbewältigung" (coming to terms with the past) is often viewed in terms of a denial or whitewashing of the willing Austrian enthusiasm for the integration of Austria into Nazi Germany in 1938 in favor of the lie of "first victim," Mitten's point about Waldheim suggests that the Austrian problem with the past is really a problem with the present and its *relation to its past*. If Waldheim's controversial candidacy for the presidency in 1986 turned Austrian "Vergangenheitsbewältigung" into a national and international scandal, the result was undue attention to often arcane legal issues at the expense of broader political and, especially, psychological and "moral moments."[18] *Die kleine Figur meines Vaters*, the first edition of which preceded the Waldheim Affair by almost ten years and which was subsequently revised and reissued in 1987,[19] scrutinizes these moral and psychological issues by focusing on Walter Henisch's "shamelessness." Rather than enabling a whitewashing of the past in favor of the present, the older Henisch's entrenched shamelessness after the war testifies to the persistence of the Nazi past into the present—in the form of a psychic defense against a past shameful self that is only too painfully present and which must be put off through an incessant postponement of a "real" present in favor of one produced through compensatory devices, such as uniforms and stories about his escapades during and after the war. If Walter Henisch is not repentant about his activities during the war, it is because he has yet to engage with the psychological reasons that paved the way for that willing participation in the Nazi war effort. For Walter Henisch, as well as for Austria itself, the past remains ineluctably present through the involuntary strategies to keep it deferred from consciousness—strategies that, in Walter

Henisch's case, leave no room for engaging with the present on its own terms. Thus, it is only by helping his father to find the present—both within his own narratives and photographic practices—that Peter Henisch's book offers an "attempt" to break past the moral irresponsibility of his father's life and art.

Towards the end of the book, Peter Henisch features his father's narratively captivating flights of escape at the end of the war: escape from the fanatical and suicidal Nazi war machine, escape from the Allied prisoner-of-war camp, and escape from the humiliating defeat of Allied victory into a career as an independent photographer. Peter Henisch recognizes a new quality of freedom to these stories of the end of the war, which seem to herald a new self of the father: "But precisely in this type of freedom my father—at least in retrospect—seems to feel most at home. And I remember very clearly that for me, as a child, the stories of a father who *maintained* himself in that sort of freedom were my favorites" (122). As Peter Henisch notes, much to his father's chagrin, this new freedom expresses itself in narrative license ("Freiheit des Erzählens"), in which consistency and adherence to logics outside the story and across stories are sacrificed to the adventurous, humorous, and heroic narratives of escape.[20] But because that freedom is always only a temporary narrative of escape, which is at the same time an escape from moral responsibility for actions undertaken in the past, it is not a true freedom. Indeed, instead of signaling the end of the war, these stories continue the same narrative of grand adventure, thereby making his adventurous activities as a freelance newspaper photographer merely a continuation of his version of the war into the Second Republic. As Walter Henisch says of one of his first assignments in the postwar period, covering the Soviet release of German prisoners of war, it "meant going halfway back into the war" (143)—a situation that Henisch clearly enjoys, since being among the Russian occupying troops meant freedom from his shameful self: "I almost felt like my old self again. Men, weapons, songs, and uniforms. . . . It didn't really make much difference *which* uniforms" (144). After all, the older Henisch has no ideological ties that would make him ashamed of being on the losing side of the war.

Though these narratives seem effective strategies at the time, the father is ultimately unable to make them work for the rest of his life. Towards the end of his career, the rise of television destroys the market for illustrated magazines, the financial basis and artistic venue for a free-lance photographer. Faced with increasing financial insecurity, Walter Henisch eventually gives up his independent status and accepts a position with the Social Democratic *Arbeiterzeitung*. Though neither Peter Henisch nor his mother fully realize it at the time, the father becomes a tragicomic figure as his attempts to continue his narrative of independence and achievement prove ever more ridiculous and unrealistic: he proposes traveling with the circus as a photographer, considers becoming a professional puppeteer, and even takes up with a younger lover for a short time. As he eventually acquiesces to his lack of independence and the limits it places on his strategies for disavowing shame, he also begins to drown his shameful self in alcohol, a support mechanism that he first uses in the war during the time he was forced to lay down his camera and pick up a gun. At the age of sixty, Walter Henisch is dying from cirrhosis of the liver.

Parallel to the father's narratives of escape in the past, however, Peter Henisch presents the attempt of both father and son to escape, if only temporarily, from their own artistic domains into the domain of the other in a kind of masculine competition. As his father recovers from his latest medical difficulties, Peter Henisch begins to have writer's block. As a result, he stops writing and begins photographing. He returns to the places of his childhood and begins taking photographs, an act that allows him to recall particular scenes from his past. Photography allows him to work through his rejection of his father's plan to have his son become his successor, which might have posed the greatest risk of resembling his father too closely. At the same time that he is photographing and not writing, Henisch becomes aware that his father has taken up writing and taping the conversations of other family members. The father, annoyed with the slow progress of the son's biography as well as with the son's explicit desire to put "that sort of gruesome stuff" (147), e.g., concentration camps, into his book, announces half-ironically—but quite competitively—that he has also begun to write. Likewise, when Peter Henisch arrives with his first roll of film for his father to develop, he lies to his father that he is planning to make a book of "photos instead of words" (150), causing the father to "growl" back that one should keep to what one is good at.

This departure from their respective realms of artistic expertise has several important consequences for the two men and their relationship to each other. On the one hand, switching roles is an utter failure for both men. The father's attempt at producing his own biography produces the biggest lie of all. Rather than beginning in the past, the father's text opens with a jokey scenario of living to 120 and then being assigned to take photographs of celebrities in Heaven. When he begins to recount a conversation he supposedly has with Joseph Goebbels, the dishonest and extremely insensitive gimmick of placing the Nazi Propaganda Minister in Heaven drives the disgusted Peter Henisch to leave his father's apartment without saying a word. Similarly, Peter Henisch's own disingenuous photographic efforts result in an embarrassing string of black prints on which no images can be made out. On the other hand, both cases are marked as successful outside the artistic realm. The father's attempt to leave behind photography for writing is clearly equated with his attempts to deal with his approaching death. Rather than the "brutal curiosity," with its photographic deferral of reality, the father begins to tape the everyday conversations in the house. As Peter Henisch notes, these recordings represent his attempts to hold onto reality regardless of the quality of the particular moment and regardless of whether holding onto such moments cancels out other potential moments. The move signals an important new openness to engaging with the present in everyday life.

In Peter Henisch's case, his failure at photography frees him to explore his past and value life differently. And, in particular, the black filmic images free him to resume work on his book about his father. Though Henisch never explicitly states why, there seem to be several reasons for his success. First, it is important that his failure at photography provides him with a new sense of his father's limited powers as a photographer. As Henisch recalls while watching his father develop the bad film: "That my father, the magician, could turn black, unrecognizable faces into white, familiar ones, had impressed me back then. Abracadabra, out of the negative comes positive. On the other hand, the work in the lab, despite all the fascination associated with it, always had a somewhat frightening aspect for the child Peter" (149-50). In this instance, however, his father's powers are incapable of making such "positive" images appear. Second, the blackness of the pictures pushes images out of the way and makes space for words. As he resumes his writing, he looks at the film again: "Now I sometimes took it out of the canister, unrolled it, held it up to the light, and tried to see through its impenetrable blackness. I wasn't so certain that there was really *absolutely nothing* on this film, but whatever *may have been there*, it was no longer recognizable" (158). The "positive" that Henisch attempted to capture on film gets produced in his writing, an act that further transfers to writing the truth that images claim to provide but which, in the younger Henisch's eyes, have become part of the lie that his father lives. Finally, the failure to produce pictures helps to stabilize his identity vis-à-vis his father. At one level, the failure suggests that the son could not be the "successor" that the father considered him to be in his youth, a recognition that begins to free him from an overpowering and debilitating fear of moral contamination. At a more important level, however, the failure produces a moment of embarrassment: "Blood shot into my face" (150). Peter Henisch's exhibition of shame in front of his father signals an important development in his own understanding of himself and the deeper roots of his relation to his father. Until now, the son has been motivated in part by his shame for the father. But this moment of shame results from the son's failure to be like his father, which is at the same time a testament of "interest" (understood as a positive, subconscious affect) in the father. Thus, rather than being ashamed by his father, his own failure to also be like the father testifies to the father's importance to the son and to the bond that the two share.

To a large extent, Peter Henisch's relationship to his father gets refigured towards the end of the book through the ambivalent metaphor of the tightrope walker. On the one hand, the tightrope walker represents Walter Henisch's life of daredevilry to capture the images that make him a manly figure in his own eyes and the eyes of the rest of the world. In fact, the recklessness connoted by the term gets concretized in the story of Eisemann, a tightrope walker on whose shoulders the older Henisch sought to cross the Danube to obtain pictures. (Instead, Walter Henisch is denied permission by the police, and he ends up photographing the deadly fall of Eisemann and his daughter.) While as a child Peter Henisch apparently shared his father's enthusiasm for tightrope walkers, he has since attempted to renounce the image by distancing himself from his father. On the other hand, the image represents the father's commitment to make his living as a free-lance photographer after the war (until finding it necessary to join the staff of the *Arbeiterzeitung*). That initial drive for personal and professional independence is clearly materially different from his position on Goebbels's propaganda staff, and thus is associated with Peter Henisch's fondness for the "free" father of the immediate postwar era. Since Peter Henisch decides to become a free-lance writer, he must now also grapple with the ambivalence of that image for himself. As he hears his father tell him in a dream: "you are a tightropewalker [*sic*], just like me" (172).

By confronting the image of the tightrope walker, Peter Henisch begins to recognize that photography and writing are not only instruments of self-escape but also ways of dealing with the world and working through it. Thus, as his wife slowly goes into labor, Henisch reaches for his notebook: "I couldn't resist the temptation to write—even, or maybe particularly, in this situation. Or maybe it wasn't a temptation at all, but simply my attempt to come to terms with the event in a way which gave me some distance from the situation" (175). The possibility that a child might emerge from the hospital just as his own father is dying in one becomes an additional spur for finishing the book and coming to terms with his father and the masculine heritage he has "inherited" and may unintentionally pass down to the next generation. If the distancing effect of "brutal curiosity" has been dislodged from an *a priori* association with the avoidance of moral responsibility, it is only by sharing the entire manuscript with his father that both reach a shift that resembles the kind of potential closure Henisch and his father have been seeking in the process of producing the book. In the final pages of the book, Peter Henisch has his father respond to the manuscript as a whole. The father claims that he doesn't know what the book stands for: is it either for or against the father? Peter Henisch responds that he has attempted to steer clear of the dictate to choose and has instead written the book "against Death and therefore in favor of Life" (178). At this point in his narrative, Henisch gives the task of writing a conclusion over to his father. When asked to close his eyes and see what is inside himself, Walter Henisch sees two balloon rides, one tragic and the other happy. By writing for life, Peter Henisch has reconfigured the two poles that the tightrope spans from a strictly moral one—the good father or the bad—across a death-defying or potentially deadly height into a balloon narrative in which the father resists the need for heights and keeps his feet firmly planted on the ground and in the present.

In both these stories about photography, Walter Henisch confronts the immediacy of the situation rather than responding through "brutal curiosity." In the tragic one, Henisch is late to a balloon ride and his place is given to another photographer. Though the ride would have taken him above the city and hence up to the heights he regularly sought his whole life for his photographic achievements and attempts to deny his shameful, lowly self, he realizes that he can pass on this adventure at his age, since the era of airplanes has inevitably denigrated the power of images taken from hot-air balloons. What is new, however, is his response to the situation on the ground, when he and the other onlookers witness the balloon launch take a tragic turn. As a dangerous wind pulls the balloon toward a tower, where it gets caught and begins to deflate, the basket carrying the passengers falls loudly to their death. Though Henisch photographs the scene, its urgent horror for him is undeferred:

> What happened next was agonizing to see, even for me, who has photographed so much death in my lifetime. . . . You know, I felt a despair that was only comparable to the one I used to feel as a child when I first heard those verses about Little Marie. The inevitability and the predictability of this event just did me in. . . . The Eisemann accident happened when I was a lot younger. This time, however, without any [prurient tinge] for the sensational, I simply felt like I had photographically anticipated my own death. (180)

Even as he photographs the deadly balloon disaster, this experience is different from the war experiences and his almost fatal encounter with death on the shoulders of the tightrope walker. Instead of deferring the horror through brutal curiosity, and thereby remaining in the realm of the sensational and impersonal, the father remains with the inevitable horror, an act that is equated to remaining with his fearful shameful self, recalled here through the reference to the "Mariechen" game.

The second, happier balloon story provides a different narrative in which the father again remains in the present in his photography—and in such a way as to give credence to his claim that he has always photographed for himself and never for his political masters. Assigned to cover a staged political event called "Children's Day," Henisch recognizes, as if aware of the dehumanizing effects of propaganda situations for the first time, the lie in the event's name, which merely instrumentalizes the attending children for political purposes. While photographing a political speech, Henisch is distracted by a charming child who, eager to release her balloon, pulls on his sleeve to ask for permission. When the child recognizes him, it offers Henisch the opportunity to reject the honors of his military past: "Papa Henisch, she said—I'm really proud that the kids know me and call me that, prouder than any possible medals and honorary awards, and possibly even prouder than

"Henisch, Father and Son" 31

of my Iron Cross First Class—Papa Henisch, is the Uncle up there a magician?" (181). Though Henisch affirms that the politician is a magician, but only a bad and unimportant one, he gives the child permission to ignore the speaker and to subordinate political and ideological activities to more basic desires for freedom and life. As Walter Henisch himself eventually ignores the speaker entirely in favor of taking pictures of the young girl, the move signals fundamental upheavals in his politics, his aesthetics, and his sense of self:

> And I too forgot about the fat Parliamentary Representative, turned my camera eye away from him once and for all [*endgültig*], and photographed the little girl. And then I lowered the camera, and just enjoyed her face as she watched the slow cheerful ascent of the balloon into the sunny autumn sky. And at that moment, for the first time in I don't know how many years, I was really happy. (181)

In this scene, the eye of the camera and the eye of Henisch the subject are unified and no longer divided. The word "endgültig" ("once and for all") is important not only in terms of its temporal dimension within his story—until this point, Henisch had been dividing his attention between the party dignitary and the young girl—but also within the narrative of his life. This sense of finality, which represents the long-awaited real beginning for the old man that never materialized in 1945, is confirmed by his subsequent interactions with an indignant functionary who attempts to berate Henisch for not having taken a picture of him with the party dignitary. Henisch responds by rejecting his career in favor of the moment, of now: "In the little time I have left I finally want to stop taking the sort of deceptive photos [*dieser verlogenen Knipserei*] that people like you have been expecting of me my whole life long. I want at last to start taking some true pictures [*wahrhaftig zu fotografieren*]!" (182). It is a confirmation of the importance of here and now, which is not opposed to but rather reconcilable with photography. The functionary's retort, which serves as the final sentence of the book, confirms Walter Henisch's transformation: "You're not the man you used to be" ["du bist auch nicht mehr der alte!"] (182). Of course, the phrase "der alte" has a double meaning that is significant for Walter Henisch. In the everyday meaning implied by the politician's sense, it means that he no longer acts like he used to in the past. But in its literal meaning, it means that Henisch is no longer old. Indeed, he has found that way to escape the constricting onset of age by coming back to a piece of youth, though not his own horrible youth—especially since the young girl represents a different kind of "Little Marie," a real one whom Henisch can smile at and remain with rather than an imaginary one whose sad tale provokes him to run off weeping. Rather than leading to an awareness of a possible masculine inferiority and a desire to expunge that self, this encounter with the girl helps him reject self-effacing political commitments in favor of a new self— one that doesn't need to flee itself out of shame. For once, Walter Henisch is shown capable of resisting the pull of manly group identifications to remain true to an independent and freedom-loving self.

By giving his father the opportunity to close the book, both father and son achieve some sense of positive closure. Portrayed as a joint ending to the book, it is created by "Henisch, Father and Son"—with the specificity of the signifier "Henisch" once again purposefully left unclear. The book does not ultimately denounce the father but rather gives him a chance to find a liberated, even shame-free, self in the present despite his politically and morally reprehensible past. Though the father never recants his involvement with the Nazis, these balloon stories offer a postwar adult Walter Henisch who reacts to death and group membership differently from Walter Henisch the scared and shameful child. Unfortunately, however, in these final accounts the book's critical exploration of the socio-psychological factors motivating Walter Henisch seems to wane, and with it the insight into the complex psychological processes that mark the "Mitläufer." Though Tomkins suggests that it is possible to overcome the stranglehold of shame and the defensive strategies individuals use for minimizing it, such transformations are "necessarily both continuous and discontinuous" (175). Since the book offers no narrative access to what might really drive Walter Henisch's epiphanic moments, we have to wonder whether these two stories are any more real than some of Walter Henisch's end-of-the-war escapades.

Yet for all its optimism, the sense of implied closure is actually neither permanent nor stable. Though the picture of the uniformed father with his unhappy son stands at the end as a kind of conclusion that predates the book itself, the real conclusion stands in the preface to the 1987 edition, in which Peter Henisch recounts a dream of his father's return. Though Peter Henisch is immediately jubilant at the sight of his father, the joy of the moment quickly sours into anxiety about the book: "To be sure, I began writing it while he was still alive, but if he hadn't died, who knows whether I would have completed it. And now that my father has returned, what am I going to do? Retract the book? Conceal my father? Or just keep on writing..." (i). These thoughts remind us that Peter Henisch's moral exploration, perhaps even the hopeful ending, requires the father's death, and that "brutal curiosity," even in the service of an ethical project, comes with its own costs since, as the author notes several times in the course of the book, the text seems to progress when his father's condition is most deleterious and seems to stagnate every time his father's health temporarily rebounds. But the threat of the father's immanent return, even after death, underlines the tenuous and incomplete process of coming to terms with the past in contemporary Austria. In the end, the book requires its readers, like Peter Henisch himself, to deal with the past within the present—without ultimate finality in terms of the moral answers that they may want.

Notes

I would like to thank Craig Decker and Susan Kassouf for responding to drafts of this article at important stages in its development.
1. Peter Henisch, *Die kleine Figur meines Vaters* (Salzburg and Vienna: Residenz, 1987). The so-called novel was first published in 1975, and then revised in 1980. The English translation of this work uses the final 1987 revision: *Negatives of My Father*, trans. Anne Close Ulmer (Riverside, CA: Ariadne, 1990). Though all quotations in the text are from the translation (except where noted), I have in some cases inserted in brackets either my own amendments to the translation or the original German wording where I thought it was necessary for the argument I am making. For those interested in consulting the German original for all quotes, add approximately five or six to the page number given in the text.
2. Though the photograph is never discussed in the text, it seems most likely that Walter Henisch took it with a self-timer, since Peter Henisch mentions several instances of the father's use of self-timers.
3. George Mosse, *Nationalism and Sexuality: Respectability and Abnormal Sexuality in Modern Europe* (New York: Howard Fertig, 1985). See especially Chapter 8, "Fascism and Sexuality."
4. Klaus Theweleit, *Male Fantasies. Vol. 1: Women, Floods, Bodies, History*, trans. Stephen Conway (Minneapolis: U of Minnesota P, 1987); *Vol. 2: Male Bodies: Psychoanalyzing the White Terror*, trans. Erica Carter and Chris Turner (Minneapolis: U of Minnesota P, 1989). Theweleit's work primarily explores protofascist Free Corps soldiers and writers who, he argues, have a pre-Oedipal need to destroy the feminine—the mother, but also the feminine within themselves—in order to maintain the psychological integrity of their identity as men. For a broader discussion of the problematic gaps between National Socialism and Theweleit's notion of fascism, see Jessica Benjamin and Anson Rabinbach's introduction to the second volume of the English translation, pp.

ix-xxv.

5. In thematizing the significant links between male subjectivity and the organization and experience of fascism in *Die kleine Figur meines Vaters*, Henisch shares important thematic concerns and rhetorical gestures with the work of his contemporary Theweleit. As products of leftist student movements, both represented new approaches to the National Socialist legacy of the fathers by providing enormous space for the "fathers" to speak, by resisting the temptation to "order" that discourse into neat explanations, and by focusing on the relationship between aesthetic production and (fascist) masculinity. Despite these similar concerns, the differences between the "fathers" are great and suggest different notions of fascism as a lived experience.

6. Silvan Tomkins, *Shame and Its Sisters: A Silvan Tomkins Reader*, eds. Eve Kosofsky Sedgwick and Adam Frank (Durham: Duke UP, 1995) 136. Additional references to Tomkins's work are cited in the text.

7. The Moscow Declaration of October 1943 officially declared Austria to be the first victim of Nazi Germany's aggression and was used by Austria after the end of the Second World War to avoid a thorough self-examination of its willing complicity in the crimes of the Third Reich. Kurt Waldheim's successful but bitter campaign for the Austrian presidency in 1986 led to the first prolonged public discussion of Austria's National Socialist past. For a good overview of postwar Austrian politics that also includes a chapter on the Waldheim Affair, see Melanie A. Sully, *A Contemporary History of Austria* (London and New York: Routledge, 1990). For a thorough treatment of the Waldheim Affair in its national and international dimensions, see Richard Mitten, *The Politics of Antisemitic Prejudice: The Waldheim Phenomenon in Austria* (Boulder, CO: Westview, 1992). Josef Haslinger also takes the Waldheim Affair as the point of departure for a thoughtful analysis of contemporary Austrian culture: *Politik der Gefühle: Ein Essay über Österreich* (1987; Darmstadt and Neuwied: Luchterhand; Frankfurt/M: Fischer, 1995).

8. Walter Henisch actually concurs with the son's choice of title, reading it as a call to retell his life story as he has

been telling it all along: "If you are going to call the book about me THE SMALL FIGURE OF MY FATHER [*DIE KLEINE FIGUR MEINES VATERS*], then people will expect something more jovial" (147) [my translation]. In the context of the book, however, the title assumes an implicit moral flavoring: the figure of someone too small to stand up for what is morally right. Though such a negative attribution of meaning to small size dangerously mirrors the same structure of Albert Prinz's early emasculation of the young Walter Henisch, the overall force of the book is much less punishing and inherently constructive.

9. During the war, Walter Henisch was briefly captured by Soviet forces, who made him an offer to join their "Operation Free Germany" as a photographer. Henisch tells his son: "I have to admit, I was of two minds—basically I really didn't give a damn which side I shot my pictures for" (87).

10. Indeed, the only ideological Nazis in the book seem to be Albert Prinz and his wife, Peter Henisch's maternal grandmother, who evinces in the present of the book strongly internalized National Socialist doctrines about Jews and German racial purity.

11. Peter Henisch quite literally owes his very existence to the war, since without the fear about what Walter Henisch might do to himself if she rejected him, his mother would probably never have married the man. As his mother confides to him: "And then he was in the war, and naturally I was worried about him then, was afraid if I hurt him in any way something could happen to him, and it would be my fault. So we got married, and so you came into the world" (95-96).

12. In contrast to the antifascist tenor of the politicized student movement of the 1960s, Henisch—along with Theweleit—does not easily circumscribe the lives of the fathers in order to make the lives of the sons free of fascist residues or contamination. For an absorbing discussion of the role exerted by concerns about fascism on the personal lives, gender identities, and sexual practices of this generation of German thinkers and activists, see Dagmar Herzog, "'Pleasure, Sex, and Politics Belong Together': Post-Holocaust Memory and the Sexual Revolution in West Germany," *Criti-*

cal Inquiry 24.2 (1998): 393-445.

13. Judith Butler's work has developed a notion of gender performativity, defined as an inescapable and involuntary chain of signification that exposes "the illusion of gender identity as an intractable depth and inner substance" (*Gender Trouble: Feminism and the Subversion of Identity* [New York and London: Routledge, 1990] 146).

14. The story also recalls Walter Henisch's response to the burly butcher in the Labor Service, who taunted him for supposedly being a Jew and who thereby became the only person in this group of men "who didn't want to accept [him]" as an equal. Walter Henisch recalls to his son: "The guy made me furious. I would have loved to open my fly. And show him my member. Look, you moron! Look at my peter. Who says I'm circumcised!" (44). Though Walter Henisch was apparently of Jewish origin, the desire to show his penis has deeper reasons than to demonstrate his Aryan heritage in anti-Semitic Vienna. Instead, it would repair the rupture that prevents him from being a full-fledged member of the group of men, something that the Labor Service uniform is supposed to guarantee. The image of the penis as evidence of a unifying masculinity that can morally corrupt the son gets emphasized in the cutesy but not fully convincing dream sequence toward the end of the book: "You realize, the doctor said, as he quickly threw back the covers and grabbed me in the groin, your father nailed this door shut?" (172). In that same dream sequence, an older woman screams just as Peter Henisch is about to put into his mouth a slice of orange dripping with blood, a likely image for the "fruits" (postwar heritage) of the Holocaust.

15. In focusing on the concept of shame, this reading parts ways with an early psychoanalytic reading of Henisch's book which focuses on "the link between political and psychological consciousness" (58) in Peter Henisch's narrative voice: Anne Close Ulmer, "The Son as Survivor: Peter Henisch's *Die kleine Figur meines Vaters*," *The Germanic Review* 61.2 (1986): 57-64. Though I find psychoanalytic readings of literary texts fruitful, I believe that there are several reasons for warily approaching this kind of text in a psy-

choanalytic framework. First, the ahistorical and universalizing tendencies of some psychoanalytic models make it difficult to produce the kind of satisfying, historically contextualized readings required by the political context of postwar Austria vis-à-vis its Nazi past. Second, any psychoanalytic reading would need to contextualize the many self-conscious Oedipal gestures of Henisch's book as part of the historical anti-Nazi, anti-authoritarian gesture of the generation of the sons and daughters (the student movement) to annoy, discredit, and overthrow the generation of their fathers (and mothers). For instance, the copy of Freud that Henisch carries with him to his grandmother's is meant to provoke her Nazi anti-Semitism as much as it is meant to indicate Henisch's own study of psychoanalytic theory. Finally, Henisch's deliberate use of psychoanalytic moments, such as dream sequences, offers the least convincing passages in the text and, as such, should make us suspicious that psychoanalytic readings might offer too little interpretive resistance to the author himself. For a cogent and provocative critique of psychoanalysis in favor of Tomkins's Affect Theory, see Eve Kosofsky Sedgwick and Adam Frank's introduction to their edited collection of Tomkins's writings: "Shame in the Cybernetic Fold: Reading Silvan Tomkins" 1-28.

16. See Craig Decker, "Photographic Eye, Narrative I: Peter Henisch's *Die kleine Figur meines Vaters*," *Monatshefte* 83.2 (1991): 147-60, here 158. Decker traces the ways in which Peter Henisch's text purposefully "thematizes how different modes of representation relate to the construction and reconstruction of history and how differing media condition the experience and depiction of social reality" (153). In Decker's reading, Peter Henisch's purposefully discontinuous narrative performs "the dynamics of rupture so lacking in Walter Henisch's life" (158), which, in the elder Henisch's unreflective narrative, mirrors his own pictures' "sense of remoteness vis-à-vis social reality" (156). Though several "fantasy sequences" in which the younger Henisch, equipped with a typewriter instead of a camera, replaces his father in the older man's wartime stories buttress the son's sense that he and his chosen art form are fundamentally different from

the father, such passages seem problematic, since the idea of typing away from inside a tank under fire is ludicrous. My reading downplays the role of genre differences in favor of the text's awareness that father and son also share similar aesthetic stances.

17. Mitten 81.
18. Mitten 81.
19. For a discussion of Henisch's more direct literary response to the Waldheim Affair, see Kathy Brzović and Craig Decker, "The Ironic Case of Austro/Jewish Identity: Psycho-Political Rhetoric in *Steins Paranoia*" in this volume.
20. For example, Peter Henisch cannot get his father to adequately explain the direction or reason why his father and friends were crossing the Elbe if their point was to get back to Austria. Peter Henisch also notes that his father's version of his escape from an English POW camp cannot account for the whereabouts of his military medals, which his grandmother is still storing.

Papa's Nazi Past and the Anxiety of Influence: Peter Henisch's *Die kleine Figur meines Vaters*

KATHY BRZOVIĆ

> Where else, if not from history, and so also from the history of our intercourse with history, might we learn how things stand with us?
>
> —Josef Haslinger[1]

In the opening pages of *Die kleine Figur meines Vaters* (1987; *Negatives of My Father*, 1990), Peter Henisch selectively records his father's own selective recollection of his earliest childhood experiences. Among these is a fairly common and much beloved experiment in which the child views the world through a cylindrically-shaped piece of paper. For most children, the first homemade telescope serves as a playful study in perspective. The standard lesson is not lost on the young Walter: "Seen through this TELESCOPE, everything was somehow more distant and more clearly delineated."[2] Yet in this case the paper telescope also serves a decidedly psychological function: "Seen through this telescope, the world, or what at that time appeared to me to be the world, didn't come too close" (16). Not only is the relative distance of objects in relation to the perceiving subject altered when they are viewed through the telescope, but the telescope itself acts as a protective physical barrier to separate the subject at a safe distance from the object world.

This parable of the telescope teaches several lessons: it points to the fact that one's perspective on the world is subject to alteration; it further indicates that the act of perception is necessarily selective; and, finally, it suggests that some things are better seen from a distance for the simple reason that close perception is fraught with danger. This latter observation especially holds true if that perception includes the witnessing of Nazi atrocities.

With these lessons in mind, Peter Henisch self-consciously approaches the painful task of writing about his personal confrontation with his father's complicity in Austria's Nazi past and his own complicity in using that past as the raw material for a work of art. While the act of writing "a book" (10) / "this book" (111) / "our book" (113) functions as a meta-literary commentary on the question of perspective and the process of perception, the "plot" of this (auto)biographical novel consists in the son's attempt to persuade his father to alter his perception of the nature and significance of the supporting role he played as photo-journalist in the Nazi propaganda machine. The tension in the text arises out of the father's concerted effort to thwart the son's aim by fashioning his autobiography into the story of the "little man as survivor." In his own words: "What can we learn from it, my son? How does one get by? Only with chutzpa and then more chutzpa![3] Put on a show, my dear boy, the world wants to be deceived!" (125).

The elder Henisch, as Austrian *magician* (141) and masterful storyteller, threatens to overshadow his son's poetic craftsmanship by endowing his oral history with what Walter Benjamin has called "the lore of faraway places, such as a much-traveled man brings home, with the lore of the past, as it best reveals itself to natives of a place."[4] As a character (in both senses of that term) whose native place is adventure and the adventure story, the little man with a lot of chutzpa fraternizes with good and evil on a grand and sometimes comical scale, thus lending just the right degree of credibility and excitement to his tale in order to hold his listeners' attention and so gain their acquiescence in his perspective on the world. The contagious communicability of his father's experience haunts the son, who fears a predictable reader-response: "In the event that I actually finish this book that I am attempting to write about you, many will say, yes, that's the way it was. We can identify with a guy like that; his humor, which shrugs everything off with a laugh, spares us the need for any soul-searching" (145).

Just as Henisch, the artist, struggles to wrest his written narrative from the powerful voice of his storytelling precursor, Henisch, the reader, struggles against a potential reader-identification with the old man's stories. The immediacy of Papa Henisch's tales of daredevilry constitute a lived experience for his imaginative son, who, on two separate occasions (90-94 and 102-6), in his mind's eye explicitly makes his father's war-front experiences his own by conjuring, out of his father's camera, his own typewriter and cassette recorder. The act of storytelling, as handed down from father to son, thus ensures a disconcerting continuity of shared experience which includes Austria's Nazi past as exemplified in the line: "My father removed his Iron Cross, First Class, from his desk drawer and pinned it to my chest" (94). From the war story emerges the war hero, and from the portrayal of heroism emerges the desire to elevate oneself through imitation. And herein lies the danger.

While forced to acknowledge the deadly allure of the past and his own creative indebtedness to it, Peter Henisch also feels that the need to break with that past presents itself as both a historico-political and an aesthetic imperative. To this end, he deliberately and self-consciously adopts the narrative strategy that Harold Bloom has termed "kenosis," "a breaking device . . . against repetition compulsions" instituting "a movement towards discontinuity with the precursor."[5] This strategy is not without danger since it involves "an 'active' repetition in order to gain mastery" over the past, so that one might then, from the vantage point of empathic understanding, embark on "'undoing' repetition."[6] So it is that only after he has twice risked entering his father's world—first behind the Russian front: "I sat in a tiger escort tank and typed on my typewriter" (93); and then in the Balkans: "As I spoke into the tape recorder I could already see H<small>IS</small> L<small>AST</small> W<small>ORDS</small> printed in the newspaper headlines" (105)—can he free himself from the repetition compulsion and declare:

> Dear Papa, I wrote, no, I don't want to become what you have become. I don't want to be what you were, although I do understand you. We all follow in another's footsteps and, in so doing, discover ourselves—that may be, but I hope not in the sense of an unavoidable identity. I don't want to follow in your footsteps, do you understand? I don't want to live my life the way you've lived yours. (106)

Henisch's declaration should not be read in simple psychological terms as an outright rejection of his father. After all, as chronicler of his father's life, if he kills his father prematurely he signs his own death sentence—an aesthetic irony that his wife, Sonja, the symbol of the sixties successor generation, cannot comprehend. "You must condemn him," she states in no uncertain terms, "otherwise you will be defending him" (154). Henisch's insistence, by contrast, on walking the dialectical tightrope of continuity and discontinuity arises primarily out of the recognition that "he who lives by continuity alone cannot be a poet."[7] However much tradition and continuity may provide a constant source of inspirational material to the poetic imagination (just as his father's life story and impending death provide the inspiration for this/our book), true poetic greatness and originality can only be achieved by breaking with tradition and inherited continuities.

Of course, within the context of Austrian tradition, the anxiety of influence reaches beyond the question of poetic creation to include the creation of alternative histories, both personal and national. Here, too, there exists a danger that an alternative history might fall prey to yet another "historical lie." For example: the tiny Austrian nation as first victim of Nazi Germany; the tiny Walter Henisch (in SS-uniform) as one of the many victims of fate. In order to counter this potential threat, Henisch adopts a strategy of forcing an inversion of the classic father/son, storyteller/listener, precursor/successor relation by challenging his father to become a reader of his son's story about his father's story.

In the act of reading, Walter Henisch's imagination must now go to work and actively "participate both in the production and the comprehension of the work's intention."[8] Because the work is so constructed as to deliberately "defamiliarize the familiar," that is to say, to call into question the normative framework within which the father has cast his own story, Walter necessarily experiences difficulty in arriving at an interpretational conclusion: "I just don't know, my father said, and laid the manuscript aside; I'm still not clear what exactly it is you're driving at. For what or against what are you writing this book? For you or against me or, in the end, the other way around?" (183). Papa Henisch is confronted with the disconcerting realization that his son's story lacks that "harmony between all the different elements"[9] of a work of art traditionally demanded by classical interpretation and with which he himself so assiduously sought to endow his own narrative.

The disruption of the normal chronology, the use of multiple and shifting perspectives, the deliberate introduction of discontinuities and breaks in the narrative[10]—all these textual aspects lead to the initial impression that the manuscript lacks the consistency necessary to meaningful interpretation. Yet these seemingly incongruous elements serve a deliberate and essential function. As Wolfgang Iser has argued in *The Act of Reading*, "modern literary works are so full of apparent inconsistencies—not because they are badly constructed, but because such breaks act as hindrances to comprehension, and so force us to reject our habitual orientation as inadequate."[11] Hence, in posing the question "for what or against what?" Walter Henisch not only asks of his son what "he never asked of himself,"[12] but he also signals his own awakening to a long dormant "impulse to question."[13] This impulse, in turn, leads him to the rejection of his habitual orientation toward existing power structures and authority in general, thus creating the "ground for forgiveness."[14]

In the closing pages of *Die kleine Figur meines Vaters*, Peter Henisch elects to record two stories selected by his father to end this book: one tragic, the other happy, to be told in that order, "so that the happy one endures" (183). The first—"the story of a prevented balloon take-off" (184)—makes the second—"the story of a premature balloon take-off" (185)—possible, indicating the very impossibility of separating life's joys from its sorrows. Walter's late arrival at a photo shoot saves him from sharing the tragic fate of those who fall to their death in an unforeseeable and, hence, unavoidable balloon accident, leaving him with the uneasy sense "that I had photographically anticipated my own death" (185). The first segment of the balloon parable creates a wholly new moral frame of reference for the aging Walter, who, for the first time in his adventuresome life, realizes the truth of all good humorists, namely, that "one cannot always put off dying until tomorrow."[15] The moral question now becomes: how should one live today, in this moment? The answer comes in the second segment of the balloon parable. A Children's Day assignment places Papa Henisch in a quandary: should he keep his camera trained on the party functionaries who have staged this balloon festival as an opportunity to create a written and pictorial record of their abiding love of children ("the children are merely there as the means to an end" [186]), or should he train his attention on an eager little girl who spontaneously expresses a "premature" desire to release her balloon into the open air and watch it gently rise into the sky? He decides in favor of youth and of joy and of life. "Stay this moment! You are so beautiful!"[16]

The storytelling journey, through repetition of the past, has now led back to a "recollection forward,"[17] to that Goethean caesura between "Stay this moment!" and "You are so beautiful!" to that decisive pause between life and death, heaven and hell. The past cannot be altered, but it is subject to a "magical undoing"[18] in the telling and the hearing of a tale—a Divine Comedy in which our hero rehearses the descent into the hell of war; cheats Death of its bounty (the Grim Reaper on the Elbe); enters a state of limbo (the Second Austrian Republic); and is transformed through the emblematic (i.e., photographic) vision of his own death. *Kenosis*, "a breaking device against repetition compulsions" (death being the final break with life), issues forth a catharsis. *Papa* Henisch is freed from the anxiety of influence (from his stepfather Herr Albert Prinz, the Hitler Youth, the SS, the Führer, the Soviet occupying power, the British and American occupying powers, the Austrian Grand Coalition) to act as a fully autonomous individual for the first time in his life, which is to say, a short time before his death.

His son Peter, in the epilogue that serves as a preface to the 1975 edition of the book, confesses to his own complicity in "cashing in" on death as a means to an end: ". . . yes, to a certain extent, when I was writing this book, I was speculating in his death" (5). The son shares his father's complicity in gambling on death to sustain his artistic production by speculating in a kind of secondary market in Nazi war stories. Yet he has good aesthetic reasons for doing so. Aesthetics is derived from the Greek word meaning perception, and the perception of Death in a climactic moment—a purely literary device—signals a radical change in essence and hence in perspective. "What, at that time, appeared to me to be the world" (16) is sublimated in the reception of the work of art, and the world now expands to incorporate alternative perspectives on human motivation and agency in personal and historical time.

The son's motive—"I transform everything into material for my work. You . . . I transform with a vengeance" (76)—reveals itself as a strategy by the successor to transform his precursor. The author fashions a magical undoing by means of an artistic repetition, that is to say, a repetition in the sense of re-creation. At the end of the book of life, he creates his father anew and, in begetting his own father in the literary work of art, attempts to free himself from the anxiety of influence and so "compose" a Self by begetting himself.[19]

This strategy is neither risk-free nor is it certain. And, indeed, the specter of the past raises itself again in the form of Kurt Waldheim to make its way into the 1987 edition of the book in which the author confesses: "To be sure, I began to write it when he was still alive, but if he hadn't died, who knows if I ever would have finished it. And now that my father has returned, what do I do? Retract the book? Hide my father? Or keep on writing . . . " (5). The act of composition is endless insofar as there is no end to the "material," to the very stuff of life and literature, to the ongoing human confrontation with the Self and the World that comes with the knowledge of good and evil.

The sons are destined to repeat the struggle of the fathers, not in the sense of an "unavoidable identity," but insofar as they are destined to be blind to their own sins, destined to fall, destined to suffer temptation and to seek their own salvation. The author represents these stages in the journey whereby the sons would clear their own path ("not follow in your footsteps") by calling upon his poetic precursors to guide him through the thicket of what, in effect, is Everyman's Pilgrim's Progress. In the process, he generates a series of thematically significant structures or moments that illustrate the symbolic or formal connection between fathers and sons.

To cite only one example: On the war front in the Balkans, Papa is temporarily blinded by a shell, while on the home front his first-born basks in the joy of his mother's full, undivided attention. Later hospitalized for a hernia operation, the now teenage Peter develops a fear of being blinded. This otherwise blatantly obvious allusion to Freud's Oedipal Complex can also be read in terms of Freud's own status as successor. Freud's discovery of the Oedipal complex is, in some sense, his own poetic misreading or misprision of Sophocles's tragedy *Oedipus the King*. The nature of this tragedy is revealed by Teiresias, the blind Seer, in two statements. The first is an admonition borne of the wisdom that comes with experience: "Ah! what a burden knowledge is, when knowledge / can be of no avail"[20]; and the second is a judgment provoked by Oedipus's dismissive arrogance: "you have your sight, and yet you cannot see / where, nor with whom you live, nor in what horror."[21] The danger faced by the successor generation, then, is that in their moral rectitude and self-righteous hubris, they murder their fathers and, so blinded, cannot see their own danger. This is the basic Oedipal morality found in traditional "Vater-Literatur" ("father literature") and the reason why it is littered with the bodies of so many dead fathers. The danger in this attitude toward history is summed up in the Biblical pronouncement: Pride comes before the Fall.

Yet the irony of life is that, in order to know, we must fall. Bloom explains this paradox when he writes of Milton's *Paradise Lost*: "Poetry begins with our awareness, not of a Fall, but that *we are falling*. The poet is our chosen man, and his consciousness of election comes as a curse; again, not 'I am fallen man,' but 'I am Man, and I am falling.'" The poet's task then becomes "to know damnation and to explore the limits of the possible within it."[22]

Milton's Satan, for example, is a strangely sympathetic character, as is Goethe's Mephisto, for the simple reason that both partake of personality traits that are human, all too human. If we look to Milton's fallen angel, we find a telling passage in which he addresses his minions before setting off to explore God's new creation with the intention of conquering the world:

> . . . Go, therefore, mighty Powers,
> Terror of Heaven, though fallen; intend at home,
> While here shall be our home, what best may ease
> The present misery, and render Hell
> More tolerable, if there be cure or charm
> To respite, or deceive, or slack the pain
> Of this ill mansion; intermit no watch
> Against a wakeful foe, while I abroad
> Through all the coasts of dark destruction seek
> Deliverance for us all . . .[23]

What do we have here but a portrayal of Satan as *paterfamilias*! And what soldier, of whatever country, cause, or clime, does not say much the same thing to his family before going off to war? Keep the home fires burning while I am abroad, fighting the enemy, conquering the world! And equally significant, what reader does not identify with our hero, fallen or falling though he may be? Through identification, the literary work of art reproduces temptation. The temptation, for example, to identify with the fleeing German soldier, Walter, in his desperate, engaging, and sometimes comical attempt to escape the wrath of the fast-approaching "enemy" is built into the very structure of the chronological and largely continuous narrative that unfolds in the final chapter of the book. We too are subject to the seductiveness of war as adventure, and through this experience of our own "brutal curiosity,"[24] through this identification with youthful exuberance, we might begin to grasp why the old man clings so tenaciously to the fond memories of his youth. Youth is so very brash and so very "free" because it is largely ignorant of moral and material restrictions. Faust, for example, must become young again—not only so that he can get the girl, but also so that he can become blind to the atrocities he is about to commit in the name of love and progress. And insight—"when he completely sees through himself"[25] as Mephisto puts it—comes only from experience. That "father literature" written by such authors as Niklas Frank (1939-), Christoph Meckel (1935-), and Brigitte Schwaiger (1949-),[26] which is based on the absolute rejection of identification with the fathers, has little to offer either as literature or as ethics, because without identification there can be no "aha! experience." And without insight, without taking that journey into our own heart of darkness, there can be no salvation.

Yet lest we end on an overly high-minded and idealistic note not evident in this novel, let it be said that, for Henisch, as for other postwar novelists such as Ingeborg Bachmann (1926-73), Thomas Bernhard (1931-89), and Peter Handke (1942-), salvation is eternally deferred. To speak in terms of the balloon parable, eternal salvation is forever "prevented" and forever "premature." It is ultimately a journey, whether taken vertically or horizontally, without end, since, "in reality," as Kenneth Burke has remarked, "we are capable of but partial acts, acts that but partially represent us and that produce but partial transformations."[27] The loss of the "Edenic moment" of absolute transformation forces upon the successor generation an eternal anxiety of influence, an eternal "coming-to-terms-with" the past. For this reason, Henisch's work has both multiple endings and multiple beginnings. Book I is titled "The Beginning of A Biography" not only because it tells the story of how the author came to write the story of his father's life (and so of his own life as well), but also because it tells the story of the narrator's repeated attempts to begin the story itself—a difficult task given the unanswered questions of whose story and what story he would and should begin to tell. More than this, however, it tells the story of the difficulty of telling this story.

In *Beginnings: Intention and Method*, Edward Said defines "*the beginning*" as "*the first step in the intentional production of meaning.*"[28] But what does it mean to come *after*, and in this specific case, what does it mean "to walk in the footsteps" of the Nazi generation? Has one necessarily inherited the "habitual orientation" of fascism in the same sense as Peter has inherited his father's artistic eye? And can one free oneself from that habit? It seems to me the successor generation's predicament is illuminated by Samuel Beckett's remark that, "The laws of memory are subject to the more general laws of habit. . . . Habit is the ballast that chains the dog to his vomit."[29] In other words, Austria is choking on its own history, and the question is: how does it free itself from this peculiar type of chain? It is a difficult proposition that the most thoughtful postwar authors wrestle with repeatedly and ironically. In *Wittgensteins Neffe* (1982; *Wittgenstein's Nephew*, 1989), for example, Thomas Bernhard discusses the precarious nature of attempting to recover one's physical strength after a prolonged, life-threatening illness. One has to begin to walk again, but only a few steps at a time, to be followed by a few steps more and then a few more, and so on, and so forth. The patient, however, anxious to achieve full recovery as quickly as possible, is tempted to overexert himself. As a consequence, "he steps out into the open air and so kills himself."[30] This is the paradox of political and personal life in the Austrian republic with which Henisch and other artists attempt to grapple and which none resolve. In the meantime, they find themselves living and working in the ironic mode, creating art out of the "material" of the fascist past. At times the past literally resonates, as in Bernhard's novel *Der Untergeher* (1983; *The Loser*, 1993), in which three young pianists, who have rented an apartment in Salzburg that was previously owned by a well-regarded Nazi sculptor, discover that the repulsive six-meter-high Nazi sculptures (*"creations of the master"*) lining the walls are, in fact, "acoustically ideal."[31] Camera, typewriter, cassette recorder, cast, piano. They all have this in common: they are artistic means—means of expression as well as means of perception, telescopes through which one perceives the world and selectively alters it.

Yet to alter the world is to have complicity in its creation, for good or for ill. And if we are co-creators through "our intercourse with history," how do things stand with us? In this sense Henisch's novel is not so much an *apologia*—a justification of his father's actions, as some would have it—as it is a call to explore our own blind allegiances, our involuntary or elective affinity with our fathers, and the extent to which we can truly claim to be authors of our own deeds and of our own freedom.

Notes

1. Josef Haslinger, *Politik der Gefühle: Ein Essay über Österreich* (Frankfurt/M: Fischer, 1995) 132.
2. Peter Henisch, *Die kleine Figur meines Vaters* (Salzburg and Vienna: Residenz, 1987) 16.
3. To Papa Henisch chutzpa signifies courage, daring, and the will to live. To his son, it often connotes "shamelessness." See Jeffrey Schneider, "Henisch, Father and Son: Masculinity, Art, and the Narrative of (Austrian) Shame" in this volume. Yet, as we shall see, to be an artist is to be shameless

in the expropriation of the material from which one creates the work of art.
  4. Walter Benjamin, "The Storyteller: Reflections on the Works of Nikolai Leskov," *Illuminations*, trans. Harry Zohn, ed. and intro. Hannah Arendt (New York: Schocken, 1969) 85. In this same essay, Benjamin observes that, "An orientation toward practical interests is characteristic of many born storytellers. . . . Every real story . . . contains, openly or covertly, something useful" (86). Papa Henisch has a very practical interest in survival and chutzpa is, for him, that character trait or useful skill that allows him to best deceive death—a character trait to which his son owes his own life.
  5. Harold Bloom, *The Anxiety of Influence: A Theory of Poetry* (London: Oxford UP, 1973) 14.
  6. Bloom 80.
  7. Bloom 78.
  8. Wolfgang Iser, *The Act of Reading: A Theory of Aesthetic Response* (Baltimore and London: Johns Hopkins UP, 1978) 24.
  9. Iser 18.
  10. See Craig Decker, "Photographic Eye, Narrative I: Peter Henisch's *Die kleine Figur meines Vaters*," *Monatshefte* 83.2 (1991): 147-60.
  11. Iser 18.
  12. Decker 151.
  13. Peter Schneider, "Vom richtigen Umgang mit dem Bösen," *Deutsche Ängste: Sieben Essays* (Darmstadt: Luchterhand, 1988) 91.
  14. The "ground for forgiveness" is, in some sense, the necessary counterpart to the "ground of infamy." Peter Henisch plays with this metaphor in *Steins Paranoia* (1988; *Stone's Paranoia*, 2000), particularly in those scenes in which Stein and Clarissa take their walking tour of Vienna.
  15. Northrop Frye, *Anatomy of Criticism: Four Essays* (Princeton: Princeton UP, 1973) 235. Frye continues: "For here as everywhere else in satire there is a moral reference: it is all very well to eat, drink, and be merry, but one cannot always put off dying until tomorrow."
  16. Johann Wolfgang von Goethe, *Faust: Der Tragödie*

Zweiter Teil, Goethes Werke: Hamburger Ausgabe, ed. Erich Trunz, vol. 3 (Munich: Beck, 1981) 384, line 11582.
17. Bloom 83.
18. Bloom 81.
19. For a psychological interpretation of the novel, see Anne Close Ulmer, "The Son as Survivor: Peter Henisch's *Die kleine Figur meines Vaters*," *The Germanic Review* 61.2 (1986): 57-64. Because the issue of identity creation is so very self-conscious and stylized, as are the multiple references to Freud, I'm reluctant to view the novel in narrow psychological terms.
20. Sophocles, *Oedipus the King*, *Three Tragedies: Antigone, Oedipus the King, Electra*, trans. and ed. H.D.F. Kitto (London: Oxford UP, 1976) 58.
21. Sophocles 61.
22. Bloom 20-21.
23. John Milton, *Paradise Lost*, *Paradise Lost and Other Poems*, ed. Edward Le Comte (New York and Toronto: The New American Library, 1961) Book II, lines 456-65.
24. This is the title of the second of three books that make up the novel.
25. Goethe, *Faust: Der Tragödie Zweiter Teil* 355, line 11811.
26. Christoph Meckel, *Suchbild: Über meinen Vater* (Düsseldorf: Claassen, 1980; rpt. Frankfurt/M. Fischer, 1983); Brigitte Schwaiger, *Lange Abwesenheit* (Vienna and Hamburg: Zsolnay, 1983); Niklas Frank, *Der Vater: Eine Abrechnung* (Munich: Bertelsmann, 1987).
27. Kenneth Burke, *A Grammar of Motives* (Berkeley/Los Angeles/London: U of California P, 1969) 19.
28. Edward W. Said, *Beginnings: Intention and Method* (New York: Basic Books, 1975) 5.
29. Samuel Beckett, *Proust* (London: Evergreen; New York: Grove, 1957) 7-8.
30. Thomas Bernhard, *Wittgensteins Neffe: Eine Freundschaft* (Frankfurt/M: Suhrkamp, 1982) 16-17.
31. Bernhard, *Der Untergeher* (Frankfurt/M: Suhrkamp, 1983) 112.

The Lizard-King Can Do Anything: Hybridity and the Cultural Logic of Globalization in *Morrisons Versteck*

FRIEDEMANN WEIDAUER

According to Pierre Bourdieu, the aesthetic preferences of a given social class mirror the manner in which it participates in other aspects of social life.[1] If this thesis is correct, then the emergence of a new social class should be accompanied by the emergence of new cultural products. Bourdieu's by now somewhat dated investigation of social classes and their aesthetic preferences did not include the connoisseurs of postmodern art simply because, when he conducted his empirical work in the 1960s, few of them were visibly present. By the 1990s, however, this group seemed to be dominating the political as well as social and artistic spheres, representing a class that can be described in a variety of ways: in terms of their age as baby boomers socialized during the sixties or, on the basis of their occupational and regional distribution, as yuppies. It is a class primarily engaged in marketing products, in managing the flow of information and capital, and in managing regionally the operations of global companies. Moreover, it is a class for which everything in this world turns into a museum. Its *modus vivendi* therefore resembles that of tourists, whether they go out to eat in refurbished warehouse districts, view the former sites of backbreaking physical labor on their vacations, or participate in spectator sports as spectators of spectacles.[2]

One could cite many reasons for the rise of such a class, including the fact that its representatives are so far removed from the actual processes of material production that even shut-down mills or defunct nuclear power plants turn into museum pieces for them. Additionally, their daily interfacing with the world through the mediation of electronic data weakens their ability to distinguish between non-electronic and electronic realities. Often, their work does not link them to any particular place, not only because they work for transnational companies but also because it does not really matter where they plug in their laptops. It is representatives of this class, Andreas Huyssen might argue, who are the consumers of postmodern art.[3]

But instead of concentrating on any one of the social factors mentioned thus far, I would like to argue that what makes this new class interesting structurally is that all aspects of the biographical background of each of its representatives form a hybrid.[4] Their lives as members of this social class are characterized by a combination—but not a synthesis—of aspects of the traditional social classes; they sell their intellectual and organizational skills, but they also play the stock market and increasingly own stock in the company for which they work. Thus, it might be in their interest as leisure-time stockholders to downsize their very own day jobs. Generationally, they are both fathers and sons, mothers and daughters, products not only of the natural reproductive cycle but also of the rebellious 1960s. By now, they have become representatives of the *status quo* and the paternalistic power of the state; former activists of the "ausserparlamentarische Opposition" (extra-parliamentary opposition) turned into "Aussenminister" (secretaries of state); "Hausbesetzer" (squatters) turned into Members of the House; boyfriends of daughters who fought for equal rights outed as intern-molesting presidential husbands. Within the cultural sphere, they have seen the culture of protest transformed into the dominant form of artistic expression, and acts of rebellion into best sellers or Grammy-winning records. As producers and consumers of cultural products they have no choice but to acknowledge what they produce and consume as commodities, regardless of the intention behind the individual work of art. Art, like all other aspects of their lives, is, therefore, above all ironic. The irony pervading every aspect of their lives forces the world to become a museum, because everything originally intended as serious has at some point been turned into a quote of its former self. The acceleration of regurgitating styles from earlier generations allows them to see the next generation walking around as quotes of their former selves. The temporal distance between fad and its reappearance as retro-fashion has shrunk to about twenty years. Having passed the mid-fifties of his own life, Peter Henisch has thus seen a subsequent generation of young people dressed the way he was when he bought his first albums by The Doors.

The irony inherent in a life characterized by hybridity (where irony stems from the contrast between what was meant to be and what actually became of it) has a certain liberating effect, because the pure life as envisioned in the 1960s (don't be commercial in your art; don't participate in the hegemonic discourse; don't be a chauvinist pig) had created a form of paranoia expressing itself in constant self-questioning. Am I already participating in the hegemonic discourse? Am I too commercial or, even worse, too elitist in my artistic endeavors? Am I helping the class enemy? This form of self-questioning led to the blossoming of Stalinist groups practicing this type of internalized self-censorship. Meanwhile, the self-questioning has not disappeared, but has turned into a form of narcissism or brand loyalty, refusing to pass judgment upon what comes under its scrutiny. Thus, we have generations identifying themselves as if christening a new product: Baby Boomers, Generation X, and, in Germany, also the generation between the two, the "Zaungäste" (those watching from the fence).[5]

For a cultural product to be truly successful commercially, however, the class of postmodern consumers is still not big enough. The culture industry—and this term is no longer the indictment it was thirty years ago—must parallel other industries so as to reach as many sectors of society as possible. Companies such as Volkswagen or Microsoft design their products for a global market. Globalization in this context means that one product platform can serve as the basis for products in all markets of the world. The VW Golf and Microsoft Office are such platforms. But to be successful these products have to be localized, adjusted to the peculiarities of the targeted regional market. The dialogue box in the software has to accommodate lengthy words in foreign idioms ("Press Shift" —> "Drücken Sie die Umschalttaste"); the homey Golf has to be sold in markets that prefer "fun" cars.

A similar process of synchronous globalization and localization takes place in the realm of culture, though localization here means something different. The global product has to fit the taste of more than one class; it has to be localized in a social sense so as to fit the tastes of as many classes as possible. The product has to please the traditional classes as investigated by Bourdieu as well as the new class of art consumers described above and partially characterized in the work of Judith Ryan and Huyssen.[6] In other words, the work of art has to be socially localized in such a way as to respond to the hybrid tastes of this hybrid class. Platforms of this sort can be existing works of art, the artists themselves, and even dead artists. Most museums now seem to be going in this direction. They already try to please the tastes of the social classes that Bourdieu has described: the owners of capital (here cultural capital in a very material sense) are given the chance to fulfill their desire for representation by inserting their names into the collection as sponsors, as owners of individual works of art, or as the people who have given the entire museum its name. The galleries themselves are the space where the middle class can put its work ethic on display by expending as much intellectual effort on interpreting a work of art as they would on a task associated with their regular jobs. Finally, the museum stores give the rest of society the chance to combine the desire for entertainment with their concept of art as something that should be useful (van Gogh paintings as neckties), those people for whom, as Bourdieu writes, the distinction between what pleases and what gratifies is an altogether dispensable idea.[7] When the new hybrid class enters these museums its members transform these different approaches to art into a hybrid itself and turn the museum into a museum of a museum by engaging and simultaneously distancing themselves from the pursuits of the other museumgoers. The transformation of classical composers into globalized cultural platforms could be analyzed in a similar fashion. But let us turn to classic rock music instead.

Jim Morrison is one such cultural platform that has been globalized and localized so as to cover as much social ground as possible. Even before the advent of the new hybrid class described above, he had been marketable to a wide array of classes characterized by their aesthetic choices. He fulfilled the desire of (mostly) male college students who wanted to fuck their parents while, at the same time, he (unconsciously) mimicked his audiences' aesthetic preferences, appearing as a rebel who is also "difficult," a rabble-rouser who is not part of the rabble. At the same time, his "difficulty" did not prevent those who experienced rebellion primarily through the music itself from consuming Morrison's art while being oblivious to the fact that he slipped words coined by the modernist avant-garde through the speakers of their pickups. In the meantime, Morrison's lifestyle helped to preserve the notion that, even amidst the anonymity of mass culture and society, it is still possible to live dangerously, thus reaffirming a special kind of humanist subjectivity gained at the risk of one's physical destruction. Accordingly, the hybrid class whose favorite trope is irony can retroactively claim to have already gotten it right when they were only twenty, having already then understood the irony of subjectivity bought at the expense of the subject, the irony of the elitist mass idol, and the irony that what then began as counter-culture came to dominate the cultural scene for the rest of the millennium—though only as a quote of itself.

Choosing Morrison as the topic for a novel/"Bildungsroman"/biography when all three genres have been declared dead or impossible to write testifies to the cultural logic that allowed Henisch, an author of the same age as his subject, to remain alive on the cultural scene from the time of Morrison's death until his rebirth between the covers of a hardbound novel. Making a living by writing novels while belonging to the generation that, in the sixties, declared literature to be dead or useless continues the hybridity and irony typical of other representatives of Henisch's generation. Indeed, it does not lack a certain logic that those who had declared themselves dead as the authors of literature, but now do better economically than ever before, feel obliged to keep alive the memory of someone who was more true to his art than they themselves. Those who sold out their integrity to the establishment (and this applies less to Henisch than to the more opportunistic representatives of his generation) must feel a certain amount of debt toward those who did not and subsequently paid for their convictions with their lives.

The author and his subject were both born in the year 1943, one in Austria, the other in Florida. Henisch's novel *Morrisons Versteck* (Morrison's Hideout) and Oliver Stone's film *The Doors* both appeared in 1991, with the former already going into its second printing one year after its publication and the latter bringing in $40 million at the box office. Oliver Stone is somewhat younger than Henisch and Morrison, but all three have one thing in common: in the year 1991 they were—or would have been—at the high, or rather, low point of their mid-life crises, vulnerable to all the ironies discussed above and possibly feeling that something might have died in the course of their continuous, though often playful, acts of self-denial and reinvention. At least financially the attempts at resuscitation by Henisch and Stone proved successful. Whether the same can be said in regard to their artistic achievements is not for me to decide. The more important question, however, is: what did they hope to achieve through their voyeuristic-vampiric endeavors? Particularly in the case of Henisch there seems to be an attempt at reinvention, an attempt prompted by the character of the Lizard-King to shed an old skin and to rejuvenate oneself through the warmth radiating from the reptile that had grown cold too early. This skewed metaphor illuminates the problem: who gives warmth to whom in this situation? A reptile lives through the warmth absorbed from its environment, and this seems to be an appropriate metaphor for Morrison who is forced by the curiosity of the media and his fans to keep wandering among them. It would be another example of the type of irony so typical of his generation if Henisch were to warm himself only by the reflected fire of Morrison's admirers, a fire reflected and focused in the concave mirror that is the object of their admiration. Like the museumgoers who enjoy the pieces of art in the reflection of how others see them, the members of the hybrid class use what radiates from mass idols only to rarify their enjoyment into a higher form of hero worship that refuses to participate in this very act. Parallel to the example of the museumgoers who turn art appreciation into the art of making the other museumgoers the objects of their appreciation, we have the logic of Henisch choosing a subject that isn't even there because all that really matters are its reflections and refractions in others.

Ironically, it is Morrison himself who in Henisch's narrative bears the attributes of a vampire. He lives on through the warmth of the curiosity and fantasy invested in his persona. But this is a reciprocal relationship. Those who try to approach Morrison have grown cold themselves and seek warmth from the fire kept burning around this figure, just like that line in one of the most famous Doors' songs which, if one chooses to believe Henisch's account, would have been turned into "Come on Buick light my fire"[8] had Morrison not preempted the particular kind of commodification in which commercials and rock songs become indistinguishable. This hints at one of the reasons why Morrison, in contrast to many of his contemporaries, might have chosen to withdraw from this branch of industry. In contrast to those who seem intent on proving that the afterglow of the "summer of love" can be made into money even after they have gained around their waistlines and lost above their brows, Morrison appears remarkably young, not only because memory has fixed him in time as a twenty-eight-year-old, but also because with him an unredeemed promise of the era lives on. While Morrison can serve as the platform for endless acts of social globalization and localization, he also keeps alive the memory of the "summer of love" whose end he seemed to have foreseen in the lyrics of one of his earliest hit songs. This is the memory of the promise of a political and sexual revolution, of the "summer of love" in the United States and the hot summer of student revolts in Paris. Revolution, after all, is war meant to destroy the enemy; it is not hybridization, the (not necessarily) peaceful coexistence of differences.

Thirty years later, however, it seems as though the real thing would be too hot to handle for Henisch and other members of his generation. Using hybridization as the dominant technique in *Morrisons Versteck* seems to offer a way out at a time when book burnings, publicly staged suicides, flag burnings, and other iconoclastic activities are no longer fashionable. What was once the cause of conflict because it could not coexist can now be juxtaposed in aesthetic form, thereby avoiding the real conflicts but also avoiding the appearance of false compromises, just as Henisch seems to avoid any synthesis or sublation of existing contradictions. Hybridity thus seems to be the literary device most appropriate and closely linked to the ironic stance that characterizes his generation. The violent attempts at reconciling contradictions back then only led to new contradictions, and the contradictions this process wedged into the autobiographies of this generation can only be borne by adopting an ironic stance toward them, a form of humor that allows one simply to smile about contradictions that formerly would have driven the same people insane. The "Bildungsroman," whose use in the guise of irony forms part of the subtext of literary traditions in *Morrisons Versteck*, has as its "Bildungsideal" to bring the narrative voice closer to this stance of humorous and ironic distance and away from the more belligerent tone at the beginning of the novel.

Achieving this ideal is the only possible way for the narrative voice (and perhaps the author behind it) to stay in business, to continue being able to write, because the conflicts of thirty years ago have created the worst-case scenario. Not only have the political and social ideas for which his generation fought lost out, but the mass culture of protest, in its commercialized form, has become the cultural norm. The aesthetic form of expression of a bygone era, emptied of its political content, has turned into a commercial automaton. A generation that had committed itself to a set of ideals whose realization it was denied had to find a form of self-expression that would allow for its survival. The publicly staged suicide and its literary form—to declare (in writing) the death of writing and to attempt to alienate one's customers through carefully orchestrated "Publikumsbeschimpfungen" (tirades against the audience)—thus seem to be the logical choice, since they stage a form of self-denial as one way to stay alive, i.e., to be reborn by the ensuing scandals the act provokes. Whether intended or not, whether playfully staged or provoked as a real-life event constituting systematic self-abuse, actual or literary suicide forms for this generation a surprisingly common way of death as a form of survival. For some it simply stood as a means of reinventing oneself (Peter Handke [1942-], Henisch, Bob Dylan, Neil Young); for others it had to be paid for in real lives (Rolf Dieter Brinkmann [1940-75], Morrison, Jimi Hendrix, Janis Joplin). This form of ending one's artistic lifeform—or one's real life—seems particularly appropriate because to stage right in front of one's audience the most extreme form of denying that very audience is to stage the contradiction between extreme elitism and admitting dependency on a mass audience. Those who had already made this contradiction productive in their former lives, e.g., Handke and Morrison, were then also more successful in the lives that followed, as they had already prepared their audiences for what was about to come.

It is precisely this dynamic that makes Morrison Henisch's muse. Morrison's ability to stay alive in the imagination of his followers—even after telling his audience to fuck itself and even after the death of the cultural turmoil that brought him to the top—provides the aesthetic model that allows Henisch to keep alive the dream of staying close to popular culture without giving up the cultural elitism one has grown so fond of. The trick lies in the ability to tell an audience to fuck itself while giving each individual member of that audience the feeling that he or she is exempt from this verdict, the feeling that even though they form a part of the masses crowding in on the stage where their hero performs he seems to have recognized in them what sets them apart from the rest—that they, too, prefer to read French poetry. Hybridity makes possible that which thirty years ago led to bloodshed, the presence of two contradictory cultural paradigms alongside each other: "Bildungsbürgertum" (the educated middle class) and "Protestgeneration" (the generation of protest); the pop biography and the "Bildungsroman"; the rebirth of the novel in the act of iconoclasm. What Henisch has in mind is to keep the promise of the "summer of love" and the hot summer of 1968 alive in a vehicle that can be parked next to the sophisticated cultural products enjoyed by the new hybrid class. Indeed, the very act of using the pop legend Morrison puts at an ironic distance earlier attempts to use pop culture as a way out of artistic dead ends. Rolf Dieter Brinkmann, another representative of this generation whose early death (or at least the story surrounding it) seems to be a radical continuation of his aesthetic experiments, wanted to use pop culture as a way to get out of history. Henisch indirectly tells us about the impossibility and naiveté of this project by paraphrasing the language of Brinkmann in a way that borders on a direct quote. This naive fascination with pop culture is projected onto the narrator's former girlfriend Petra, who follows Morrison in order "to leave all that behind. The weather, relationships, my job, the political constellations" (70), i.e., all those things that in Brinkmann's words "continue to continue," constituting a process he would like to stop through the immediacy of poems constructed like pop songs.[9] In contrast to Brinkmann's poetry, to Petra's naive attempts, and to Morrison's manneristic excesses, Henisch's narrative apparently is supposed to serve up a version of pop culture that is loaded with historical significance. The interviews that Morrison grants Petra are perceived as too simplistic, and so are given the depth of intellectual history by the narrator Paul. The works cited in the course of the narrative and listed in the middle of the book (168-69) include everything from William Blake to Jean Baudrillard, from Mao to Marx and Marcuse, as well as Freud, Reich, and Bachofen, and, of course, Rimbaud, Artaud, and Cocteau. By nodding in the direction of scholarly writing through the playful placement of the bibliography in the middle of the book instead of at its end, Henisch adds another element to the hybrid that is his style of writing. At the same time, this allows him to take stock of the corpus of works that was on every good baby boomer's reading list, the works that formed the groundwork for the cultural revolution that was supposed to accompany the social one, the works that were supposed to infuse intellectual depth into the attacks on bourgeois high culture. This bibliography forms the link to intellectual history. Petra and her contacts with Morrison underscore the fascination with pop mass culture. And Morgenrot, Paul's publisher, grounds the narrative in economic reality, as he, though often reluctantly, supplies the cash for Paul's investigations. Thus, in addition to the meta-narrative on the contemporary difficulties of writing a novel or a biography, we find a meta-narrative about the economic predicaments of the author, thus forming a link to a tradition that goes back to writers such as J.R.M. Lenz (1751-92) and Goethe (1749-1832). In this attempt to rewrite the history of an era, Henisch wants to avoid the mistakes the iconoclasts made back then, but the reader who manages to stay alert soon becomes suspicious that the base of popular culture cannot carry this top-heavy construct.

Henisch himself, however, seems optimistic that he can achieve what he sets out to accomplish, namely, the formation of a new hybrid incorporating European intellectual history into American pop culture in accordance with his protagonist's pronouncements at the outset of the novel: "Because nowadays what else links . . . us authors to the people? . . . I've tried, my dear lady, to reestablish this link . . . Rock music, I thought, is the golden bridge" (68). This is Morrison's program, the program of a man who would have preferred to become a poet rather than a rock star. But towards the end of his American career we must hear the ugly words addressed to his audience, the people: "You're all a bunch of fuckin' idiots" (287). So it didn't work. "The alchemist process, set into motion with insufficient means, went awry, and the gold turned into shit" (68). But Henisch is not intimidated by this assessment. By retelling the story of this failure he is simultaneously attempting to establish a new link between the two poles. Having read Friedrich Schiller (1759-1805), he seems to be aware of the two ways of doing this, i.e., either pulling the masses up to one's own elevated position or lowering oneself to the intellectual lowlands. Henisch, however, wants to do neither. The multipolar oppositions introduced on various levels in this novel (narrative, cultural, gender-related, etc.), including the one between myth, poetry, and rock music, do not seem to be moving in the direction of a synthesis. No mediation is taking place; Henisch strives to come up with a new form that leaves intact the elements from which it is constructed. It is characteristic of Henisch's approach that he never stops at introducing only one dichotomy so that the reader is not tempted to anticipate a Hegelian synthesis from the interplay of just one thesis and one antithesis. There are always at least three poles between which the narrative moves. A synthesis does not seem desirable, as it often makes invisible the traces of the old in the new object it produces. Henisch takes care to preserve these traces as the lengthy quotes from his sources take on a life of their own—at times even to the point of testing the reader's patience.

A synthesis is often less than the sum of its original components. Henisch's efforts are not about a synthesis of the "summer of love" in places like San Francisco and the hot, political summer of 1968 in places like Paris, a synthesis that would combine the revolutions of the spirit in Europe with the revolutions of the body in the United States. The answer to what Henisch has in mind is again the creation of a new fourth element, and this particular example demonstrates what is always present as the third factor among the fields of tension in the narrative, namely, an element of tradition as historical depth. In the discussion above, this element was present as myth, as a form of narrative that goes back to the roots of all narrative traditions. We now find alongside the sensual-psychological and political components the entire and, one has to admit, predominantly European cultural history that is supposed to prefigure a new form of revolution. The unredeemed promise of the two revolutions cannot be fulfilled by adding one to the other; the vision of a different kind of revolution must include a continuation of everything that went before it. "If the hippie movement . . . really had encompassed the entire United States, you could have closed down the shop America" (196), we read in the novel about the "summer of love," on the one hand. On the other, we read about the hot summer in Paris: "Just imagine if this May here in Paris had been followed by a June" (196). In addition to these two components, the narrative contains a parallel history of the cult of Dionysus, whose last embodiment, Jim Morrison, makes the narrator confident enough to proclaim: "And as far as the social conditions, which are such that we didn't make them dance in '68, are concerned—well, the last word hasn't been spoken yet" (180).

But these examples—as well as Henisch's overall narrative form—also show the limits of his attempts to create something new out of what he has found. In the first case—a new form of culture—the predominantly European mythology provides the component of historical depth; in the second instance—a new form of revolution—the figure of Dionysus, who represents the same tradition, is supposed to play a similar role. In the case of the narrative form, that again is intended to prefigure something new generated out of the tension between at least three poles, and we once again find a European element meant to anchor it in history. The narrative is partially constructed out of the forms most appropriate to the era of mass media: the interview (that is, the fictional interviews Morrison grants Petra); the pop biography; and the golden oldie of European literary history, the "Bildungsroman" (i.e., the element that is to provide historical depth). The first two forms already combine aspects of popular and high culture, as historical curiosity and mythologizing fascination with celebrities cross-pollinate and also impede each other. The "Bildungsroman" is introduced by the narrator himself, whom his former girlfriend calls "a not quite successful attempt at being a writer" (139). Of course the narrator is intent on demonstrating the opposite, and wants to do so using Morrison's biography as his subject. We, in turn, have to admit that he has succeeded, since we do hold the result in our hands. The form of the biography is, according to the narrator, "a narrative alibi" (6), because today it is virtually impossible to write a novel "unless one is completely naive" (6). Of course it is obvious that he nevertheless wants to write a novel and, in his own opinion, he is successful: "While the advance that the publisher projected upon receiving half of the manuscript wouldn't get me all that far, a few days of rest that had nothing to do with the environment of *the novel* would do me good" (299). Despite the doomsaying of the publisher and the narrator's ex-girlfriend, something has come about that can, in fact, be called a novel. The "Bildungsroman" does not only relate the story of how the novel comes about and how the narrator learns to understand the object of his curiosity. On a structural level it is also about the attempt to find a form appropriate to this content. And this, too, Henisch believes he has accomplished. The novel begins with something the publisher has said, "I never really liked Jim Morrison, he said" (5), and ends with the narrator installing himself, with the help of his advance, in the hotel next to the park in which Morrison is hiding. Put quite simply, the first half of the manuscript must have convinced the doubting publisher.

One has to grant Henisch that he develops a way of writing that goes beyond the more traditional forms of collage and montage, and that he blends quotes and his own text in a way that maintains the autonomy of all of the constituent elements while creating something new as a result of their unique combination. The descriptions of pictures; the retelling of passages from movies; quotes from other biographies of Morrison; a commentary providing the perspective of intellectual history; the fictive elements telling the story of the narrator and his ex-girlfriend; and the meta-commentary about the problems of writing blend into one another in such a way that the reader is drawn unsuspectingly at first from one level to the next and accordingly becomes disoriented. In retrospect, however, one is always able to reconstruct the elements out of which the passage was built. At the same time, one begins to recognize the new way of writing that can grow out of this, a form of biography or historiography that seems to attribute to literature the new function of experiencing historical processes beyond the dichotomy of myth (which, in a sense, is an ancient form of pop biography) and scholarly writing.

This literary form of processing history does not depend

upon proving certain sources to be wrong or privileging others. It is neither about the representation of historic truth nor the repudiation of myths, but about a particular form of truth that offers an approach to a media phenomenon like Morrison. The most appropriate metaphor for this particular kind of historic event is the interdependence of voyeur and exhibitionist to which Henisch devotes most of his attention. It is the interdependence of rock star and admirer, each of whom cannot exist without the other. It is the tension between these two penchants—for observing and for being observed—that produces the milieu of the pop spectacle in all its aspects. If there is any truth to be found here, then it is a truth that is constantly being produced by this tension.

This interdependence finds its parallel in the relationship of the narrator to the subject of his narration. The novel unfolds out of the tension generated by the exhibitionist art of seduction practiced by Morrison and the voyeuristic desire to observe on the part of the narrator. By reenacting in his own narrative the process by which pop spectacles are being produced, Henisch provides the reader access to how this process works in other instances. This is precisely the narrative level on which Henisch also introduces his experiments with new gender relations that try to go beyond the usual dichotomies of male/female and homo/heterosexual. Within the fields of sexual charge generated between the four main characters of the text (the narrator, Morrison, Petra, and the publisher) various combinations of gender-specific attributes are enacted for each person as well as mixed forms of relationships between the genders. Here, too, we find the elements of the "Bildungsroman" as the narrator, who at first feels repelled by the unequivocally homoerotic signals emanating from Morrison and by the combination of gender attributes he embodies, opens himself towards the end of the novel to the attraction of Morrison on a video that he, out of what only looks like a coincidence resulting from the narrative, is only able to view in the cabin of a peep show. The video culminates in a shot in which Morrison's mouth draws near the microphone erected in front of him in a way that needs no further interpretation (211). In contrast to his initial homophobia, the enraptured narrator now calls Morrison a "tender blasphemous lover" (211). But he still recoils from the imagined invitation by Petra to a triangular relationship (257-58), though of course his imagination now speaks a different language. The narrator's slowly and painfully acquired openness toward gender relations that go beyond his fixation on Petra positively influences his writing. As he notes concerning the status of his text, "things are perking up" (271).

The mixed forms of gendered attributes in each character and the mixed forms of attraction between the genders are mirrored in the mixed forms of narrative voices in the text. These voices work through the entire spectrum of narrative perspectives, from the omniscient to the first-person narrator. In the process, these different narrative voices break up not only the gendered dichotomies but also the limits of individual identity and subjectivity because, although they all have equal weight, they do not add up to one collective voice. Henisch again creates a hybrid form in which the individual voices are not drowned out by the chorus of all the others. On yet another level, this narrative dynamic refers back to Henisch's visions of a new form of revolution, one that does not get bogged down by the contradictions between individual and collective political liberation.

Finally, there is a geographic, cross-cultural dimension to these attempts at hybridization. It is, after all, a book about the attraction between an Austrian and an American. Here, too, Henisch seems to attempt to break out of preconceived dichotomies. The characters of the novel represent the entire spectrum of Austrian/European attitudes toward American pop culture, from arrogant rejection to uncritical embrace. These attitudes, in turn, have been the driving force behind cultural politics in the German-speaking countries, accounting, on the one hand, for the stubborn insistence to keep the modernist avant-garde alive through public subsidies (and thereby save the culture of the Occident) and, on the other, for the euphoric imitation of boundless cultural commercialism, for the transformation of neo-liberalism into cultural marketing epitomized by the new phenomenon of commercially run musical companies on the outskirts of major European cities playing the canon of global Broadway hits several hundred times in a row while the avant-garde productions of classic plays in the inner cities draw fewer and fewer spectators. To do justice to Henisch's book, a stage production based on it would have to appeal to both audiences, playfully engaging the mental capacities of the "Cats" and "Phantom" fans while intellectually seducing the Peymann devotees and allowing them to enjoy themselves.

In this respect, the new hybrid type of cultural product exemplified by Henisch's book breaks up the traditional divisions between classes and disrupts the established practices of how they enjoy aesthetic objects as outlined in Bourdieu's study. Just as the new class has begun to blur the lines between the owners of the means of production and those who can only sell their labor to them, a book like *Morrisons Versteck* confuses any neat distinctions about how art is being enjoyed by different social classes. To the hard labor of the aesthetic asceticism of the middle classes has been added an element of playfulness; the education of the reader that is supposed to parallel the educational goals of the protagonist in the "Bildungsroman" does not so much require discipline as the willingness to put playfully at risk elements of the reader's identity—for example, his or her gender attributes. The upper classes' ownership of cultural capital in the literal sense, i.e., the actual ownership of works of art, has been turned into a repertoire of "quotables" that is supposed to attest to the owner's knowledge of aesthetic traditions but does not require a firsthand knowledge of them, a tradition reflected in the "reading list" in the middle of *Morrisons Versteck*. The only requirement is that one drops these names without revealing the lack of any further acquaintance with them. Finally, the issue of the use value of aesthetic objects important to the aesthetic preferences of the lower classes is here taken over by the function of the text as a form of biography and a new type of historiography. In short, then, the aesthetic preferences identified by Bourdieu for the three traditional social classes have been mixed and modified to meet those of the new hybrid class. In a very graphic sense, the order of the traditional bookstore or library is being disturbed. While *Morri-*

sons Versteck has, I assume, been designated as a "novel" for marketing purposes, without this marker a bibliographer would have difficulties in assigning the proper Library of Congress classification to the book.

But this disruption of established categories is itself only the reflection of a shift taking place beneath the surface, a shift in what it means to be a subject in the global marketplace. The blurring of the social borders that used to mark class differences is only the beginning of a redefinition of individual subjectivity in all its aspects, including those thematized in *Morrisons Versteck*: the new social mapping of cultural identity as well as a new view of cultural traditions; a mixing of gender attributes and forms of relationships between the genders; and new ways of expressing these new identities as reflected in the variety of narrative voices present in the text. As has often been the case, literature provides a kind of training ground for trying out these new subject positions. As it turns out, the individual subject, in its many transformations and in its ability to adapt to new social conditions, proves to be much more long-lived than one thought at the time when attempts to deconstruct it were first undertaken. The new subject does not fall apart as a result of contradictions, but rather emerges stronger from the process of playfully engaging them.

But this is also a case in point for Terry Eagleton's observations on the double-edged character of the sublime in bourgeois culture. The sublime serves to introduce the risks and, thereby, the fears associated with real dangers—for example, to one's subjectivity. It thus activates and keeps them alive but, at the same time, it tames them as an aesthetic construct.[10] Hence, the danger that is evoked is simultaneously represented as being subject to aesthetic control. As the worlds in which the new hybrid class moves are increasingly of a virtual nature, this latter aspect of the sublime seems to absorb the elements of risk and danger. "Let's run . . ."

Notes

1. Pierre Bourdieu, *Distinction: A Social Critique of the Judgement of Taste*, trans. Richard Nice (Cambridge: Harvard UP, 1984), here especially pp. 1-7, 22-35 and 39-63.

2. On the ubiquity of the tourist experience and its connection to the emergence of a "new leisure class," see Dean MacCannell, *Empty Meeting Grounds: The Tourist Papers* (London and New York: Routledge, 1992), especially Chapter 9, "The Desire to be Postmodern," and Chapter 10, "Spectacles"; and his *The Tourist: A New Theory of the Leisure Class* (New York: Schocken, 1989), especially Chapter 1, "Modernity and the Production of Touristic Experiences," and Chapter 4, "The Other Attractions."

3. See Andreas Huyssen, *After the Great Divide: Modernism, Mass Culture, Postmodernism* (Bloomington and Indianapolis: Indiana UP, 1986) pp. 15, 171-73, and especially 179-82, 196-98 and 216-21.

4. It should be obvious that my use of this term is very different from the ways in which, for example, Edward Said (in *Culture and Imperialism* [New York: Vintage, 1994] 317) or Homi Bhabha (in *The Location of Culture* [New York: Routledge, 1994] 38, 114, 242 and 251-52) use it. The main characteristic of the hybrid as used in this essay is the presence, within one aspect of an individual identity, of the juxtaposition of two elements structurally opposed to each other (for example, the juxtaposition of employee/shareholder) that have led earlier generations to some form of identity crisis. More examples will be discussed in the course of this essay.

Subsequent to the completion of this essay, a book-length study of this new hybrid class appeared: David Brooks, *Bobos in Paradise: The New Upper Class and How They Got There* (New York: Simon & Schuster, 2000). "Bobo" is short for "bourgeois-bohemian." Brooks uses the term "hybrid" very much in the sense that I do here. However, I locate the "bohemian" aspect of the hybrid identity more specifically in the rebellions of the 1960s, and I do not consider the marker "bohemian" to be specific enough, as it alludes to a lifestyle that already could be found in the nineteenth century.

5. The cover of Reinhard Mohr's book *Zaungäste: Die Generation, die nach der Revolte kam* (Frankfurt/M: Fischer, 1992) promises that this generation "will decisively participate in shaping the fate of the Federal Republic by the year 2000."

6. See note 3 and Judith Ryan, "The Problem of Pastiche: Patrick Süskind's *Das Parfüm*," *The German Quarterly* 63.3/4 (1990): 396-403.

7. See note 1.

8. Peter Henisch, *Morrisons Versteck* (Salzburg and Vienna: Residenz, 1991) 282.

9. Rolf Dieter Brinkmann, *Westwärts 1&2* (Reinbek bei Hamburg: Rowohlt, 1975) 6.

10. See Terry Eagleton, *The Ideology of the Aesthetic* (Oxford and Cambridge: Blackwell, 1990) 373.

"The Inner Movie Screen": Film in/and *Hoffmanns Erzählungen* and *Morrisons Versteck*

JENIFER K. WARD

The medium of film is a prevalent trope in several of the novels of Peter Henisch. His own father was a photographer for the National Socialist Party, and his early novel *Die kleine Figur meines Vaters* (initially published in 1975; *Negatives of My Father*, 1990) is an attempt to confront his father's role in the life and legacy of the Third Reich. In the first pages of that novel, Henisch describes the way the past and present are structured in his own mind as events played out on his "innere Leinwand" (inner movie screen). Combining his father's tool of the photographic image with his own tool of the written word, Henisch proceeds to produce narratives in subsequent works in which cinematic references reflect the importance of *both* image and text in his artistic endeavors. Whether exploring the interconnections between his father's past and his own present—as in *Die kleine Figur meines Vaters*—or seeking to create hagiographies of icons of Western culture, Henisch's narrative style in the two novels I will discuss in this essay,

Hoffmanns Erzählungen: Aufzeichnungen eines verwirrten Germanisten (1983, Tales of Hoffmann: Notes of a Confused Germanist) and *Morrisons Versteck* (1991, Morrisons Hideout), reveals a continuing preoccupation with the visual, both in form and content. After a very brief introduction to the two novels, I will begin my discussion by exploring in general some of the textual strategies common to the two works, with an eye toward whether they are truly filmic or simply a new feature of fiction writing. I will then discuss some of the strategies common to cinema, highlighting why these typically visual techniques are particularly interesting when applied to Henisch's verbal projects. Finally, I will discuss specific examples of the use of film and the use of the visual in the two texts themselves.

Both of these novels are fanciful and quasi-fictional accounts of the legacies of two eccentric figures in Western culture. *Hoffmanns Erzählungen* introduces us to a German professor who encounters a man claiming to be the reincarnation of the Romantic poet E.T.A. Hoffmann (1776-1822). *Morrisons Versteck* considers the proposition that Jim Morrison (1943-71) of The Doors is still alive and well—albeit elusive in a vampirish kind of way—and interacting with a photojournalist in Paris. In these two works, Henisch creates complicated structures to tell his stories. Using verbal equivalents of cinematic narrative strategies such as crosscutting,[1] Henisch mirrors the content of his stories, which themselves use screenplays, moviegoing, movie houses, and references to films to shape the landscapes in which the characters move. These landscapes—or "sets"—are decidedly postmodern. Marked by the suspension of spatial and temporal boundaries, the intersection of high cultural and pop cultural icons, and by a general fascination with schizophrenia and various hybridities, the worlds in these two novels constantly cross-pollinate one another, yielding works that, for the reader, are quite labyrinthine.

To say that a narrative is more like a film than a novel, however, is to assume an intact category of "novel structure." Furthermore, the kinds of strategies that appear filmic or cinematic in these narratives could just as easily be seen as symptomatic of postmodern fiction in general. Edward Branigan summarizes Sergei Eisenstein's description of the logic of cinema as one in which film data is arranged neither vertically nor horizontally, but "might be perceived as arranged vertically in matrix form, exhibiting a multiplicity of criss-crossing relationships in an instant."[2] But consider the way in which multiple levels of narrative are presented in postmodernist fiction. As Brian McHale has argued:

> Postmodernist fiction shares with classic modernist fiction an affinity for cinema (and more recently for television), drawing on it for models and raw material. . . . The movies and television appear in postmodernist writing as an ontological level: a world-within-a-world, often one in competition with the primary diegetic world of the text, or a plane interposed between the level of verbal representation and the level of the "real."[3]

McHale argues further that the kinds of temporal/chronological and spatial displacements we will explore in these two novels by Henisch are as symptomatic of postmodernist writing as they might be of cinema. And so, between the conventions of narrative cinema and the trends in certain kinds of recent fiction writing, both of which play with deconstructing easy notions of time and space, Henisch's work is located.

Expectations about the articulation of linear time, then, are of no help in Henisch's novels. Even such conventional devices as flashforward and flashback assume a single strand of time (x happened before or after y). And yet in these novels it is just as likely that a particular part of the story will be emplotted in a parallel world altogether. By this I do not mean that different parts of the story are hinted at simultaneously ("meanwhile, back at the ranch"), but that different parts of the story inhabit *one another* at one and the same time. In this way, the story moves not only chronologically but also spatially. A visual medium such as film allows the movement between different time and space planes to be executed more elegantly. Consider, for example, the recent example of the film *The Matrix* (1999). In this film the Keanu Reeves character is fundamentally transformed by his location in the respective "worlds" he inhabits onscreen. When in the pod, he has one physical appearance, and when in the matrix, he looks another way. Similarly, he is seen physically moving through barriers or falling through chutes as editing devices to move him between these worlds and to move the spectator from one scene to the next.[4]

It is the use of these *visual* cues that signals the move into a parallel world. No narrator or voice-over tells us in words what is happening, illustrating that film at least has the potential to destabilize our concept of linear time and unity of place in favor of simultaneity and multiple locations. The logic of the filmic experience—its ability to present concurrent actions simultaneously—is a paradox: on the one hand, chronology is suspended by the structuring of scenes and sequences. We are familiar with the example of crosscutting between the woman tied to the railroad tracks, the approaching train, and the hero barreling along on his horse to save the woman. It is clear to the viewer that these scenes represent actions that are occurring at the same time. On the other hand, the story is ultimately presented to the viewer in a sequential piece. There is, after all, a beginning, middle, and end to the physical strip of celluloid.

By the same token, time in the cinematic experience depends on our acceptance of a film world in which not all moments are documented. Indeed, film sequences shot in "real time" appear unnatural to us as spectators. In a verbal medium, one in which we can no longer rely on our eye ("seeing is believing"), we would expect to be given some sort of verbal guidepost to signal our location in time and space. In Henisch's novels this is achieved by a variety of means, which will be explored in the discussion of the individual works. One of the challenges of working with Henisch's texts, however, is that these changes in course—which are so negotiable in film—are sometimes *not* clearly marked in these novels, or are marked not by narrative clue but by visual hints (punctuation, unconventional spellings, etc.), leading to a reading experience in which nothing can be taken for granted.

But why employ this particular emphasis on film as narrative strategy and as content in these novels in the first place? Eva Schobel, in her 1987 dissertation on Henisch, argues that his difficulty in finding a mentor in his own emotionally unavailable father led Henisch to turn to so-called "geistige Väter"—spiritual and intellectual fathers who were also cultural figures of times past—to provide him with a model of how to be in the world.[5] E.T.A. Hoffmann's emphasis on the "Befreiung der Phantasie" (the liberation of one's fantasy from externally imposed influences) in his own life and work certainly applies to the cultural legacy of Jim Morrison and to Henisch himself. And both Hoffmann's work—in its "visualness"—and Morrison—as a cult figure—evoke the notion of spectacle, in the sense of visible and visual excess. Film, then, as a hybrid between the visual and the verbal, serves logically as the bridge on which Henisch stands to link him to these "fathers"—both real and "spiritual."

Indeed, as Craig Decker has pointed out in his discussion of *Die kleine Figur meines Vaters*, Henisch and his father found it difficult to get the "snapshots of memory" into any helpful chronological sequence, much less to get them to lead to any helpful understanding of a lived present.[6] Photographic images, by their nature, are static, frozen in the time that produced them. Film, on the other hand,—"moving pictures," "the movies"—is by nature dynamic, and allows sequences of static images to come to life, even if only as illusion. Thus, film not only serves as a hybrid between Henisch's tool (words) and that of his father (images), but film's dynamic nature also allows past, present, future, and parallel worlds to be grouped together in a single work.

Perhaps the multiple meanings of the word "projection" are helpful here. Projection in the psychological sense is certainly taking place in these novels, and in multiple ways: Henisch projecting his own identity questions onto his father(s); Henisch projecting himself onto his fictional characters—Kreisler, Hoffmann, Morrison, etc.; Henisch's fictional character Kreisler projecting himself onto the fictional character of Kowalsky who projects himself onto Hoffmann. There are more examples, to be sure, but even this brief list reveals the degree to which the projection of identity—and the instability of these projections—govern Henisch's narrative project. And what better way to cast light onto one's project than to *project*—in the filmic sense? Projection in this sense is to pass light through an image, using a mediating apparatus, onto a screen for all to see. In the case of Henisch the mediating apparatus is the written word rather than a film projector. And according to Schobel, these projections have their ultimate source in Henisch's unresolved issues with his father. Referring to *Hoffmanns Erzählungen*, she asks:

> Was Henisch, therefore, in pursuit of his own history as he wrote the Hoffmann story? Did he project in an uncritical way onto his esteemed colleague those things he believed to have found in himself, from childhood on? Once again, it would be too simple to see it that way. Because Hensich does project onto Hoffmann, but he projects logically what one would expect. That is, the projection does not lack a relationship to reality. Certainly, Henisch resonates with Hoffmann, and such resonance usually stems from a (real or imagined) similarity. Henisch believes he has discovered a soul mate (he says that he was not allowed to choose his own biological father, with whom he had a falling-out ten years ago, but that spiritual fathers are freely chosen).[7]

Whether or not Schobel is correct in her assessment of the close link between Henisch's father-issues and his choice of subject matter in his novels, the question is begged: did Henisch choose to use filmic form because he was dealing with "spectacular" protagonists? Or was he drawn to spectacular protagonists because film and spectacle were organic to his sensibilities? He was raised in a household, after all, where the image—the visual—was valorized over the verbal. One could say, therefore, that his epistemological "Bildung" (education) was steeped in the visual—and that, whereas these sorts of connections are addressed overtly in *Die kleine Figur meines Vaters*, they remain as residue in Henisch's subsequent works.

HOFFMANNS ERZÄHLUNGEN

The exposition of *Hoffmanns Erzählungen* foreshadows the many layers of narrative we can come to expect in this novel. Conventionally, we expect an exposition to provide us simply with an entrance to the narrative, and we further expect that subplots, additional characters, narrative emphases, etc., will be introduced gradually as the narrative proceeds. In *Hoffmanns Erzählungen*, however, the first several pages contain references to virtually all of the thematic and formal concerns that will structure the unfolding of the work. This stylistic approach—presenting multiple strands of a narrative side by side—is evocative of E.T.A. Hoffmann's own work as it is described by the protagonist Kreisler, and also mirrors one of the strengths of cinematic form: its ability to present simultaneously occurring strands of narrative by targeted use of editing strategies, particularly crosscutting (that is, editing between two or more lines of narrative that take place in different locations). These narrative threads, presented in epistolary form, comprise a complicated fabric in which stories contain other stories. These stories relate intertextually to one another as well, so that the reader encounters a textual structure in which linearity plays only an occasional role, and even the "layers-of-an-onion" approach normally associated with frame narratives falls apart.

The novel begins by signaling its epistolary form through the use of a greeting to the recipient of a letter. Within the title and the first few paragraphs, we learn that the writer is a confused Germanist named Kreisler who is a scholar of the Romantic poet E.T.A. Hoffmann, and that he is writing to a psychiatrist who is also a parapsychologist in order to unravel in his own mind the events he will describe. What is clear to him is that he is having a twofold crisis of identity. As a professional, he finds that he is unable to write easily and confesses to the doctor: "You might be thinking that, as a Germanist, writing—or at least transcribing—should come easily to me, or at least not be difficult. But you are reading—if, in fact, you wish to continue reading—the notes of a *confused* Germanist."[8] Personally, he has a sense that he has fallen into a sort of schizophrenia; that through his loss of critical distance he has allowed his own (auto)biography to merge with that of his object of study; and that the events he wishes to recount are "para"-normal in some way, occupying a hybrid space between fantasy and reality. Given the characteristics of his "case," therefore, he feels that a single therapist with expertise both in psychiatry and the paranormal will be most appropriate to offer him a diagnosis.

As Kreisler begins to try to explain the intricacies of his experience to the doctor, he finds that he is unable to tell his story in a conventional way. He states a desire to "write it all from beginning to end," but he feels that this structure would not be appropriate and that he should write it like "him" (Hoffmann). Unable to describe even the very dilemma of time and chronology without reference to past images ("rückblickend") and future narrative pieces ("vorgreifen"), he demonstrates the impossibility of writing about Hoffmann in an un-Hoffmann-like way. He likens the experience to existing outside of time and space: "I imagine myself to be a lost astronaut, falling out of the time and space continuum, no: more like floating" (12).

This crisis in chronology is no less troubling than Kreisler's conundrum with medium. He asks the doctor to lend him his ear, but then quickly replaces "ear" with "eye":

Simply write everything down, I thought, from beginning to end in a linear fashion. Although, even here at the beginning, I have the urge to violate this principle and get ahead of myself, like *him*, like the one you'll hear more about, the one who approached me after my lecture here in Berlin, that is, if you'll lend me your ear, or—more precisely—your eye, for a while. But no, the story, *my* story with Hoffmann, begins much earlier. You might think I'm taking this kinship obsession too far, but when I look back on it, it really seems it all began when my father, Anton Kreisler, married my mother, Gunda, and conceived me legitimately, resulting in my name also being Kreisler, not Johannes, of course, but Franz. I can't emphasize that enough, in spite of the fact that Julia, I mean Kitty, could not be deterred from calling me Johnny, but I really don't want to leap ahead. (6)

Here Kreisler also mentions the possible role his own name has played in the slippage of his identity into a Hoffmannesque world. Noting that he is Franz—and not Johannes Kreisler, Hoffmann's friend—he points out that even his paramour Kitty (whom he interchanges with Julia Marc, Hoffmann's music pupil and lover) will come to refer to him as Johnny. In this same opening section of his letter, he goes on to say that he had intended to write Hoffmann's biography and not his own, and yet he admits that it has become increasingly difficult to keep them separate, in spite of his doctoral advisor's admonition to beware of losing his critical distance.

Kreisler reveals that his particular interest in Hoffmann had already yielded a scholarly presentation, the occasion of which had brought him to Berlin. The description of his work, titled "On Late Romanticism and its Relationship to the Present, with Particular Emphasis on Schizoid Structures in the Work of E.T.A. Hoffmann," sounds ironic, especially given the constellation of concerns he has just outlined. He refers to the "zwiespältige Existenzform" (dual ontological nature) of the human condition and the literary products emerging from it. Referring to Hoffmann's style, he illustrates: "But you see, the placing together and then moving apart of two or more parallel strands of narrative is typical of his work. Here we have a rare coincidence of form and content. What usually does not come about (although this is principally what the works are about) is identity. One could say that Hoffmann's figures are always in search of themselves" (16). Indeed, this quest for identity comes to trouble Kreisler the more he enters into Kowalsky/Hoffmann's world. At first, it is simply a matter of losing his passport, but as the novel proceeds this practical "loss of identity" is accompanied by ever more confused references to Kowalsky as either Kowalsky or Hoffmann.

In a visual medium these confusions of identity would be easily marked. Perhaps we as spectators would see Kowalsky/Hoffmann from Kreisler's perspective through particular lens filters, or an editing device would aid us in discerning who was who at a given moment. Henisch has no such luxury. And still, since we as readers tend to *see* the print in front of us, Henisch has used visual cues to help us along. For example, Kowalsky as Hoffmann has a tendency to use antiquated language: "Aber wenn Sie mehr erfahren wollen, kommen Sie morgen zum Thee zu mir" (But if you care to learn more, please come to my house tomorrow for tea [30]). The addition of the "h" in the spelling of the German word for tea is an economical way of letting the reader in on the identity dynamics at play between Kowalsky and Kreisler. Furthermore, Kreisler indicates his confusion by referring to his new acquaintance as "Hoffmann-Kowalsky"; by admitting in his letter to the professor that, for simplicity's sake, he will refer to Kowalsky as Hoffmann; or by correcting himself: "'And at the same time,' said Hoffmann (I mean Kowalsky)" (72). Perhaps the most interesting *visual* cue, however, comes as Kreisler begins to lose track of where Kowalsky-Hoffmann ends and he, Kreisler, begins in the recounting of the following story:

> THE CAT and I, Professor—me and the cat . . . I, the way I write, he, the way he walks onto the lambskin rug in front of Kitty's bed with his large front paws, his eyes thoughtfully turned toward the ceiling . . . Me and the cat, Professor—the cat and I . . . He, the way he sits on the windowsill, his neck stretched out, his lower jaw twitching excitedly as he meows at the pigeons on the roof across the way, I, the way I write, the way I still write my (Hoffmann's ((Kowalsky's))) story, with which I want to be done, with which I must be done. (210)

The use of the triple parentheses indicates in a concise visual way the tangled interrelationship between the different strands of the narrative. In this example, we understand something about form—that several planes of the story are referred to at once—and we also learn something about content—that Kreisler has lost his critical distance so fundamentally that he no longer recognizes who he is or whose story he is telling. A summary of the rough contours of the narrative structure is as follows: Kreisler's letter to the psychiatrist serves as an outer frame device and positions him as a kind of "metanarrator." Contained within this frame is the story of Kreisler's relationship with the character Kowalsky, who believes himself to be the reincarnation of E.T.A. Hoffmann. Within this story is Kowalsky's reflection of his own awareness of himself as Kowalsky, but also of his "Hoffmann" self. Already we can see the "frame-within-a-frame" strategy collapsing, as we now have a bifurcated-schizoid level of narrative. As Hoffmann, he retells key events in the actual biography of Hoffmann. But as Kowalsky, he and Kreisler view a film he has made recounting this same biography, with himself playing the role of Hoffmann. Complicating the narrative further is the fact that Franz Kreisler begins to believe, as we saw above, that his own identity is being confused with the identity of Hoffmann's friend Johannes Kreisler. In addition, ancillary characters such as Kitty begin to merge with the women in Hoffmann's biography, Misha and Julia. Even the fictional "Kater Murr" (Tomcat Murr) appears both as Kitty's cat and as a reference in the recounting of Hoffmann's biography. At the same time, other uncanny occurrences serve to add to the narrative confusion and to Kreisler's growing identity crisis. For example, he discovers a photo of himself at Kitty's apartment, a photo of himself as a child in front of his childhood home, complete with house number. Seated next to him is Kitty, also as a child. Of course, Kreisler has only just met Kitty, and he is at least twenty years her senior. These "uncanny" occurrences are evocative of Hoffmann's stories, of course, and signal the dissolution of the boundary between the real and the fantastic, but they also serve as examples of the way in which different narrative worlds inhabit one another—as opposed to merely existing side by side—in Henisch's work.

In short, we are confronted with a narrative in which worlds lose both their temporal and spatial boundaries: past, present, and future are fluid, as are the boundaries between physical and psychic identities. In this sense, Kreisler's fear that he is beginning to suffer a kind of schizophrenic lapse is mirrored both by the schizophrenia of other characters on the level of content and by Henisch's employment of a "schizophrenic" narrative strategy on the level of form. And as I argued at the outset of this section, this strategy is evocative both of E.T.A. Hoffmann's own style and—most pertinent for this essay—also reminds us of some of the conventions of cinematic form. It is important to stress here that the use of what I call a verbal approximation of filmic crosscutting does not make this novel just like a film; it does not, in other words, simply adopt film form. And certainly I am not arguing that Henisch necessarily set out with the intention of finding a form that was somehow "filmic." Rather, I am pointing out that this particular narrative strategy has its most elegant expression in cinema; that cinema as a visual and verbal medium resonates with an author like Henisch for reasons discussed elsewhere in this essay; and that cinema as an imagistic medium is particularly logical as a modern way to approach the essence of E.T.A. Hoffmann's art. Indeed, both Henisch and Hoffmann could be described as verbal artists whose works contain particularly "visual" images. Recall, also, that Henisch frequently refers to his own mind as an "inner movie screen" on which these images are constructed; this reference appears in *Hoffmanns Erzählungen* (12) and in other works by Henisch as well.[9] Thus, while Henisch chooses to communicate his art through a verbal medium, it is always mediated through a visual sensibility and comes as the result of a creative process that owes much to cinema.

The strands of narrative hinted at above in terms of content are formally communicated in a variety of ways. As I mentioned, one strategy Henisch uses is to incorporate punctuation and archaic spellings as visual/verbal indicators of time and identity. In addition, film language is used to introduce and describe new scenes. Rather than having a prose narration outlining what a scene looks like and what action is contained within, we encounter a kind of storyboard style to situate us: "Extreme close-up of Julia. Extreme close-up of the consul's wife. Extreme close-up of Mischa. Graepel's fists clutching fork and knife. 'How do you mean that?' Then, coming to his senses, grinning again: 'Oh! You're referring to other circumstances'" (168). Unfortunately, it is not the case that these are stable markers. One might expect, for example, that these "storyboard" directions would always and only signal when part of Hoffmann's biography was being recounted. But Henisch is just as likely to usher in a narrative segment where Kowalsky and Kreisler are interacting in such a way, or when Kreisler is recounting part of the story to the doctor: "WELL, PROFESSOR ... here are a few childhood memories. For example, this one: it's Sunday morning. Characters in the scene: my father, my mother and me" (47).

I want to mention one more striking way in which film is present in *Hoffmanns Erzählungen*: by virtue of part of a screenplay which is inserted into the text. Kowalsky urges Kreisler to view with him the film he has made about Hoffmann's life. Leading up to the screenplay is Kreisler's depiction of his experience as a spectator. He recalls, for example, what the walk was like to the video studio and the experience of seeing the first images flicker on the screen. More importantly, he acknowledges the identificatory feelings he has as he watches Kitty and Kowalsky onscreen:

> Shot-reverse shot Hoffmann and Julia, Julia and Hoffmann. While playing four-handed piano his little finger diverges from the instructions in the sheet music and brushes hers. This ends in an almost lascivious embrace. Cut: her face in extreme close-up, her eyes closed, her nostrils vibrating, her lips parted. What did Hoffmann do? One did (she did) not see it. She dreamed, she fantasized, she wasn't there. Oh Julia, Käthchen, Kitty, you terrible angel! She was seductive, without meaning to seduce. (162)

Why is this particular scene so crucial for getting at the importance of film for *Hoffmanns Erzählungen*? If we accept that the fascination of this novel lies in the "schizophrenic" rendering of a Germanist's slip into the identity of his object of study, then the fact that it happens *here*—at the articulation of desire for the woman onscreen in a spectatorial experience—makes sense. Two of the most popular film theories circulating in the 1970s and 1980s concern themselves with just this intersection of issues: identity formation, on the one hand, and voyeurism and desire, on the other. Jacques Lacan's famous "mirror stage" in identity development—that moment in which a child is able to distinguish its own separate identity by seeing its image in a mirror—was adapted and adopted by film theorists. The movie screen became the mirror, and the spectator "became" the protagonist in a complex process of identification. At the same time, this process was only possible through voyeurism, and the object of sight was generally a woman. As the male spectator experienced his desire for the object of his vision, then, he identified with the male protagonist, thus allowing him to "possess" the woman.[10] And sure enough, Kreisler begins here to question himself. Whereas before he was only unsure of the boundary between Kowalsky and Hoffmann, he now begins to stumble in reference to himself and the degree to which a boundary exists between himself and Kowalsky and Hoffmann.

Ultimately, the novel ends with yet another letter to the professor. Kreisler does not recant having "met" Hoffmann, but rather relates the ways in which his encounter with Kowalsky led him out of a kind of identity crisis and into more clarity. Ironically, it took a total immersion in fantasy to lead him into a more realistic relationship with his wife and a recognition that writing biography was perhaps a better vocation for him. Looking forward to his next project, the subject of which he was already considering, he writes to the doctor, "Whether or not his reincarnation will also cross my path, that is certainly the question. But maybe I won't find that necessary, since I have accomplished one thing to a certain extent. With Kowalsky's help I have been able to liberate my fantasy, at least from the shackles of literary scholarship" (241).

Perhaps *Hoffmanns Erzählungen* can best be read as a "filmic" novel, or perhaps—following the maxim of E.T.A. Hoffmann/Kowalsky/Kreisler to liberate one's creativity from all strictures—simply as a prose narrative lifted from the authority of genre. At any rate, both in content and in form, the many visual images, instances of film language, and conventional film strategies in this novel contribute to a world in which an "inner movie screen" is perhaps the only place where the dreamlike quality of the narrative can make sense. Henisch's style, taken together with his employment of filmic imagery, reminds one of an old 16mm projector which, having encountered a technical glitch, begins spewing forth tangled cascades of film. The task for the reader of this novel, then, is to get at the way in which stories are nonetheless contained in those linear strips of film, in spite of the chaotic heap of "celluloid" on the floor.

MORRISONS VERSTECK

According to the dust jacket of the hardback edition of *Morrisons Versteck* (published in 1991 by Residenz Verlag), this novel is a "relationship-rich tapestry of parody and seriousness, fantasy and reality, irony and deep meaning."[11] Appearing several years after *Hoffmanns Erzählungen*, we recognize nevertheless one of the earmarks of that earlier work: a focus on the hybrid spaces between opposite poles— parody and seriousness, fantasy and reality, irony and deep meaning. In addition, we know that the subject of this novel, Jim Morrison, dead former lead singer of the rock band The Doors and one-time UCLA film student, represents for his era what E.T.A. Hoffmann personified as a nineteenth-century icon. Both figures were spectacular; both figures refused to be hemmed in by societal expectations; both searched for ways to free themselves from inhibitions to their considerable creativity and fantasy, and—in these characteristics—both resembled the author who would come to resurrect them in novel form, Peter Henisch.

Earlier in this volume, Friedemann Weidauer discusses the usefulness of the term "hybridity" for understanding what is at stake in *Morrisons Versteck*.[12] Indeed, the concept is relevant for *Hoffmanns Erzählungen* as well, both in its treatment of content and in its formal qualities. As a kind of intermediate genre incorporating aspects of screenplay, film, and novel, the text and its narrative strategies reflect the ways in which Kreisler and Kowalsky find themselves to be hybrids: embodying characteristics of multiple personalities and eras within their own ever-shifting identities. *Morrisons Versteck* employs similar strategies. The novel makes frequent references to film, but it also uses film language, snippets of screenplay, and actual instances of film screenings to reflect Jim Morrison's affiliation with film and the visual. Perhaps both novels also contain the implicit acknowledgment by Henisch that one genre, either verbal or visual, is simply inadequate for treating the kinds of larger-than-life, "spectacular" figures he wishes to represent. At any rate, the similarities between the two novels are notable, and I will discuss them in the pages to follow. Since I have already outlined the so-called filmic strategies in *Hoffmanns Erzählungen* in some detail, I will simply remind the reader that they are repeated in *Morrisons Versteck*. My treatment of this novel, then, will concentrate more fully on the ways in which the content—Jim Morrison's powerful legacy—intersects intertextually with another image-rich narrative of a charismatic figure, namely, the New Testament of the Christian Bible. The similarity in meaning between Weidauer's use of hybridity, on the one hand, and the etymology of the very visual Biblical genre of parable—the parabola—on the other, will serve as the bridge on which I will consider *Morrisons Versteck*.

I agree with Weidauer that hybridity is helpful in understanding Henisch. Certainly the understanding of the hybrid as being comprised of two phenomena or entities is interesting in the context of Henisch's repeated use of all manner of dualities: the use of the verbal and the visual in his narrative style; his discussion of schizophrenia; his bridging of English and German, Europe and America, and popular and high culture; describing characters like Morrison as vampire-like (a being both dead and alive) or Christ-like (a being both worldly and heavenly). But Henisch's idiosyncratic style also gets at another aspect of hybridity: its function as the new space created by the melding of two *or more* characteristics or valences or objects. Here the emphasis is on a transcendence of dichotomy, on the hybrid thing as a whole being more interesting or revealing than its constituent parts. It is this sense of hybridity—its dialectical features—that dovetails with one of the ways in which the use of film and the concept of hybridity intersect in a particularly interesting way in *Morrisons Versteck*.

Clearly Jim Morrison has been deified by many fans and admirers of his own and subsequent generations. Weidauer recalls in his treatment of *Morrisons Versteck* that Oliver Stone made a major motion picture in tribute to him at roughly the same time Henisch wrote his novel. And the continuing throngs of mourners and gawkers at his grave in Paris bear witness to this deification. I want to suggest, then, that in light of the deification of Jim Morrison we think of the intersection between film and hybridity as evocative of *parable*. According to the definition of "parable" in the *Theological Dictionary of the New Testament*, parable is related to the geometric term "parabola," which denotes a figure with two sides that move toward and away from each other. This is akin to Kreisler's description of E.T.A. Hoffmann's writing style (the two strands of narrative); reminds us of the dual nature of the dialectic and its synthetic impulse; and is also representative of Henisch's own style—both in *Hoffmanns Erzählungen* and *Morrisons Versteck*. Parable is also typically understood as a "scene" within the Gospels that serves to illustrate a particular point, in contrast to a verbal recitation. In German theological parlance, the illustrative and figurative nature of parable is even referred to sometimes as "Bildersprache" (literally, picture language).[13] The twofold connotation of parable also reminds us of one of the recurring motifs in *Morrisons Versteck*, namely, that of a statue of Janus, the two-headed god of doors and gateways who looks in two directions at the same time. Moreover, it is also the case that Morrison is likened to Christ in a number of passages in *Morrisons Versteck* (for example, 178-79, 194, 277-78, 281, 294). The parables in the Bible are often used to direct us to eschatological concerns (the end time),[14] which also becomes relevant given the final pages of *Morrisons Versteck*. But perhaps most importantly, the very act of retelling a story—as Paul does in this novel with Morrison's biography—is parabolic.

In what follows, then, I will summarize the narrative project of *Morrisons Versteck* and then turn to a discussion of the "parable" of Jim Morrison. Finally, I will return to the formal affinities—as well as the many comparisons on the level of content—this text shares with *Hoffmanns Erzählungen*, particularly in regard to the use of film metaphors and attention to the visual. Since the narrator of *Morrisons Versteck* sums up the nature of the novel himself on more than one occasion, I will offer one of those instances here. In a conversation with Morgenrot, a friend who might be helpful in publishing his project, the narrator—a journalist—Paul writes:

> Have you still not given up that Morrison project?
> You don't look well. That story is eating at you.
> Of course. The question is, which story. The one with Morrison or the one with Petra.
> But for me the stories couldn't be separated.
> Okay, listen, I said: the female protagonist (Petra) imagines she has found the supposedly dead Jim Morrison in his hideout.
> And the male protagonist (Paul), who receives her letters, doesn't quite know what to make of them, but the content of the letters, regardless of whether his rational consciousness believes it or not, haunts the inside of his head day and night. (48)

What is not clear from this passage is that the recounting of this conversation with Morgenrot, as well as the letters Paul receives from Petra, are part of a larger story in which Paul chronicles his own involvement with the biography of Jim Morrison. Essentially, the story is simple. Paul reconnects with Petra after many years as she begins to send him letters about her encounters with Jim Morrison, whom she believes to be alive. As Paul recalls the times he had spent with Petra—recalling the plots of favorite films while together in the bathtub, for example—he also becomes seduced by the fantastic stories she recounts about Morrison. Whereas Paul began as a skeptic, we see him becoming increasingly interested in the myth of Morrison, so much so that he eventually embarks on a journey to discover the "truth" about Morrison—even if, at first, only to appease Petra and assist her in her own research. Paul's travels take him to Paris and to America, from where he corresponds all the while with Morgenrot, educating the reader, in the meantime, about Morrison's life. As he moves deeper into Morrison's biography, he becomes more and more obsessed with him, an obsession that corresponds to a crisis in writing: "I have to bring order into my thought processes. I have to bring order into my notes. I have to hold onto what is threatening to derail" (181).

Moving back and forth between diary entries and letters (both by Petra and Paul), straight narrative, film scenes, verbatim English passages from other published biographies of Jim Morrison, and text from The Doors' album covers and the like, the novel is a pastiche of fragments from multiple layers of time, extending from Morrison's birth in the 1940s to the time of Paul's narrative (presumably in the late 1980s). In terms of space, the text traverses the Atlantic Ocean and goes from Paris to the entirety of North America, from California to New Mexico to Florida, and to many places in between. As evidenced by the passage above, dialogue and narrative in *Morrisons Versteck* do not always stem from a clearly identifiable point of view and often combine thoughts or quotes from a variety of characters into one utterance. For example, a common feature of *Morrisons Versteck* is its hybridization of English and German and narrative voice. Consider the following:

> On December 8, 1943, James Douglas Morrison joined the wartime baby-boom, so ein haarsträubender Blödsinn!
> I joined nothing. Ich bin überhaupt nicht gefragt worden!
> Wie kommt man dazu: eine Seele, herumflanierend, free & easy, in so was hineingezogen, hineingesogen zu werden: eine American-way-of-life Umarmung?

Und dann aufzuwachen in Melbourne, Florida, near what is now Cape Canaveral: Da kannst du tatsächlich nur schreien, bis der Kopf rot wird!
Jim's father left him at six months to go back to the Pacific to fly Hellcats—wäre er doch gleich zur Hölle gefahren!
Die nächsten drei Jahre putzteufelte die Mutter in Clearwater, Florida, das hieße weit treffender Aqua Destillata.
Noch cleaner als sie waren nur meine Großeltern, Queen Victoria und ihr vertrocknender Prinzgemahl.
Rauchen: verboten; trinken: verpönt; Sex: völlig indiskutabel—mein Dad ist, das sieht ihm ähnlich, durch Knospung entstanden. (7)

(On December 8, 1943, James Douglas Morrison joined the wartime baby-boom, what hair-raising nonsense!
I joined nothing. I wasn't even asked!
How does one get to that: a soul, sauntering along, free & easy, to get pulled into such things, to get *sucked* in: embracing the American-way-of-life?
And then to wake up in Melbourne, Florida, near what is now Cape Canaveral: you just want to scream til you're red in the face!
Jim's father left him at six months to go back to the Pacific to fly Hellcats—if only he had gone straight to hell!
His mother spent the next three years hanging out in Clearwater, Florida, a more fitting name would be Aqua Destillata.
Only my grandparents were cleaner than her, Queen Victoria and her dried-up prince consort.
Smoking: forbidden; drinking: prohibited; sex: completely unmentionable—my Dad, that would suit him, came about through budding.)

Combining bits of Morrison's biography in English with Paul's musings about him ("How does one get to that") and Morrison's fictional commentary about his own life history, Henisch yields up a narrative ball of yarn in which the reader has no easy time untangling the strands. Ironically, the passages in which film language is inserted into the text appear as a relief: "*Outside. Still nighttime.* She (Petra) flying through the park" (108). This, by the way, is one of the striking characteristics of Henisch's style. By offering standard verbal narrative in such a complicated—and, thus, alienating—form, Henisch's divergences from standard verbal narrative come to appear natural and seamless, as welcome smooth strands in an otherwise tangled weaving-together of multiple elements. Hence, the use of film references—which should be the alienating formal element—ultimately provide clarity and stability to the text. In other words, this fairly simple story as outlined above (what happens) becomes quite complicated as a plot (how the story is told).

I want to highlight only two aspects of the story for discussion here, because they strike me as indicative of the way in which Henisch's interest in the power of the visual and his search for "spiritual fathers" intersect. The first instance occurs when Paul is in California working on the Morrison biography. He has concerned himself with Morrison's beginnings as a film student at UCLA and has interviewed former instructors, looked over Morrison's required student film project, and the like. He then comes across a copy of a documentary video on the history of The Doors. Since Paul is staying in a cheap motel, he has no access to a videocassette player in which to play the tape, so he heads out in search of one to rent. However, he stumbles across a pornography store advertising video booths, and so he asks the store clerk to let him watch the video in one of the booths. The clerk is understandably quite perplexed that someone would want to forego the available videos at the store and would be willing to pay money to watch rock concert footage instead. Still, he agrees, and Paul enters the booth. The experience of watching the video is recounted in pages and pages of detail. We have described for us the action on screen, certainly, but also the ambient sound of other videos and their spectators in the neighboring video booths as well as Paul's increasing sense of fascination and concurrent discomfort as he looks at the sensual and androgynous images of Morrison. Paul returns to the store more than once to watch the film, and then something curious happens:

> It was different than the last time, this time the tape didn't begin running from bottom to top, but simply went dark. It must have turned itself off, because the screen suddenly seemed like a mirror, in which I saw my own image. I didn't like the way I looked, my hair was even more unkempt than I had remembered it. And I had deep, dark rings under my eyes.
> But I didn't have much time for self-pity, because in the next moment the locked door opened behind me, and a second person, namely, Petra, squeezed into the booth meant for one. (231)

Again, let us recall Lacan's mirror phase as it applies to film theory and Mulvey's theory of identification and voyeurism in the narrative cinema. As was the case with Kreisler in *Hoffmanns Erzählungen*, the protagonist in *Morrisons Versteck* has a moment of identification in the context of a cinematic experience. Paul's desire for Petra is mediated by his desire for the image of Morrison, even as he recognizes himself in the fading image of Morrison on the video screen. Shaken and alienated by this experience, he leaves the store, gets drunk, and returns to sleep in his motel room. When he awakens, he has an epiphany as he realizes the seductive power of the self-constructed spectacle of Morrison: "And I didn't want and don't want my soul to be led by (seduced by) Morrison. I wouldn't play his little game" (236-37).

This sense that Paul has become aware of having fallen under the spell of Morrison coincides with his sense of resolve that he will write this story and have it published. Up to this point, Paul has been ambivalent about what his research will lead to; he vacillates between thinking that he is working on his own project and thinking that he simply wishes to help Petra with her search for information about Morrison.

Ironically, the point in the story where Paul gains this resolve is near the end of the recitation of Morrison's biography. In the novel, he is already in Paris in those last fateful days before he was found dead in a bathtub. So as Morrison is about to die on one narrative plane, and even though on another plane Paul has claimed not to want to give up his soul to Morrison, we see Paul coming to terms with his newfound sense of himself as a quasi-disciple.

Jim Morrison as Christ; the traveling apostle Paul writing epistles about him; Petra—in a reversal of the story of Peter's denial of Christ—asking people if they have seen Morrison ("Do you know this man?") and being told, no, they do not know him (for example, 13, 41, 43). These adaptations of Biblical references are peppered throughout the novel, and certainly evoke recollections of other "spiritual fathers" and messianic narratives. Indeed, the moments in the text leading up to Morrison's death remind us of the crucifixion of Christ as depicted in the Gospels and end with the description of Morrison's dead body cast in the image of the body of Christ on the cross: "His arms resting on the porcelain sides, his head leaned back, his long wet hair matted against the rim, a boyish smile across his clean-shaven face" (295).[15] The parable of Morrison in this text, then, is one of a media spectacle, whose charisma and androgynous appeal have led countless numbers to follow him, to continue to believe in his power, to keep watch by his grave, and to write biographies about him. Even the objective journalist's critical distance is no match for the magnetic draw of his timeless legacy. In a passage recounting Paul's travels in a manner evocative of the Book of Acts, the novel ends with Paul leaving Paris after the completion of the Morrison project. He travels by train to a destination elsewhere in France—which he believes will afford him much needed rest and no memories of Morrison—and rents a car. He drives only a short while before realizing that he has lost all orientation. He circles around, passing things he has seen before, and then finds himself in unknown territory again.[16] Finally, he stops in a bar for a bite to eat and inquires about a hotel. He is told that he is, in fact, already there, and that the entrance is around the corner:

And not at all far away. Here in this house, to be precise. The entrance is right around the corner.
   Sure enough, I now noticed that the name of the hotel must have once been on the peeling wall of the house over the veranda you could still sit on, even though it was winter according to the calendar.
   But most of the letters were only present as shadows, and only an A and an O remained. (300)

Paul checks into his room and falls into a heavy sleep. When he awakes the next day, he throws open the window. The final sentences of the novel read: "The next morning I threw open the window. There I saw the wall. And behind it the garden" (300). After all his attempts to flee from Morrison, he has ended up at the beginning, at the place described by Petra as the "Versteck" (hideout) of Jim Morrison. On the last page of the novel, then, just as the hotel's name with its A and O reminds us of the last page of the Book of Revelation in the Bible, we face the end time, the eschaton, which is also a beginning:

   See, I am coming soon; my reward is with me, to repay according to everyone's work. I am the Alpha and the Omega, the first and the last, the beginning and the end.
   Blessed are those who wash their robes, so that they will have the right to the tree of life and may enter the city by the gates. (Rev. 22.12-14)

Henisch thus ends his novel with a passage that points to one of the most visual of all the books in the Bible, to the last page of the last book of the New Testament, reinforcing the image of Morrison as someone whose mythology has escalated to the point of being compared to a living Messiah. The ordering of the New Testament does not follow a linear chronology, and some sections of the New Testament were written after the Book of Revelation. So even the formal structuring of what we think of as "first" and "last" in the narrative about Christ recalls Henisch's own narrative tendencies in *his* telling of parables of other "spiritual fathers." And finally, the Revelation reference points back, in circular fashion, to the Henisch text with its use of the image of gates.

CONCLUSION

Janus, god of gates and doors, depicted with two faces looking in opposite directions, also forms the root of the word January, the month that looks back to the previous year and forward to the new one. It is perhaps no surprise, then, that Henisch uses Janus as a recurring motif in the Morrison novel, since it is such an apt symbol to represent the bridging of the two sides of this particular parabola: a novel comprised of spatial and temporal dualities, certainly, and filled with visual and verbal references to characters and occurrences marked at every turn by the way in which they defy unitary understanding.

Janus might be considered an appropriate symbol for *Hoffmanns Erzählungen* as well. As we saw in the discussion of that text, many of the "hybridities" at work in *Morrisons Versteck* were already present in that earlier novel. Both works are concerned formally with depicting action on multiple planes of time and space. The beginning of *Hoffmanns Erzählungen*, let us recall, refers to Kreisler's confusion as to whether to look backward or forward, and the end of *Morrisons Versteck* invokes the beginning and the end, the Alpha and Omega, as well. And both novels attempt to bridge the space between visual and verbal varieties of mediation, as Henisch uses film references, film language, and sometimes even film form to communicate the stories he wishes to tell.

In addition to the concentration on hybridities, though, the novels mirror each other in other ways as well. Both novels are "epistolary"—using letters to structure much of the narrative—and biographical. Moreover, both novels wrestle with the problem of identity, which leads to a crisis in writing. And with both protagonists, the crisis comes to a head in a moment of identificatory desire while confronting a cinematic image. Kreisler's triangle with Kitty and Kowalsky mirrors Paul's triangle with Petra and Jim. What I want to highlight here, therefore, is that in Henisch's texts the notions of interweaving parallel strands of narrative, of the primacy of the visual, of the bridging of hybridity, and of temporal movement into the past and toward the future find expression in multiple stories. Henisch repackages them, to be sure, in ways that are unique to the subject matter he explores. But they are nevertheless images composed visually, albeit in a verbal medium. And in the two cases under discussion here, the "spiritual fathers" E.T.A. Hoffmann and Jim Morrison, although eras apart, come to show themselves in these narratives in ways that evoke the "inner movie screen" Henisch first came to articulate in reference to his own biological father, the photographer.

Notes

1. David Bordwell and Kristin Thompson, *Film Art: An Introduction*, 4th ed. (New York: McGraw-Hill, 1993) 493.
2. Edward Branigan, *Narrative Comprehension and Film* (London and New York: Routledge, 1992) 35.
3. Brian McHale, *Postmodernist Fiction* (London and New York: Routledge, 1996) 128.
4. *The Matrix*, dir. Larry and Andy Wachowski, Warner Brothers, 1999.
5. Eva Schobel, *Peter Henisch: Eine Monographie*, diss., U Vienna, 1987 (Vienna: Verband der wissenschaftlichen Gesellschaften Österreichs, 1988) 482.
6. Craig Decker, "Photographic Eye, Narrative I: Peter Henisch's *Die kleine Figur meines Vaters*," *Monatshefte* 83.2 (1991): 147-60. See especially pp. 156-57.

7. Schobel 481-82.
8. Peter Henisch, *Hoffmanns Erzählungen: Aufzeichnungen eines verwirrten Germanisten* (Munich: Nymphenburger, 1983) 5-6.
9. This reference also occurs in *Die kleine Figur meines Vaters* (Salzburg and Vienna: Residenz, 1987 [for example, pp. 33 and 47]) and in *Vom Wunsch Indianer zu werden: Wie Franz Kafka Karl May traf und trotzdem nicht in Amerika landete* (Frankfurt/M: Fischer Taschenbuch, 1996 [16]).
10. For a discussion of film theory, desire, and identification, see Laura Mulvey, *Visual and Other Pleasures* (Bloomington and Indianapolis: Indiana UP, 1989), especially 14-29.
11. Henisch, *Morrisons Versteck* (Salzburg and Vienna: Residenz, 1991).
12. See Friedemann Weidauer's essay "The Lizard-King Can Do Anything: Hybridity and the Cultural Logic of Globalization in *Morrisons Versteck* " in this volume.
13. For a discussion of the etymology of parable, see "Parable," *Theological Dictionary of the New Testament* (Grand Rapids, MI: Eerdmans, 1967) 744-61. For a description of parable as "Bildersprache," see 752, note 55.
14. *Theological Dictionary of the New Testament* 758. My thanks to Faith Kirkham Hawkins and Brian T. Johnson for their considerable help in discussing the New Testament with me.
15. This scene also evokes Jacques-Louis David's famous painting from 1793 depicting the death of the revolutionary Jean-Paul Marat.
16. See The Book of Acts for a discussion of Paul's travels.

A Morphology of Fragments in *Hoffmanns Erzählungen*

BOHDAN BOCHAN

> Everything is a seed.
> —Novalis[1]

Among the many prose works of Peter Henisch, one that merits special attention is the novel *Hoffmanns Erzählungen: Aufzeichnungen eines verwirrten Germanisten* (1983, Tales of Hoffmann: Notes of a Confused Germanist), not only because of its labyrinthine narrative itinerary but also for its curious, if not bizarre, subject: retelling the life of the writer E.T.A. Hoffmann (1776-1822). A scholar named Franz Kreisler chronicles fragmentary reminiscences from Hoffmann's life told by an actor who believes he is a reincarnation of the nineteenth-century writer. As the title suggests, the novel will describe the narrator's encounter with this pseudo-Hoffmann. A series of forty-two fragments, the authorship of which alternates between the narrator and his interlocutor, results from this encounter. These shifting viewpoints form a structural fissure within the novel which is maintained through the ambivalent use of the name Hoffmann, a name denoting not only the historical person but also the actor impersonating him. This initial ambiguity intensifies when the narrator introduces himself as Franz Kreisler, using the same last name the author E.T.A. Hoffmann used for a main character in a collection of stories as well as for signing his own famous music reviews in journals. In both instances, the name Kreisler intimates characteristics of E.T.A. Hoffmann himself. By using these two names, Peter Henisch, in turn, thematizes a twofold world, i.e., that of the historical E.T.A. Hoffmann intertwined with the contemporary one, both of which are authored by Kreisler/the narrator and Hoffmann/Kowalsky. While following these shifting points of view, the reader journeys through a space in which both realms interact.[2]

By virtue of this organic ambiguity embedded in the novel's texture, one is tempted to conclude that Henisch is intentionally rewriting the biography of a known literary figure in order to explore the phenomenon of ambiguity and its diverse modalities in relation to the human condition.[3] This objective seems to be his primary concern, especially if we think of the background events prompting the composition of the novel. Elaborating his reasons for writing the novel, the scholar-narrator provides some information about himself and his interest in E.T.A. Hoffmann. The reader finds the narrator in a very precarious mid-life crisis. Confused and dissatisfied with his university career, he changes course by becoming a free-lance writer working on a biography of E.T.A. Hoffmann.[4] For this purpose he leaves the city of his employment, travels at first to Königsberg and later to other cities where E.T.A. Hoffmann resided, and finally moves to Berlin to deliver at the university a lecture entitled "The Relationship of Late Romanticism to the Present with Special Consideration of the Schizoid Structure in E.T.A. Hoffmann."[5] It is here during the lecture that he meets Lescek Kowalsky, a former actor who thinks of himself as the reincarnation of E.T.A. Hoffmann and behaves accordingly, reenacting and recounting in detail episodes from Hoffmann's own life. The narrator becomes so fascinated by this conscious identification with the historical writer that he writes a letter—the novel—to a parapsychologist asking him about the possibility of such an event occurring.[6]

Already here at the outset begins the circular movement of the narrative with the narrator masterfully widening its orbit in order to bring into relief the chasm separating the nineteenth century from the last quarter of the twentieth. The storyteller appears to be particularly drawn to the rift separating these two epochs, a rift reflected not only in the schizoid being of Hoffmann the imposter but also markedly grafted upon the social body of modern times. Speaking of his lecture in Berlin, the narrator comments: "My fundamental thesis actually dealt with the schizoid existence imposed on the sensible spirit (ha, ha, spirit!) by certain societal conditions" (16).[7]

Instead of limiting his discussion to the seminar, the narrator develops it into the actual project of the whole novel. Not only does he delve into the split personality of the protagonist, but he also concurrently investigates the chronic breaks occurring within human history. Thus, the initial signs of ambiguity contained in the title of the novel foreshadow an overall climate of disjunction that will permeate subsequent happenings. To be more precise, the element of ambiguity, confined at first to the framework of the story, eventually will give way to open dichotomies whose territory will be markedly enlarged as the novel proceeds from an individual to a more universal dimension. The immediate outgrowth of these dichotomies will be the possibility of change in the seemingly immanent history of the contemporary world. What immobilizes history is the human tendency toward uniformity and security as mirrored in the powerful concept of identity with its monolithic constitution. *Hoffmanns Erzählungen* attempts to dismantle such a notion of identity fostered by logocentric categories of the past. Retracing the past, the novel will reassemble known facts into hitherto unknown configurations.[8]

Of course, this attempt is not new, especially in light of Romantic predilections for dealing with the archeology of the past. However, what is new in the novel is a historically motivated need to deconstruct the authority of the concept of identity on behalf of an experience of difference. In contrast to the Romantics' infatuation with historical continuity, Henisch stresses the significance of alterity, adumbrated already in the idea of ambiguity which is present not only in names but also in the semantics of human language: "But you see, the placing together and then moving apart of two or more parallel strands of narrative is typical for [Hoffmann's] work. Here we have a rare coincidence of form and content. What usually does not come about (although this is principally what the works are about) is identity" (16). This critical remark about E.T.A. Hoffmann's metamorphic writing style, wedged between proximity and distance, emphasizes the centrifugal forces in his texts which refuse any convergence of life's properties into a single, finite center invested with a firm identity.[9] A similar attempt to undermine identity is made in *Hoffmanns Erzählungen*, as the protagonist's life becomes severed from a familiar environment and he himself floats adrift in a threshold situation with a dichotomized identity, belonging neither to the past nor to the present: an outsider *par excellence*, inventing himself in the course of narration!

The lack of a cohesive identity accelerates the flow of events in the novel, starting with the location in which events come into being: the ambiguous postwar status of the divided city of Berlin with its inhospitable and uniformed opaque appearance. Everything and everyone residing in this metropolitan twilight bear traces of a lifestyle suspended between bleak everydayness and the desire to break out into the open, into freedom. Hoffmann the actor reminds Franz Kreisler of the shifting ground beneath the city dwellers whose mask-like appearance is concealed in innumerable hidden layers: "I saw him double. 'Oh yes, my dear!' he said, as if he had guessed it. 'Sometimes dear reality appears multiple to us. And believe me, it not only appears that way, it *is* so! In wine lies the truth. For sure. In this I am an expert. Look around. The faces. Behind each one there is another! At least one. Among them, animal faces. And plant faces'" (22). To undermine the concept of identity further, a moth with which the narrator spends the night after his first meeting with Hoffmann the actor takes away his passport. The narrator's inordinate reaction to this loss is indicative of the pivotal role the concept of identity plays in human affairs: "I needed my passport. The proof of my identity" (30). This statement implies the importance attached to the concept of identity throughout history, in spite of its lack of a substance. Its real value amounts to a piece of administrative paper. Instead of liberating the subject, identity papers in this instance lead to confinement. The narrator is forced to stay in Berlin, becoming the captive of a captive city: "I had resisted this psychopath and this city, both in vain. I? That was funny—without proof of my identity in my pocket I really had a feeling of a kind of depersonalization" (31).

Returning to the question of identity on several occasions, the novel initiates a process deconstructing traditional, categorical ways of thinking which, in alliance with the ubiquitous presence of ambiguity, aims at loosening the soil of rigidly organized institutionalized life. Feeling himself depersonalized, the author will un-define his immediate world, making the normative fabric of his environment more open and flexible so that it will permit centrifugal forces of life to proliferate. The extent to which he succeeds in this task can be measured by his ability to surreptitiously implant into the texture of the novel from the very beginning the idea of a migrating, porous identity caught in an endless process of alteration and becoming. Expanding the novel's narrative space, the narrator simultaneously broadens the scope of man's thinking to accommodate the ambiguous adventures of a mind within boundless horizons.[10] What will progressively evolve from the relentless movement of deconstruction will be the sweeping dynamics of a creative fantasy which will underpin and direct human endeavors. It is fantasy in the sense of a spontaneous, formative force of thinking that fashions out of nothing a figurative representation of objects and material for the make-up of a new world. Peter Henisch fully avails himself of this organ to reconfigure the past by letting fantasy intervene in the survival effort of E.T.A. Hoffmann's great mind. But even more so, he uses the same force of fantasy to oppose any social order conceived by teleological thinking, which always terminates in catastrophe—e.g., the Napoleonic Wars, as well as more recent ones.[11]

Before the narrator embarks on these liberating movements of fantasy, he describes the reasons for his own departure from the university and explains his decision to write a biography of E.T.A. Hoffmann. The narrator sees this project as an escape from the daily inertia of his teaching profession: "my fantasy is fettered in every respect by this type of life, and probably not only mine" (9). Alluding to the decline of his creative power, the narrator touches upon a main concern of Henisch himself: the ominous flight of fantasy from the contemporary scene.[12] By resurrecting the historical E.T.A. Hoffmann in a novel, Henisch endeavors to regenerate the power of fantasy inasmuch as it safeguards human freedom and directs its meaningful employment. What the twentieth century lacks, according to Henisch, is precisely fantasy and, consequently, freedom: *"Modern man does not even make any demands on his fantasy. He does not notice the terror perpetrated [against him], he allows himself to be hooked. Whereas, I believe, all the way up to Romanticism, the connection between freedom, fantasy, and life was, to a large extent, taken for granted"* (ZS 154). In writing *Hoffmanns Erzählungen*, Peter Henisch stresses the essential responsibility of a writer vis-à-vis his or her readership to defend and promote the work of fantasy from a personal as well as social standpoint. It is for this reason that the author-narrator retraces the footsteps of E.T.A. Hoffmann's life, focusing especially on episodes where the play of fantasy performs a liberating role in the life of the narrator as well as in the life of two other protagonists, Lescek Kowalsky and Kitty.

To appreciate the scope and significance allotted to fantasy in *Hoffmanns Erzählungen*, a few additional remarks by Henisch on this subject will be very helpful, especially since the role fantasy plays in the novel is not only aesthetic but also epistemological. Revealing the productive quality of fantasy, the novel performs a double function: it entertains while simultaneously advocating a new, creative way of thinking,

A Morphology of Fragments 107

one unencumbered by any dogmatic weight. Henisch defends this position in his critical observations: "*In the past people waited until someone stopped by and performed a concert. Today people turn on the radio. But instead of enrichment, this is an impoverishment. Curiosity is completely blunted, information dwindles away, every form of productivity is lacking, and the vacuum is replaced by a mentality of consumption*" (ZS 140). This emptiness of modern life can either be perfunctorily alleviated by a shopping spree or it may solicit a new power to emerge, since the phenomenon of emptiness is not just a passive state but also a state of receptivity in which fantasy may take root and grow into a legislative force of openness. For Henisch the critic, this second possibility is urgently needed: "*To restore power to fantasy means that creativity comes into politics again. The success of 1968 was insufficient. But still the separation of the real from the possible was perceived as false, because n o t h i n g is p o s- s i b l e once fantasy is eliminated*" (ZS 155). The possibility of any development and change is predicated on the creative power of fantasy because the real harbors within itself the matrix of the possible, in the sense that the real is always subject to metamorphosis.

Transforming things and issues, the power of fantasy is capable of delivering freedom precisely because of its ability to carve fissures and rifts into the homogenized world view of modern man, replacing his categorical univocal norms with a transparently plural and, therefore, alterable constitution. Fantasy engages a productive freedom that has to labor in order to free itself from the seduction of immanence and security which today reign supreme. As Peter Henisch observes, "*You no longer need fantasy for freedom. It is given. Freedom implies fantasy. However, the freedom they try to talk us into is none. It is a freedom to consume, a passive and illusory freedom*" (ZS 155). What is missing in the exercise of freedom today is its internal *élan* which, according to Henisch, manifests itself in the work of fantasy. Enacting freedom, fantasy also keeps it alive by meandering through the realm of the real and the possible, through explorations of the unknown. Thus, fantasy also creates the ambiguous, the indefinite so much avoided by modern man: "*Consequently, this fear of change, of more freedom which change could contain. That is, people exchange freedom for security so that security is ultimately thought of as freedom, while fantasy, which could have brought more freedom, withers away*" (ZS 155).

To prevent this withering away, the narrator deliberately keeps the gaps open, those hollow spaces produced by the ambiguous title of the novel—*Hoffmanns Erzählungen*—because the ambiguity contained there is potentially a source of change. The element of indecision and suspense harbored by ambiguity between an either/or choice resembles the transparent fabric of fantasy which participates simultaneously in the realms of the real and the possible, in presence and absence. Both concepts—fantasy and ambiguity—are operative concepts in the sense of expressing possibilities; as such, they are harbingers of change. The trajectory of *Hoffmanns Erzählungen* spans the space between two poles, between the immanent world and the realm of possibilities, between the actual and the potential, with all the intervening forms of transformation emanating from the use of creative fantasy. Since E.T.A. Hoffmann's life has been written about and documented extensively, the narrator will attempt from the outset to submit all authenticity to doubt and rewrite this very life. By altering the historical date of E.T.A. Hoffmann's last diary entry, the narrator starts his biography from a new calendar date. Reading an excerpt from Hoffmann's biography, Kowalsky asks the narrator to observe the date: "It was March 7, 1815." But the scholarly annotated diary of Hoffmann ends with an entry on March 3, after which date he stopped writing: "Thereafter he noted nothing more (that, at least up until my meeting with him—I mean Kowalsky—was the accepted thesis)" (62).[13]

This valid thesis, corroborated by critics, will intentionally be overturned and reconfigured to articulate in its new format major concerns of Peter Henisch: how to safeguard and promote the faculty of imagination—fantasy—in light of indisputable facts verified by history. The devices Henisch chooses to undo the signature of history are the fragment, irony, and humor, all three of which, if not constitutive ingredients of fantasy, are at least its indirect offspring. Precluding the idea of wholeness, correctness, and completion, the rhetorical devices of the fragment, humor, and irony contaminate the narrated episodes with omissions, breaks, and outright lacunae, addressing only parts of a conspicuously absent totality.

This is obvious in the case of the fragment, which always remains in a state of expectation in the sense that it harbors in its own being the idea of absence and openness.[14] Kowalsky's retelling of Hoffmann's childhood; his affair with Julia Marc; and the scenes from the Napoleonic Wars in Dresden and Leipzig function as metonymic abbreviations of a life's journey frequently cut short, detoured, or abandoned. The narrator displays only fragments, yet they are marvelously integrated into the narrative network, haunting the reader with their deliberate torso-like quality of incompletion. It is in this fragmentary mode that Kowalsky narrates his previous life as E.T.A. Hoffmann. And even the film portraying E.T.A. Hoffmann's affair with Julia Marc is made from this perspective: "The film is a fragment!—As every living artwork! As every life!" (152). The dominance of the fragment (and not only in terms of the novel's structure) becomes visible in the aphoristic thematic currents the narrator adopts. Not only does he frequently interrupt the narrative flow when addressing himself to Professor Salaban, but even the sequence of the chapters lacks any chronological order: events overflow following a stream-of-consciousness technique. The reader is witnessing an enhanced polyphony in the fashion of Dostoevsky, but with a pronounced counterpoint technique. Stories are told, suddenly discontinued, and then revisited from a shifting temporal as well as spatial dimension. No wonder Kowalsky comments to the narrator: "Time, my dear Doctor, is relative. Says, as you know, Einstein. Einstein is right!" (62). In addition to temporal fragmentation, the spatial breaks are likewise frequent, so much so that the entire landscape of the novel appears to be in kaleidoscopic motion. The narrator is constantly on his way, starting with his search for his passport to his later walks with Kowalsky through the city of Berlin: "Now the city of Berlin, as you probably know, is a city without a center due to the division. So I had the impression I was walking in circles" (49). The upshot of this feeling is the absence of spatio-temporal causality which dominates the narrative strategy of the entire novel, and for good reason. As Kowalsky tells the narrator when asking him to read excerpts from his manuscript about the life of E.T.A. Hoffmann: "It is an experiment, a fragment, as so many a thing of mine" (197). The narrator reads it several times, only to be astonished at its sequestered patterns of composition which repeat themselves throughout the novel. "I read and reread. I was confused and shaken. *The Golden Pot* [*Der goldene Topf*] and 'Three Fateful Months' ['Drey verhängnisvolle Monathe'], each one cut apart to a certain extent and reassembled into a new totality" (197). Following this remark are "excerpts" the narrator relates to Professor Salaban.

Quoting fragments from two important works written by E.T.A. Hoffmann—one dealing with the genesis of poetry in mythical terms, while the other relates the Napoleonic Wars from the pages of Hoffmann's diary[15]—Kowalsky/Hoffmann relives in these quotations several episodes in fragmentary fashion. At first he sees himself as the author of *Der goldene Topf* pursuing the itinerary of Anselmus, the protagonist in the novel. Later he describes his relationship to his wife Mischa. And finally he witnesses the havoc wrought by war and the political tyranny of Napoleon, summarized in Hoffmann's own diary as "Drey verhängnisvolle Monathe." Two domains are specifically discernible in this segment of the novel alluding to the works by E.T.A. Hoffmann. Passages taken from *Der goldene Topf* and from the diary are deliberately fragmented; in particular, references to the Napoleonic Wars are quasi-synecdochic, articulating again isolated fragments. For example: "Complete dead silence. The student Anselmus felt seized by an instinctive dread. Complete dead silence. An infinite multitude of wounded were brought inside on wagons and wheelbarrows, one of them wore a face without eyes" (198). Against this historical background of the battlefield, the narrator masterfully introduces the theme of division and separation, which contrasts sharply with Napoleon's desire for the opposite—absolute power.

A Morphology of Fragments 111

In this particular instance, the focus on the outright decimation of war illustrates the reality of periodic breaks and discontinuity in the course of history. The strewn remnants of what used to be indivisible—*individuum*—subverts Napoleon's claim to absolute, systematic power in a Hegelian sense. As an eyewitness, Kowalsky/Hoffmann scans the movement of breaking apart on two tracks: individual fragmentation of the victims as well as universal disorder—chaos—among nations. He provides a suitable background for this process of disintegration by letting his own language *literally* fragment itself. He purposefully reedits a quotation from *Der goldene Topf* portraying the rustling of the golden waves of the Elbe, "behind which the magnificent city Dresden boldly and proudly raised its bright towers into the fragrant sky. Which bent down. Upon the bloody meadows. And out of deep dusk. Gave the jagged mountains. Tidings" (199). The passage in Hoffmann's text reads as follows: "on the other side rose lordly Dresden, stretching, bold and proud, its light towers into the airy sky; farther off, the Elbe bent itself down towards flowery meads and fresh springing woods; and in the dim distance, a range of azure peaks gave notice of remote Bohemia."[16] When compared to the original, Kowalsky's version is very revealing; it illustrates concretely the unbridgeable chasm separating our century from that of E.T.A. Hoffmann.

As the truncated syntax in Kowalsky's statement so vividly expresses, a fragment is constitutive of human reality. Whether it remains in isolation or is incorporated into a larger enterprise, it always is informative (tidings) of the precarious, fragmentary human condition. According to Friedrich Schlegel's formulation, a fragment is "complete unto itself like a hedgehog."[17] It has multiple meanings and can either stay intact, thereby contributing contiguously with other elements to the welfare of its environment, or it can remain as a part among parts, creating havoc in its tendency to control its own territory. In times of conflict it is the second tendency that surfaces. A countess just about to enter a carriage that would bring her to safety fails to do so because: "in the same instant she was . . . literally *torn apart* by a grenade. As she looked out of the window in the Pirna suburb, a midwife's head was snapped away; while sitting in his *comptoir*, a clerk lost his arm as well" (204). The fragments speak of the end of the wishful romantic dream of safety and peacefulness in the face of a reality whose make-up always remains fragmentary, that is, in a state of growth or decline. For the speaker, and thus also for the reader, the fragments quoted above succeed in riveting attention to decimated and decapitated victims who, through their ineffable silence, generate revulsion to absolute power. The fragments become seeds in Novalis's sense of the word, not only fertilizing the battlefield with blood exuding from dismembered body parts but also nourishing the human mind with resistance to the Hegelian totalizing system:

> And then I encountered Napoleon . . ., whom Hegel had interpreted as the incarnation of the world spirit, on the Elbe Bridge on his historical journey. Well, I had already seen him on several occasions and, by the way, he never impressed me (this, too, sets me apart from Goethe). But this time he appeared to me as an incarnation of the apocalyptic rider. . . . Hence, I, and people like me, could only get out of the way of his cyclopic walk as quickly as possible. (208)

Napoleon's one-dimensional view of the world fails due to his disregard for the fragment that resists assimilation into a system, in this specific case, the Hegelian system. At this advanced stage of the narrative, we witness the danger of the Napoleonic look of power affiliated with the center of an institution. It is not just Napoleon that is in question here, but the entire edifice of social structures that, in their totalizing effect, consume human freedom on behalf of a supreme order. The universality of this project is parenthetically inserted into the novel as a dangerous undercurrent that attends most forms of human interaction. There is always a tendency in history to collect fragments on behalf of a collective goal, in other words, to establish a hierarchy of values that monitors adherence to or deviation from the center of power: "By the way, Mister Hegel also perceived the Prussian state—with which I have had my dealings, believe me—to be the highest stage of interpersonal life up until that point in time. I tell you, the man had a visual defect" (208-9). What Hegel failed to see is, "The look of a man in boots who sees a troublesome insect. Then I also *saw*: I became aware: I realized" (208). Henisch italicizes the verb "saw," implying a difference between Hoffmann/Kowalsky's perception of power and that contained within the Hegelian hierarchy. The Hegelian concept of power implies an accumulation of life's forces into the body of an organized system whose power depends on the powerlessness of the others, just as the notion of totality, in like manner, overwhelms its parts.

Peter Henisch restores some balance into these disequilibria by subverting the whole concept of power, not only through redeeming the strength of the fragment but also by animating its movement through the vehicle of humor.[18] The narrative texture is saturated with laughter, occasioned by frequent incongruities within the atmosphere of the story. From the seesaw that resonates in the neighborhood of the hotel while the exhausted narrator looks for sleep to the "Kater Murr" relative who silently speaks of adventures of a bygone age, the story is replete with humor, a peculiar Hoffmannesque type of humor that Baudelaire characterized as "the power of being oneself and someone else at one and the same time."[19] This type of humor conditions laughter with an unmistakable critical twist enabling one to differentiate between servile submission to and autonomy from one's own environment. It is a peculiar humor that evokes a laughter that disempowers any ambition to excel and climb the social ladder at the expense of another; it is a redemptive laughter in the sense that it echoes the carnival-like free spirit that provides hope in hopeless conditions, such as a state of madness. But, above all, it is an enlightening laughter orienting the reader to encounter both humanity's deficiencies and its surplus of wealth.

Consequently, the narrator's humor is two-pronged. On the one hand, it frequently deals with the fragmentary, and thus deficient, individual state in which humor functions as a corrective to an oppressive situation. On the other hand, it becomes a device for dismantling institutionalized precepts governing modern society. In both instances, we also encounter slight traces of a Sternean social humor which, however, is less intrusive and more entertaining due to its spontaneity enlisted by events themselves rather than thoughtful deductions. When purchasing a tape recorder in order to record verbatim Hoffmann/Kowalsky's story, the latter admires the records available in the store and then comments to the clerk: "Do you know, Miss . . . what you are guarding here? You don't know!—Food for the soul from the kingdom of the infinite! Of course, in tin cans" (67). The refined lightness of the narrator's humor, although not lacking in Sternean biting effect, is evident even in traumatic situations which otherwise would call forth sarcasm and the outright rejection, rather than understanding, of human foibles. When Julia decides to marry Graepel on account of his wealth and Hoffmann finally realizes that his affair with her has ended, he comments: "'Understand me correctly. What happened between us was poetry, not prose. Don't you ever forget that!'—'No,' Julia sighed, 'how could I ever!' But obviously she was also interested in the prose" (166). Humor for both the narrator and Hoffmann/Kowalsky is an outgrowth of incongruous fragments that refuse to coincide with fixed patterns of thought. Something is missing and out of joint. Therefore, the fragments remain fragments, as in the case of Julia's fainting spells à la Kleist:

> One day Käthchen, who, in the meantime, was well trained in somnambulism, fainted altogether. What to do? Hoffmann opened her laced bodice; Kitty at least blinked. And Hoffmann (as I said, a Kleist fan) suddenly found himself in the sweet temptation of the Russian officer in the novella *The Marquise of O.* Dea ex machina, her mother entered the room. Mrs. Marc, whose bosom even under normal conditions was inclined to quake. Now it shook even stronger than usual. "Mister Music Director, what are you doing?" He gesticulated defensively. "Yes, yes, always these unexpected accidents." (164)

Whereas in Kleist we are dealing with an existential contingency, the seriousness here is prevaricated by Julia's own disposition, as Hoffmann/Kowalsky already stated earlier: "She was seductive, without wanting to seduce. That is, without letting it be known that she wanted to" (162). The reference to Kleist is a fragmentary reference, leaving behind the entire context in which the Kleistian event took place. Hoffmann/Kowalsky's allusion to Kleist is funny because it is fragmentary, devoid of the background to the situation; it is simply an opportunity for seduction delivered by a feigned chance occurrence that is always fragmentary and, therefore, open. The unexpected break in the action brings with it an unexpected righteousness, from without and not from within. Frau Marc enforces it, in spite of the silent agreement of the two lovers.

The main feature of humor in *Hoffmanns Erzählungen* is not so much the juxtaposition of two unequal elements or the contradiction between two issues or ideas, but rather the undermining, and sometimes reorienting, of an entire habitual mode of thinking. At first, the use of humor proceeds in simple terms of contradiction. The humor of Hoffmann's aunt is seen in this light: "Actually she was the only one in the family who was funny" (77). She is the one who teaches him to laugh by introducing him to the possibility of change that laughter entails: "'Little Ernest,' she sometimes said, 'Little Ernest, what's wrong? Have we given you the wrong name? Can't you be funny because of your name?' While saying this she laughed in such a way that I had to laugh, too" (77). Her lessons on laughter are very well assimilated by Hoffmann, who goes a little bit further than her harmless humor of simple opposition: "And if *my* humor, as problematic and, as you know, as contradictorily skittish as it is, was able to develop at all, I have her to thank to a great extent. To be sure, her cheerfulness was, if I understood it correctly, simply an affirmation. Mine was frequently a negation, right from the beginning" (77). The immediate example of his humor's negative undercurrent very appropriately is linked to light, candlelight, to be precise, illuminating the salon where weekly concerts are given in the house of his uncle: "One evening—and this was the first confrontation of my kind of humor with the world—I could no longer bear the tension, no longer resist the temptation and started to blow out the candles" (78). The punishment for this act must have been inordinate, because the reader can synesthetically hear and see the color of the "resounding slap in the half or three-quarter darkness" (78). In spite of the consequences, Hoffmann/Kowalsky notices the reward humor brings. His aunt responds to his punishment with amusement, "Only auntie laughed a counterpointed laughter" (79).

Her counterpointed response widens in the course of the story, in which the humor of the narrator as well as that of Hoffmann/Kowalsky create wider gaps by crossing from opposition to outright negation. Hoffmann's infatuation with Jadwiga, whom he compares to Botticelli's Venus ("Well, Jadwiga, born out of foam" [88]) fails to materialize because of his physical insufficiency, pointed out in his reference to phallic dwarfishness: "there I was a dwarf like Little Zaches" (88-89). This stunted growth, however, does not prevent him from intensifying his humor into a form of social criticism in which humor serves as a tool to uncover shortcomings of the state—for example, the notorious portrayal of Prussian officers in occupied Poland. In his second year in Poznán, "that carnival affair took place. . . . Carne vale—the contradictory connection between carnality and abstention, between life and death, laughing in the face of transitoriness has something really intoxicating about it if one understands the deeper meaning of this feast of farewell and renewal. But at precisely that time I was quite sober" (112). For the historical Hoffmann, staying sober during carnival was already an extraordinary feat, but to be able to laugh and draw caricatures of the dissolute officers was, according to Kowalsky, to become a lifelong mission for Hoffmann: "But to unmask this thoroughly masking society . . . was not only the hoax my friends had in mind, but a dead serious need, too. . . . It had to do with the pervasive wretchedness of the gang" (112-13).[20]

As Hoffmann/Kowalsky's stories continue, humor begins to play an increasingly functional role, not only as a device to alleviate social problems but also as an existential medium to cope with the human predicament as described by Hoffmann/Kowalsky in a "scenic fragment." In this dreamlike fragment Hoffmann/Kowalsky gets lost in the city of Plock and asks an old Jew for a way out. After the Jew suggests to Hoffmann that he ought to find his own way, they both begin to laugh at being God's fools. And it is here that the Jew casually explains the existential significance of humor: "After all, you got humor, Mister, even though, forgive me, you are a goy" (117). Hoffmann is not only a stranger who has humor but, at this moment, also a survivor who resides in the most backward city of his Polish journeys: provincial, isolated, and depressing. It is in this very city that his humor flourishes, so much so that he even writes a comedy. As the narrator informs us: "In any case, one day or perhaps even gradually he must have thought about his humor there in the middle of that desolate Plock" (117).

The reason behind this awakening of humor comes from the Jew who sees in humor the only existential exit from being and feeling lost. The creation and preservation of humor assumes a messianic purpose in light of the universal plight of man: "By the way, the Jew mentioned something about the fundamental sadness of the world and the fact that one could counteract it through a cheerful soul. If everything remains silent and all hope dies, then perhaps a single song full of life could bring forth the Messiah" (117). Although the Messiah is absent in this story, the redeeming quality of humor is evident across the entire novel. Humor saves Hoffmann from the haunting thoughts of insanity, but even more so, it makes life bearable in dire circumstances—for example, during the needless slaughter witnessed in the city of Dresden: "The goblet was quickly passed around, and under the thunder of the cannons, under the crackling of grenades, we were all absorbed by a cheerful humor. Which always results from a mood heightened by danger, and on such occasions one easily lapses into the fantastic and romantic" (203).

Hand in hand with the use of humor goes the employment of irony which lets the jagged contours of the fragment stand out, thereby preventing its assimilation into a larger design. When pseudo-Hoffmann is concerned with his depressed existence and mentions his talent for madness, the narrator observes how his face reached "that peculiar movement which, starting as it were under the skin, *announced the spirit of irony*" (86). Italicizing the last part of the sentence—i.e., a fragment—Henisch highlights the crucial function of irony in the structure of the novel. The narrator and Hoffmann/Kowalsky are masterful dissemblers; speaking in fragments, they withhold information by frequently covering it up or dissimulating it. The presence of irony becomes especially pronounced as a countermeasure against a mindset that dictates a convergence of interests and aspirations. To prevent this homogeneity from spreading its power, the narrator will resort to irony as a force of displacement or as a catalyst for bifurcation into extremes. As an ironist, he will always speak in fragments because he will say less than what he actually thinks. Irony functions for Henisch as it does for Kierkegaard, leading to a "collision with actuality."[21] Irony sustains life by creating new possibilities. As Kowalsky observes, "Yes, I avoided injury (and later very frequently the nonsense) from reality by sensing and fantasizing behind it another (deeper, higher) reality" (190). A "non-concurrence of points of view" takes place.[22] The common and customary assume a new appearance and function when reedited by the ironist; they become intentionally distorted and thus no longer correspond to their preordained context. A new world comes into being, the world of the possible created by an author in a state of constant transitions:

> So I am to some extent a free-floating fool, a kind of descendant of the great Till Eulenspiegel, whom I admire very much. Or the ancestor of a kind of fool who does not yet exist. A transforming, eating, drinking, loving, hating, music-playing, writing anachronism. . . . One who notices how strange that which appears familiar to others is. And who does not feel at home where others settle down, those broad-assed narrow-minded people. (158-59)

Hoffmann/Kowalsky's tendency to transform his immediate condition is especially visible in terms of his childhood, which he remembers vividly after having read Sterne's *Tristram Shandy*. "Then I already had developed my talent for laughter" (72). He even goes on to identify his uncle with the rigid world of Sterne's Sir Ott, who is not only an obtuse provincial pedant but, with his lethargic behavior, also immobilizes the flow of events. Something similar occurs in our novel with pseudo-Hoffmann's uncle; he is only concerned with preserving the *status quo*: "Man, was his motto, man needs order and planning. He lived according to a timetable" (73). It is not only that he himself lived this way, but he also expected everybody else to follow suit. The extremity of his proposal borders on the absurd because, he claimed, "everything (be it even nothing) had to follow the hands of his repeating watch" (73).

This imposition of absolutes, of a normative code of behavior, upon the child is accompanied by ironic understatements culminating in outright criticism when, as a student in Königsberg, Hoffmann/Kowalsky comes in contact with the philosophy of Kant. He sets the tone in his ironic remark that, "the future lies in his philosophy" (91), and then proceeds to cancel that judgment:

> You know, Kreisler, such providers of imperatives always did get on my nerves. Those who want to prescribe to others how they ought to live intend, consciously or unconsciously, to hinder them in their [enjoyment of] life. My being protested so to speak against categorically formulated moral demands. This resistance went . . . so far as my falling asleep. I frequently searched the starry heavens above me, but only rarely did I find within myself the moral law. (92)

To refute this prescriptive ideology, we find the description of his passionate illicit affair with a married woman called Dora. From the very beginning, Hoffmann/Kowalsky details how the categorical imperative is overwhelmed by the imperative of the body: "'Dora seduced me,' he said, fired up in spite of the cold weather, 'after I had heroically resisted her for several hours'" (92). Of course the seduction is mutual, and Hoffmann's short-lived resistance gives way to a scandalous affair such that Sir Ott "believed all of Königsberg was scandalized on our account" (95). Of greater importance here is the ironic subversion of the Kantian normative principle and its claim to universality. The story of adultery shows how the protagonists interact in a given situation that determines its outcome from within. Kant's autonomy of human judgment, of human reason, is the result of tradition and social institution that Hoffmann/Kowalsky and, for that matter, the narrator (through his own severance from his wife Sophie) are reluctant to accept: "One did not have to be productive but *re*productive, had to do what generations before him had done, to behave properly and to propagate the nonsense, today still considered to be sensible, of starting a family" (97). The thrust of Hoffmann/Kowalsky's criticism is directed toward foundational epistemology which affirms *a priori* universal guidelines founded on rational principles. Dora's behavior, like that of Kitty/Julia, highlights the prerogative of the individual to choose as she pleases. With regard to Dora's getting herself a new lover, Hoffmann/Kowalsky ironically states: "Needless to say, she disliked all along my too short, all too dark, hairy legs (she already had a blond friend with longer ones)" (96). Trivializing the institution of marriage through Dora's libertine behavior, Hoffmann/Kowalsky continues to chip away at the entire edifice of Western civilization, but primarily at its hierarchical structures geared to produce power centers—be they ethical, as in the case of Kant, or ideological, in that of Hegel, or sexual, as in the tradition of the family. According to Henisch, modern man is the executor of this legacy, for better or for worse; it is up to him to embark upon new pathways: "You people of today must do something against it, if you want to see a tomorrow" (235).

Peter Henisch responds to this challenge of his protagonist. By evoking and recasting the past in *Hoffmanns Erzählungen*, he simultaneously channels the present course of history into a new direction. His prime concern seems to be the opening of long forgotten avenues for man's routine existence paved by the inexhaustible source of human fantasy. To prepare the groundwork where fantasy could thrive, the author plows the soil of the novel into fragments where the seeds of fantasy can take root and initiate slow growth, thereby generating, uplifting, and solidifying man's presence in a meaningful world. With this objective in mind, Hoffmann/Kowalsky sees his own task within the framework of the novel: "What *I* tried to do, undermine the deadly play of the powerful with vivid irony, was, after all, a contribution, but in those days it was easier" (230). Whether it actually was easier in those days or not is a rhetorical question. However, the fact remains that because of today's rule of immanence, the space of fantasy is continuously shrinking. The homogenized one-dimensional way of thinking in contemporary society, epitomized by the university in the novel, prompts the narrator to disconnect his career from a life of sterility and nurtured detachment. He embarks on a crusade to redeem the power of fantasy because:

> Again and again they try to fetter our fantasy. Through schools, in which one unlearns more than one learns; through jobs, for which one does not feel any calling; through scholarship, which for a long time now has not been *for* humanity; and through politics, which for a long time now has been *against* humanity, etc., etc. So that it (fantasy) seems to stagnate; soon one won't even be able to imagine anything except the universal rule of the narrow-minded. (229)

Instead of an identification with the immediate world, which would close off horizons and thus impoverish and confine the human faculty of thinking, a sense of openness-in-the-world is needed, an openness that would bring with it new possibilities, new ways of looking at the world. It is significant that Hoffmann/Kowalsky defines the work of fantasy from this operative perspective: "But Kreisler, I tell you, fantasy is the great artist of unchaining" (230). Fantasy works to dissolve the immanent, familiar reality surrounding man, enabling him to metamorphose it into new configurations. In this sense fantasy is revolutionary because of its inexhaustible energy to produce new worlds, new dwelling places for humanity. It is powerful because of its boundlessness; it can be everything and, even more importantly, it can grant the experience of nothingness: "It rises unexpectedly, naked and beautiful as it is, and sets itself—now it must equalize its long silence—into motion. Do you know the painting by Eugene Delacroix—'La liberté guidant le peuple?' If I were a better painter, I would paint a picture in which fantasy leads the people!" (230).

Albeit not as a painter, the author vividly depicts, even if in hyperbolic terms, the danger man faces in the absence of fantasy. The world of consumers along with the producing power centers could eventually broaden their network around the globe, suffocating it with their own success. Once everything is known, explored, and preserved, it becomes sealed with the signature of permanence. For Peter Henisch, this would mean the end of the world as we know it: "'On the other hand,' Kowalsky said, 'I am afraid that they will suffocate fantasy, gas and poison it, simply explode it into the air! Burn it down worldwide, even if they were to destroy themselves in the process. (Since they are without fantasy, they obviously cannot imagine this or, at most, only insufficiently!)'" (230). *Hoffmanns Erzählungen* alludes to the possibility of such a catastrophe if a uniformity of thinking and a lifestyle of immanence continue to hold sway over modern man. But the real significance of the novel lies in its deconstructive narrative strategy which, while disassembling the finite shape of the past, invests it with a new meaning. From the beginning of the novel until its end, the reader witnesses the creation of a *joie de vivre* which overcomes all the hardships and disappointments to be encountered in life. What carries the day in the novel is the hope that survives personal as well as social turmoil. Although it may seem that the novel deals largely with the past, its actual thrust is the future, as reflected in the dialogic form of letters sent to a distant recipient. Even Hoffmann/Kowalsky resorts to this medium to spread the news of his "manifesto to liberate fantasy" (241). He asks the narrator to disseminate his ideas about a liberating fantasy in a "chain letter." His commitment to the future is motivated by his successful reshaping of the past because, as he says, "my name is Hoffmann: a man who (in spite of everything) never gives up hope" (230).

The hope that Hoffmann/Kowalsky envisions is future-oriented if we keep in mind not only the aesthetic pleasure derived from reading the novel but also the epistemological insights we gain by doing so. The rhetoric of the fragment, humor, and irony bear directly on our modes of thinking to the extent that they enable us to relate to reality from very different vantage points. Henisch appropriately calls this a "multilayered" method of thinking (ZS 8), inferring by this a direct encounter with reality in its forms of diversity. All three rhetorical devices are means for prismatically interacting with the external. They thus enrich our experience of a manifold world characterized, according to Henisch, as "polydimensional" (ZS 140). To cope effectively with this plurality of spheres, a correspondingly heterogeneous way of thinking is needed. Peter Henisch succeeds in maintaining this heterogeneity of thought throughout the novel by fostering a conspicuously liberating openness that depreciates the value system of tradition. The conditioned madness of Kowalsky after his failure as an actor becomes the unconditional freedom of Kowalsky/Hoffmann. This is not to imply that he is cured, but the question does arise as to whether he needs to be cured at all since, in the course of the novel, "madness" has been domesticated. Moreover, what really counts is the colorful blending of order and disorder, of sanity and insanity, to the extent that closures that have existed for centuries are broken down, closures that even today, according to Foucault, are normal: "We have now got into the habit of perceiving in madness a fall into determinism where all forms of liberty are gradually suppressed; . . . for madness threatens modern man only with that return to the bleak world of beasts and things, to their fettered freedom."[23]

Henisch transforms this fear of marginal existence by bringing it into the open, by using humor to metamorphose threats into laughter and to replace life's risk and danger with the advent of hope. His concern is to keep the doors of human enterprise wide open: "*Keeping the contradictions comically open with a certain concurrent human hope, well, you know, that's my idea of irony*" (ZS 9). In other words, it is a productive way of thinking that emerges at the end of the novel, a thinking that evolves from the situation rather than being determined *a priori* by it. It is a powerful thinking that never ebbs but always grows. As Henisch, in conjunction with Nietzsche's *Vom Nutzen und Nachteil der Historie für das Leben* (1873; *On the Use and Abuse of History*, 1911) writes of this freedom in *Steins Paranoia* (1988; *Stone's Paranoia*, 2000): "I mean (Nietzsche means) the power to grow singularly out of yourself, to refashion and incorporate the past and the foreign, to heal wounds, to replace what is lost, to reconfigure broken forms from within yourself."[24]

The broken forms, the fragments transformed as they are, remain fragmented in *Hoffmanns Erzählungen*, but Henisch makes sure that they stay discursive and thus accessible to the reader who, at the end of the narrated stories, is left with the blank pages Franz Kreisler is sending to the addressee of the novel, the parapsychologist. Indirectly, the reader is summoned to sow his or her own fragments on the surface of these blank pages, his or her own seeds derived from the discourse of the novel and, above all, from the ideas planted in the seminar the novelist delivered at the beginning of the stories. The central theme there, we remember, is the schizoid structure of thought, whose colorful constitution the novel embroidered into its own texture. These patterns of fissured thought are seminal—as a seminar should be—because they give birth to a polydimensional reality commensurate with a human mind that thinks through a discourse animated by "the continually self-generating interchange of two contesting thoughts."[25]

> Grains of mustard seeds
> we have planted
> . . .
> Don't you notice
> how they live
> and move

and how they strive
toward the sun
a tiny bit

day by day   (ZS 208-9)

Notes

1. Novalis, "Neue Fragmente," *Werke und Briefe*, ed. Alfred Kelletat (Munich: Winkler, 1968) 451.

2. In some respects the structure of the novel resembles Sterne's *Tristram Shandy* where conflicts are frequently left open, despite Sterne's ironic claims to the contrary: "By this contrivance the machinery of my work is of a species by itself; two contrary motions are introduced into it, and reconciled, which were thought to be at variance with each other. In a word, my work is digressive, and is progressive—at the same time" (*Tristram Shandy* [Indianapolis: Odyssey, 1976] 73). The question of openness in *Tristram Shandy* is so pervasive that critics are still debating its "unity." See Wayne C. Booth's remarks in this regard in *The Rhetoric of Fiction* (Chicago: U of Chicago P, 1961) 221.

3. Since Henisch's intent in the novel is to promote a new way of thinking, his choice of the notion of ambiguity is essential, especially if we accept John Dewey's hypothesis that, "Thinking begins in what may fairly enough be called a *forked-road* situation, a situation which is ambiguous, which presents a dilemma, which proposes alternatives" (*How We Think* [Boston/New York/Chicago: D.C. Heath, 1910] 11). With regard to ambiguity in general, see the fourth and sixth types of ambiguity as discussed by William Empson, *Seven Types of Ambiguity* (New York: New Directions, 1966)

133-54 and 177-91.
  4. The subtitle of the novel sheds some light on the role of the author/narrator in this work. It sounds puzzling and strange at first reading: "Notes of a Confused Germanist." The subtitle seems to me to anticipate the overall problems the novel treats; it is of a preparatory nature as far as the reader is concerned. Novalis's thoughts on the issue of confusion may help us to understand the tendency of the author-narrator: "The more confused a man is—people call the confused ones stupid—the more he can make of himself through diligent self-study; in contrast, the smart heads have to desire to become true scholars, thorough encyclopedists. The confused ones have to struggle with powerful obstacles; they penetrate only slowly; they learn to work with difficulty: but then they become sovereign and masters forever. The clear [smart] ones enter quickly [into the subject matter], but they also exit quickly" ("Blütenstaub," *Werke und Briefe* 350).
  5. Peter Henisch, *Hoffmanns Erzählungen: Aufzeichnungen eines verwirrten Germanisten* (Munich: Nymphenburger, 1983) 15.
  6. The problem of credibility arises not only on account of the schizophrenic condition of Kowalsky/Hoffmann's mind but also due to the fantastic element disseminated throughout the novel—for example, the appearance of the cat in the footsteps of E.T.A. Hoffmann's "Kater Murr" (Tomcat Murr). With regard to the conflict between the fantastic and reality, see Tzvetan Todorov, *The Fantastic* (Ithaca: Cornell UP, 1975) 38-40.
  7. The theme of schizophrenia is also present in the political dimension of the novel; it runs as an undercurrent throughout the whole work. When Kreisler visits Kowalsky's apartment he hears next to it the noises of a demolition team—"Abbruchskommando"—clearing the dilapidated buildings. Kowalsky comments: "'Well, the demolition . . . we all live subject to recall.' (He laughed in a tone that almost hurt me). 'Yes, yes, my dear. We are in an area in need of reconstruction'" (228). Kowalsky uses the polysemous term "Sanierungsgebiet" which can refer to prophylactic treatment in terms of both health and social politics.

8. Of course, the question of split identity is one of the central motifs in Hoffmann's stories. As E.F. Bleier rightfully observes in his introduction to Hoffmann's works: "Hoffmann's work is permeated with the concept of personality fragments coming to separate identity and acting as characters" ("Introduction," *The Best Tales of Hoffmann,* ed. and intro. E.F. Bleier [New York: Dover, 1967] xix).

9. As to the genesis of E.T.A. Hoffmann's style, see the informative chapter by Harvey W. Hewett-Thayer, *Hoffmann: Author of the Tales* (Princeton: Princeton UP, 1948) 140-65. The interesting feature of his style seems to be the fragmentary leaps derived from the *commedia dell'arte*.

10. When Hoffmann/Kowalsky observes that reality is "multiple," he implies also that the cognitive capacity of man ought to be diverse. In the course of the novel we witness a "multilayered" way of thinking exemplified in Kowalsky's simultaneous and manifold perception of reality. The epistemological issues in the novel come very close to what Heidegger describes as "thinking": "[M]ultiplicity of meanings is the element in which all thought must move in order to be strict thought. To use an image: to a fish, the depths and expanses of its waters, the currents and quiet pools, warm and cold layers are the elements of its multiple mobility. If the fish is deprived of the fullness of its element, if it is dragged on the dry sand, then it can only wriggle, twitch, and die. Therefore, we always must seek out thinking, and its burden of thought, in the element of its multiple meanings, else everything will remain closed to us" (*What Is Called Thinking?*, trans. Fred D. Wieck and J. Glenn Gray, intro. J. Glenn Gray [New York: Harper & Row, 1968] 71).

11. The subversive nature of fantasy has been treated by Gianni Rodari in his pedagogical investigations: "A mind that is always at work is creative, a mind that always asks questions, discovers problems where others find satisfactory answers. It is a mind that prefers fluid situations where others only sense danger, a mind that is capable of making autonomous and independent judgments (also independent from the father, the professor, and the society), that rejects everything that is codified, reshapes objects and concepts without letting

itself be hindered by conformist attitudes" (*The Grammar of Fantasy*, trans. Jack Zipes [New York: Philmark Lithographics, 1996] 114).

12. Throughout his long interview in *Zwischen allen Sesseln: Geschichten, Gedichte, Entwürfe, Notizen, Statements 1965-1982* (Vienna: Hannibal, 1982), Peter Henisch advocates the need to think "colorfully." In my understanding of the adverb, it means to think freely rather than prescriptively, the latter being the case with traditional categories of logic. Subsequent page references to *Zwischen allen Sesseln* will be provided in parentheses with the initials ZS.

13. See E.T.A. Hoffmann, *Tagebücher*, ed. Hans v. Müller (Munich: Winkler, 1971) 266.

14. The impact the fragment has exerted on modern times has been very well assessed by Deleuze and Quattari and shares an affinity with Henisch's "preference for periphery" (ZS 91). Hoffmann/Kowalsky moves all the time on the edge of boundaries, a position Deleuze characterizes as follows: "We live today in the age of partial objects, bricks that have been shattered to bits, and leftovers. We no longer believe in the myth of the existence of fragments that, like pieces of an antique statue, are merely waiting for the last one to be turned up, so that they may all be glued back together to create a unity that is precisely the same as the original unity. We no longer believe in a primordial totality that once existed, or in a final totality that awaits us at some future date. . . . We believe only in totalities that are peripheral. And if we discover such a totality alongside various separate parts, it is a whole *of* these particular parts but does not totalize them; it is a unity *of* all of these particular parts but does not unify them; rather, it is added to them as a new part fabricated separately" (*Anti-Oedipus: Capitalism and Schizophrenia*, trans. Robert Hurley, Mark Seem and Helen R. Lane [Minneapolis: U of Minnesota P, 1983] 42).

15. The excerpts from Hoffmann's diary which Henisch incorporates into the novel are noteworthy because they describe the horror of war aphoristically and with a Hoffmannesque touch of humor. See "Drey verhängnisvolle Monathe!," *Tagebücher* 269-77.

16. "The Golden Flower Pot," trans. Thomas Carlyle, *The Best Tales of Hoffmann* 2. Of course, the difference between the two passages is even more striking when compared to the German original. See E.T.A. Hoffmann, *Der goldene Topf, Werke*, ed. H. Kraft, vol. 1 (Frankfurt/M: Insel, 1967) 127.

17. Friedrich Schlegel, *Athenäum Fragments*, trans. Haynes Horne, *Theory as Practice: A Critical Anthology of Early German Romantic Writings*, ed. Jochen Schulte-Sasse (Minneapolis: U of Minnesota P, 1997) 322.

18. Henisch's overall disposition toward the world is very much akin to Bakhtin's conviction that a meaningful life correlates with one's ability to laugh: "It is precisely laughter that destroys any hierarchical . . . distance. As a distanced image a subject cannot be comical; to be comical, it must be brought close. Everything that makes us laugh is close at hand, all comical creativity works in a zone of maximal proximity. Laughter has the remarkable power of making an object come close, of drawing it into a zone of crude contact where one can finger it familiarly on all sides, turn it upside down, inside out, peer at it from above and below, break open its external shell, look into its center, doubt it, take it apart, dismember it, lay it bare and expose it, examine it freely and experiment with it. Laughter demolishes fear and piety before an object. . . . Familiarization of the world through laughter and popular speech is an extremely important and indispensable step in making possible free, scientifically knowable and artistically realistic creativity in European civilization" ("Epic and Novel: Towards a Methodology for the Study of the Novel," *The Dialogic Imagination*, ed. Michael Holquist, trans. Caryl Emerson and Michael Holquist [Austin: U of Texas P, 1986] 23).

19. Charles Baudelaire, "On the Essence of Laughter," *The Painter of Modern Life and Other Essays*, trans. Jonathan Mayne (New York: Phaidon, 1965) 164.

20. The distortion of the norm that occurs in the grotesque has a direct impact on the reader: the narrator wants him to form his own point of view and thereby become critical of the "military" norms. See Boris Uspensky, *A Poetics of Composition*, trans. Valentina Zavarin and Susan

Wittig (Berkeley: U of California P, 1973) 127.

21. In some respects, Henisch's use of irony is as refined as Kierkegaard's, although it lacks the latter's tendency towards transcendence of a given situation. Henisch's ironist remains immanent and connected to the world, unlike Kierkegaard's who "stands completely above his environment" (Søren Kierkegaard, *The Concept of Irony*, trans. and intro. Lee M. Capel [New York: Harper & Row, 1965] 298).

22. For the ideological implications of the shifting perspectives of the narrator-author vis-à-vis the reader, see Uspensky 103.

23. Michel Foucault, *Madness and Civilization: A History of Insanity in the Age of Reason*, trans. Richard Howard (New York: Vintage, 1973) 83.

24. Henisch, *Stone's Paranoia*, trans. Craig Decker (Riverside, CA: Ariadne, 2000) 83. *Steins Paranoia* situates the experience of the "rift" in the present haunted by the past. In *Hoffmanns Erzählungen*, in contrast, the Hoffmannesque past is being haunted by the present. In this respect the novels complement each other.

25. Schlegel, *Athenäum Fragments, Theory as Practice* 321.

The Ironic Case of Austro/Jewish Identity: Psycho-Political Rhetoric in *Steins Paranoia**

KATHY BRZOVIĆ and CRAIG DECKER

> We should note that only through an internal and external experiencing of folly could we possess (in our intelligence or imagination) sufficient "characters" for some measure of development beyond folly.
> —Kenneth Burke[1]

In the *Kleine Zeitung* of March 27, 1986, Austrian journalist Kurt Vorhofer diagnoses the partisan attacks on the "non-partisan" presidential candidate as symptoms of a diseased mind: "Even in our most vehement condemnation of the methods used to attack Kurt Waldheim and Austria, we should make allowances for the fact that these Jewish functionaries, like so very many Jews, are profoundly psychologically damaged people."[2] Max Stein, the protagonist in Peter Henisch's *Steins Paranoia* (1988; *Stone's Paranoia*, 2000), represents the fictional realization of the psychically disturbed

Jew whose faulty sense of perception and memory lands him in the madhouse. The rather sudden and fleeting encounter that gives rise to Stein's paranoid delusion that anti-Semitism is abroad in the land is the utterance of a certain type of sentence by a certain type of man on a certain Monday evening shortly after six o'clock in a certain newspaper kiosk on the corner of the subway stop Wien-Schottenring. Although Stein vividly recalls the exact time and place in which the alleged insult was hurled, he cannot recall the exact words uttered, but only has some vague sense that they were anti-Semitic in their import and that they resembled, after a fashion, other words often heard, or sometimes not heard, around this same period of time or sometime shortly thereafter.

Those readers who, untutored in questions of individual and social psychology, are puzzled by cases like Stein's paranoia, need only consult Walter Schwimmer, People's Party functionary and President of the Austro-Israeli Society, who tells us in "Zum Vorwurf des Antisemitismus im Wahlkampf" (Charges of Anti-Semitism in the Election Campaign): "The giddy pace of political discussions and the understandable forgetfulness of all those not directly involved in the dispute produce a common reaction: Yes, yes, there was something, he or she said this or that in this or that way, and so, especially when one wants to believe something, it becomes in one's mind an example of anti-Semitic agitation."[3] The Jewish Diogenes, in search of truth and honesty, is proclaimed by the Austrian Abderites to be mad. Symptoms of the disease, according to journalist Peter Gnam: "hatred and blind rage."[4] Clinical history of the disease as proclaimed in a March 28, 1986 headline in the *Neue Kronenzeitung:* "SINGER'S FATHER FORCED TO 'CLEAN' STREETS WITH TOOTHBRUSH IN 1938 VIENNA!"[5] Barring a complete cure, such cases, according to Walter Schwimmer, are to be handled by non-Jews with understanding and compassion: "[We should] bear in mind that to those who have been persecuted all too often simply because they were Jews, an attack on a single individual appears threatening to all of them if it is coupled with the adjective 'Jewish,' even though such an attack appears to us to be a far cry from any type of anti-Semitism at all."[6] Fortunately for our fictional character, the psychiatrist assigned to his case is as perceptive as his real-life counterparts and is able to diagnose his pathology: "That someone like [Stein] goes decidedly too far in his interpretation of reality."[7] A partial cure of the patient is effected such that, although upon leaving the hospital and believing that he sees a swastika, Stein at least is able to recognize: "I am . . . just imagining things again" (97).

The purpose of this introduction is not merely to illustrate what Schwimmer has called the "admittedly difficult psychological situation,"[8] but equally to illustrate the rhetorical situation in Austria of which Henisch's novel is a part. In the course of the 1986 presidential election campaign, political rhetoric quickly shifted from deliberative, future policy-oriented discourse to forensic or judicial discourse as a consequence of accusations that Dr. Waldheim had not been completely honest about his activities in the German Wehrmacht. The defense strategy adopted by the Austrian People's Party was based on the contention that the accused was not guilty of any crime but had been framed, the victim of a vicious "smear campaign" ("Verleumdungskampagne") perpetrated by "certain individuals" ("Einzelpersonen") living on the East Coast of the United States of America whose primary organ was the World Jewish Congress. The defense argued that the motive for the frame was a desire for revenge; Jews are "vindictive," whereas Christians are "forgiving." In the post-election phase of the rhetorical proceedings, the defense sought to counter the prosecution's charge of anti-Semitism—and thereby rescue Austria's image as a magnanimous and compassionate nation—by granting the Jewish conspirators a reprieve on the grounds that they suffered from a psychically traumatic persecution complex.

At this point we enter the ironic phase of the dispute in which Peter Henisch becomes a participant. Allen Tate characterizes irony as "that arrangement of experience, either premeditated by art or accidently appearing in the affairs of men, which permits to the spectator an insight superior to that of the actor."[9] The doubly ironic pose adopted by the defense is achieved by virtue of the assumption that the non-

Jew is a non-participant in the tragedy of the Jewish people. The defense views and judges the tragic irony of the Jew as persecuted persecutor from the superior position of the outside spectator. It should be clear that this stance is not merely a function of a simple "perpetrator"/"victim" inversion. It is made possible by the so-called grand Austrian delusion ("Lebenslüge"/"Überlebenslüge"), a delusion deemed by some to have been a survival mechanism that continues to survive, and one that can be better appreciated if we translate "the myth of Austria's victimization by Nazi Germany" into the following statement: After 1938 Austria did not exist; therefore, Austrians did not participate in the Holocaust. Consequently, the Austrian of the Second Republic is twice removed from any identification with the affairs of the Third Reich: first, insofar as the Austrian does not share an identity with the Jew and, second, insofar as the Austrian does not even share an identity with himself as German.

In *Steins Paranoia,* Henisch counters the ironic condescension of the defense with what Kenneth Burke has called "true irony" or "humble irony," which is "based upon a sense of fundamental kinship with the enemy, as one *needs* him, is *indebted* to him, is not merely outside him as an observer but contains him *within,* being consubstantial with him."[10] In the act of writing *Steins Paranoia,* Henisch does not overcome the division created by the rhetoric of identification ("us and them"), but he does present us with a quintessentially ironic situation narrated in an ironic mode that calls attention to the fluidity and friability of identification and division. He creates a fictional character who, as an Austrian Jew, is a figure with whom he can identify,[11] yet with whom he is not strictly identical. And, in a further ironic twist, although Henisch writes as an act of therapy, he does not heal the patient but narrates him into a state of obsessive neurosis, precisely because both author and character are Austrians caught in a quintessentially neurotic national predicament. "Rhetorically," Kenneth Burke tells us in this regard:

> the neurotic's every attempt to legislate for his own conduct is disorganized by rival factions within his

own dissociated self. Yet, considered Symbolically, the same victim is technically "at peace," in the sense that his identity is like a unified, mutually adjusted set of terms. For even antagonistic terms, confronting each other as parry and thrust, can be said to "cooperate" in the building of an over-all form.[12]

In the case of Stein's paranoia, the over-all form is the Austrian nation. As an Austrian and as a Jew, Max Stein is doubly consubstantial with the enemy whether one defines the enemy as the Jew or as the Austrian. As a consequence of his inability to react to an anti-Semitic statement, Stein becomes an unwitting and unwilling actor in the political wrangle over identification with a much maligned and beleaguered little Austria. Meanwhile, the anti-Semite who inflicts the psychic wound in the novel's opening pages completely vanishes from the scene to become the non-participant in the Jewish affliction.

With Stein in the role of "jüdischer Mitbürger" (Jewish fellow-citizen)—a phrase that simultaneously captures identification with and division from a predominantly German and Catholic Austria—Henisch satirically reproduces the rhetorical rivalries, strategies, acts of persuasion, and ambiguities found in the national argument over Austrian identity that arose out of the 1986 election campaign and carried over into and beyond the so-called "Bedenkjahr"("Year of Remembrance and Reflection") of 1988. One of the novel's more subtle ironies is that Stein, this dissociated self, is the embodiment of the Austrian nation. If his memory is poor, it is only because Austria's memory is poor. If he is at war with his past, it is only because Austria is at war with its past. If he feels uneasy about the present, it is because the nation as a whole is uneasy. His internal dispute as to his own identity symbolically and necessarily mimics the nation's public dispute. In this respect it is important to note with Kenneth Burke that:

> In pure identification there would be no strife. Likewise there would be no strife in absolute separateness, since opponents can join battle only through a media-

tory ground that makes their communication possible, thus providing the first condition necessary for the interchange of blows. But put identification and division ambiguously together, so that you cannot know for certain just where one ends and the other begins, and you have the characteristic invitation to rhetoric.[13]

In other words, the rhetoric in Austria became so very heated precisely because the lines of division and identification were so ambiguously drawn.

What is the difference between a Christian and a Jew? a citizen and a Jewish fellow-citizen? an Austrian and a German? a perpetrator and a victim? a war survivor and a concentration camp survivor? What is the difference between voluntary complicity and forced compliance? between an attack and a defense? an anti-Semitic remark and an explanation? an explanation and a rationalization? a rationalization and a lie? a lie and a memory lapse? It is into this rhetorical whirl of confusion that Henisch introduces Stein, the personification of rhetorical rivalry who must learn to "thrust and parry" in a battle of "antagonistic terms," whether spoken, written, or represented by other figures he meets along the way. His Jewish father and his Nazi father-in-law; his indigenous wife and his foreign girlfriend; the chauvinistic taxicab-driver and the neo-Nazi youth; the president and the psychiatrist; the living and the dead; all are rhetorical terms or figures that appear on the narrative scene, enrolled in an immense and complex national act of persuasion that is at once a sign of identification and division, cooperation and confrontation.

In order to appreciate the nature of the personal and national trauma depicted in *Steins Paranoia*, one must understand that the protagonist belongs to that younger generation of Austrians who fulfill the promise of the Second Republic, founded on a national identity distinct from that of Greater Germany. Whereas the First Republic expressed in its name, "Deutsch-Österreich" (German-Austria), and in its constitution a longing for eventual unification with Germany,[14] the Second Republic sought to forge a positive sense of a separate

The Ironic Case of Austro/Jewish Identity 137

Austrian national identity in its citizenry. Stein's marriage to Brigitte is an act of rhetorical persuasion that seeks to overcome the historical divide separating the Christian and the Jew, negating in their union the antagonisms of their ancestry. The marriage between Brigitte, the daughter of an illegal Nazi, and Stein, the son of a Jewish exile and grandson of a concentration camp victim, represents a form of transcendence that gives birth to hope in a better future as embodied in their daughter Marion. This nuclear family is the literal objectification of the new nation, the new Austrian family, adding its voice to a new national narrative.

The single—but in no way singular—anti-Semitic remark that sets the novel in motion confronts Stein, for the first time since his migration to Vienna, with Jewish identity as division, as separate and apart from Austrian identity, and thus shatters his belief in transcendence. A stone is hurled and falls to the ground; Stein falls from a state of grace. The force of the anti-Semitic utterance ruptures his sense of well-being, of being at home in his Austrian skin, and he is left with a feeling of the uncanny. Freud distinguishes between two forms of the uncanny; the one of primary interest to us here is that form "associated with the omnipotence of thoughts, . . . with secret injurious powers and with the return of the dead."[15] Freud writes:

> The condition under which the feeling of uncanniness arises here is unmistakable. We—or our primitive forefathers—once believed that these possibilities were realities, and were convinced that they actually happened. Nowadays we no longer believe in them, we have *surmounted* these modes of thought; but we do not feel quite sure of our new beliefs, and the old ones still exist within us ready to seize upon any confirmation. As soon as something *actually happens* in our lives which seems to confirm the old, discarded beliefs we get a feeling of the uncanny.[16]

For Freud, the process of human development that leads to the establishment of a higher order of social and political relations, and which we call civilization, occurs through enlightenment whereby mankind surmounts primitive modes of thought. Racialist ideology, however, is based on the primitive belief in the possibility of tribal cleansing through ritualistic purgings. In the Nazi state, the sacrificial pyre is transformed by means of modern technology into the gas chamber, a purified form of the act of purification. In viewing old newsreels of the death camps, one is struck with a sense of the uncanny, a terrifying feeling that although we have surpassed our fearful forefathers technologically, we have not transcended their mode of thought.

If enlightenment entails clarity about these historical processes, then the figure of Clarissa, this latter-day Jewish prophet, appears on the scene to bear witness to this uniquely modern form of primitivism as a threat to civilization. Clarissa is on a pilgrimage from the New World to the Old World of her persecuted forefathers in order "to investigate, to analyze the malevolent development" (29). She is an archaeologist of knowledge who unearths the gravesite lying below the surface of Stein's beloved Austrian home. The familiar Vienna in which he happily passed thirty-six years of his life becomes uncanny as she furnishes him with the material evidence that his anxiety over the reemergence of anti-Semitism is not groundless.

The very ground beneath their feet has a story to tell of fear, of hate, of death and destruction. Although, on the surface, Stein and Clarissa trace the path mapped out by the standard tourist brochure, they are guided by another book on Vienna between 1938 and 1945. It is not the "Grand City Tour [of] Court Palace & Stables, Belvedere Castle, Schönbrunn ... Spanish Riding School, Vienna Boys Choir & Tombs of the Habsburgian Emperors" (35), but the grand tour of the tombs of those who fell victim to the Gestapo and the SA troops. Not only are their graves unmarked by any commemorative tablet, but the very foundation of their life and identity—the synagogue—has been demolished, not once, but twice over.

If history is written for the purpose of identification, what do these two very different books tell us about identity in postwar Austria? Neither book tells an entirely false history and neither tells an entirely complete history. One appropriates the glorious past of Imperial Vienna and its symbolic successor UN-City, the other the inglorious past of the "Anschluß" and the Third Reich. The first book invites identification as inclusion on a grand scale ("Vielvölkerstaat" [multiethnic state] and global diplomacy); the second represents identification as exclusion, expulsion, and extinction. Strictly speaking, chronology demands that the second book be contained within the first. However, since the period between 1938 and 1945 is not consonant with the inclusive identity narrative of a peace-loving Austria, it is excluded. In blocking out this historical period, it blocks out the light (as Henisch would say), the light that sheds understanding on human behavior and interaction. It does not admit of the insight that cooperation can run amok.

It is in this light that the anti-Semitic "us-and-them" discourse of the election and beyond takes on significance—or, to use another Henisch metaphor, anti-Semitic rhetoric sends shock waves into the earth opening up cracks in the foundation of the Second Republic that threaten its present stability as a republic. The tectonic movement wakes the dead and the ghost of Stein's Grandfather appears on the scene. Although cooperation on behalf of identification and division has prematurely and brutally separated him from the living, he nevertheless represents a rhetorical alternative to Clarissa's agonistic response to the antagonistic rhetoric of identification. He possesses the ironic humor of the dead, of those who are cognizant of the dialectical tension between life and death, affirmation and negation. He teaches the lesson of the satirist who holds up the mask of death to the living as a reminder that they must look to the present for there may be no tomorrow. The Grandfather thus admonishes his grandson to not merely "suffer the slings and arrows of outrageous fortune," but to embrace life as affirmation, to participate in life, and to take some kind of positive action: "To *us*, of course, it makes little difference. Dead is dead. There's not much you can do about that. But as long as you're alive things are different. You should *do* something . . . and not just *suffer!*" (61).

Stein's late father, resigned to a bitter fate; Clarissa, full of clairvoyant rage; and the ghost of Stein's irrepressible Grandfather represent three distinct rhetorical figures in a deliberative debate over how to respond to the rise of anti-Semitism, their disagreement giving the lie to the notion of a unified Jewish conspiracy. The father, as the embodiment of the Wandering Jew, sought to persuade his son to remain in the Jewish fold, to remain in a constant state of readiness, in short, to keep his bags packed. Clarissa, the witness and sign of remembrance, "she who sees too clearly," seeks to persuade Stein to save himself from a repetition of the same through emigration. Finally, the Grandfather seeks to persuade his grandson to remain by his side in Vienna, to keep him company, and to do justice to the dead by doing justice to the living; Stein should act to resist destructive forms of division by identifying life-affirming possibilities.

The rhetorical noise and confusion is so great that a befuddled Stein finds himself persuaded by all three arguments, and he acts on all three. He keeps his "Jewish bag" packed; he decides to emigrate to America, but gets only as far as London; the very next day he returns to Vienna to keep his Grandfather company and to *do something*. Yet given the general lack of agreement over the rules governing speech-acts in Austria during this period, his newfound determination to do something merely results in a series of infelicitous acts. He temporarily relieves himself of the guilt of non-resistance when he runs to the rescue of a handicapped beggar about to suffer a blow from an irate shopkeeper, but to Stein's surprise the disabled man jumps up and runs away. He writes a letter of reconciliation to the newly elected president, but it is doubtful that the president ever reads his letter and it is certain that he never answers it. He attempts to compose a few words to commemorate the demolished synagogue, but the story is too long and tortuous and hence the words are far too many to fit on the surface of a small plaque.

Because Stein cannot change the world—either by his actions or through the art of persuasion—he decides to stop it. To arrest the backward flow of history, to prevent the present form of anti-Semitism from assuming its past form,

Stein determines to take a stand, to *literally* stand his ground as a living memorial, as a watchman at the newspaper kiosk on the corner of the subway stop Wien-Schottenring. This is the scene of the fateful anti-Semitic utterance that, once hurled, splits Stein's identity in two. It is the scene of Stein's petrified non-resistance that burdens him, as an Austrian and as a Jew, with personal, national, and historical guilt. It is the scene of his encounter with Clarissa and of his courtship with Jewish identity that dissolves the bonds that tie him to family and nation. And it is the scene where, pursuing or pursued by his *idée fixe*, Stein is bowled over by that slow-moving streetcar that lands him in the madhouse.

Mad though he may be, Stein does have the good fortune to live in a Republic that operates according to the rules of parliamentary democracy. One could easily take one of J.L. Austin's tests of an illocutionary act as a test of the most basic rule governing democratic life, namely, "when we adopt a verbal means of doing something instead of a non-verbal means, when we talk instead of using a stick."[17] The anti-Semitic battle fought in the Second Republic foregoes the field of war and the concentration camp; in its stead the battle is carried out on a rhetorical field. The consequence is not death, it is only madness.

It is the madness of a split identity, of a nation not at peace with itself because it has not made peace with its past. It is a nation divided between those obsessed with recovering the past and those obsessed with denying the past, or at least denying its significance for the present. It is a Republic founded on an Austrian resistance in an Austria that did not resist. It is a Republic whose politicians of whatever stripe, from Kreisky to Waldheim, cannot resist the temptation of evoking anti-Semitism for the sake of an election victory. And at such times, it is not at all clear whether Austrian national identity should be seen as a cure for fatal antagonisms or as a *"disease* of cooperation"[18] which promotes animosity and division. In the heat of battle, in the desire to win at all costs and to save one's own skin, one invariably reverts to old modes of thought. The rhetorical success of anti-Semitism is undeniable. If it brings advantage in the field of political battle, it will be used, almost casually, as a kind of Mephistophelian sophistry:

> True enough! But one shouldn't be overly plagued by scruples
> Because exactly where ideas are absent,
> A word appears just in the nick of time.
> We can strike a blow in a dispute with words,
> We can fashion systems of meaning from words,
> We can have sure-fire faith in words,
> And words will never lose one jot.[19]

But then again, Faust may well have been right to suggest that words do have meaning and force, that words are a kind of action.

In *A Grammar of Motives* Kenneth Burke proposed the development of an analysis of drama that "treats language and thought primarily as modes of action" (xxi) and characters as "the scenic condition or environment of one another" (7). His project was not solely a literary one, but one that would allow us to "study and clarify the *resources* of ambiguity" (xix) upon which so much political rhetoric relies and which, given the nature of human relations generally and the rise of mass party politics specifically, has led to so much human misery, grief, and destruction in the twentieth century. *Steins Paranoia* is a fiction built upon the premise that language and thought are modes of action that have consequences; in this case, the dissolution of a marriage, a traffic accident, and a term in the mental ward. Stein's paranoia is a condition that says as much about the state of political rhetoric in Austria as it does about his state of mind. Like many of his fellow countrymen, he is the victim of rhetorical ambiguities that he can neither clarify nor resolve. Charges of a "Jewish conspiracy" or remarks concerning the existence of a "Jewish persecution complex" are met with accusations of "anti-Semitism" that are, in turn, dismissed as a sign of "paranoia" to be treated with the aid of psychopharmacon, shock therapy, and, particularly relevant to this case, talk therapy. Because the determination as to what constitutes a delusional fear of persecution, as opposed to a well-founded one, is not always clear-cut, it is a rich source of psycho-political indeterminacy.

Henisch spins a complex narrative structure out of this central ambiguity: Did a given speech-act occur in fact, and, if so, was the meaning attached to it the correct one? When communication once misfires, it leads to further communicative and interpretive uncertainties. Did the attempt at communication actually succeed or fail? Were the conventions invoked in the performance of the speech-act valid for *both* the speaker and the recipient? If the speaker has fled the site of the original utterance and it therefore proves impossible for the recipient to ask for clarification, is it legitimate to attempt to clear up any questions regarding "misunderstandings, indeterminacy or obscurity"[20] by appealing to the situational context in which the statement was issued, such as the 1986 presidential campaign; the 1987 "Mahnwache" (Memorial Watch) and the placement of the Austrian President on the Watch-List; and the 1988 "Bedenkjahr" (Year of Remembrance)? Yet even if the recipient correctly construes the utterance as an anti-Semitic remark, is the utterance significant or insignificant? And if it is significant, what is the correct response? As it transpires, there is no single conventional response, but rather a series of possible conventional responses that the recipient enacts in quick succession and that only lead to further confusion and ambiguity.

If Henisch writes this novel in the ironic rather than the tragic mode, it is only because the rhetorical situation, albeit threatening, remains safely within the bounds of parliamentary discourse. But is the Republic, based on mutual respect and tolerance, truly safe? In answer to this question, Henisch ends *Steins Paranoia* with a deliberate ambiguity: "I set foot in the house that I'm still inhabiting. I close the front door behind me. The roof across the way reflects the twilight" (97). Twilight, to be sure, but is it dawn or dusk?

In considering this final, ambiguous image, it is important to remember that, in the ironic mode, the pair "dawn-dusk" can no more be separated than the equally "reversible pairs . . . disease-cure, hero-villain, active-passive."[21] To this series of politically and rhetorically charged pairs, we could also add "perpetrator-victim" as yet another set of terms acting as the mnemonic source of Stein's befuddled state of mind and also of Austria's continuing political contention and national confusion.

Notes

*An earlier version of this essay appeared as "Waldheim's Austria and the Rhetoric of Identification: The Case of *Steins Paranoia*" in *Rhetoric in German Contexts*, special issue of *Carleton Germanic Papers* 23 (1995): 43-52.

1. Kenneth Burke, *A Grammar of Motives* (Berkeley/Los Angeles/London: U of California P, 1969) 512.
2. Reprinted in Ruth Wodak, Peter Nowak, Johanna Pelikan, Helmut Gruber, Rudolf de Cillia and Richard Mitten, *»Wir sind alle unschuldige Täter!«: Diskurshistorische Studien zum Nachkriegsantisemitismus* (Frankfurt/M: Suhrkamp, 1990) 119.
3. Walter Schwimmer, "Zum Vorwurf des Antisemitismus im Wahlkampf," *Die Kampagne: Kurt Waldheim—Opfer oder Täter? Hintergründe und Szenen eines Falles von Medienjustiz*, eds. A. Kohl, Th. Faulhaber, G. Ofner (Munich and Berlin: Herbig, 1987) 315.
4. Wodak, et al. 119.
5. Kurt Steinitz, "Weshalb der Jüdische Weltkongreß und dessen Chef Israel Singer jetzt so zornig sind," *Neue Kronenzeitung* 28 March 1986, reprinted in Helmut Gruber, *Antisemitismus im Mediendiskurs: Die Affäre "Waldheim" in der Tagespresse* (Wiesbaden: Deutscher Universitäts-Verlag, 1991) 251.
6. Schwimmer 323.
7. Peter Henisch, *Stone's Paranoia*, trans. Craig Decker

(Riverside, CA: Ariadne, 2000) 95.
8. Schwimmer 316.
9. Burke, *A Grammar of Motives* 513-14.
10. Burke, *A Grammar of Motives* 514.
11. In his essay "Warum ich nicht will, daß Österreich untergeht" (Why I Don't Want Austria to Sink), written while he was working on *Steins Paranoia*, Henisch refers to Max Stein as an "Identifikationsfigur": "The . . . identification figure is called Max Stein; he is approximately my age. However, on account of circumstances that, until recently, we considered to be passé, he was born in Quebec, Canada. Stein wants nothing more than to be a good Austrian, but one day in our oh so present past he begins to realize that he can no longer easily do so" ("Warum ich nicht will, daß Österreich untergeht," *Reden an Österreich: Schriftsteller ergreifen das Wort*, ed. Jochen Jung [Salzburg and Vienna: Residenz, 1988] 90).
12. Burke, *A Rhetoric of Motives* (Berkeley/Los Angeles/London: U of California P, 1969) 23.
13. Burke, *A Rhetoric of Motives* 25.
14. Article 1 of the Constitution of Austria's First Republic reads: "German-Austria is a democratic republic," while Article 2 states: "German-Austria is a constituent part of the German Republic."
15. Sigmund Freud, "The Uncanny," *The Standard Edition of the Complete Psychological Works of Sigmund Freud*, trans. and ed. James Strachey, vol. 17 (London: Hogarth, 1955) 247.
16. Freud 247-48.
17. J.L. Austin, *How to Do Things with Words*, eds. J.O. Urmson and Marina Sbisà, 2nd ed. (Cambridge, MA and London: Harvard UP, 1975) 130.
18. Burke, *A Rhetoric of Motives* 23.
19. Johann Wolfgang von Goethe, *Faust: Der Tragödie Erster Teil, Goethes Werke: Hamburger Ausgabe*, ed. Erich Trunz, vol. 3 (Hamburg: Wegner, 1949) 65, lines 1994-2000.
20. Wolfgang Iser, *The Act of Reading: A Theory of Aesthetic Response* (Baltimore and London: Johns Hopkins UP) 56.
21. Burke, *A Grammar of Motives* 512.

The Collective Nature of Subjective Crisis: Peter Henisch's *Der Mai ist vorbei*

HELGA SCHRECKENBERGER

> Schizophrenia
> is a deficiency disease
> of our time:
>
> the deficiency
> of identity
> —Peter Henisch[1]

In Germany, the events of the student protest movement of the sixties emerged as a significant literary topic already in the early seventies. In particular, those authors who were a part of the movement or had in some way been connected with it soon began to work through their experiences in their literary works.[2] Initially, such texts concentrated on the influence of these turbulent times on the political and personal development of the main character.[3] In subsequent, primarily autobiographical texts, the focus shifted from the political events to the subjective state of mind of the protagonists, exploring their confusion and resignation in view of the disappointing political and social developments following the initial euphoric feelings of change and progress.[4]

Peter Henisch's novel *Der Mai ist vorbei* (1978, May Is Over), the first work to deal with the student movement in an Austrian context, falls into the latter category.[5] Taking place in April of 1977, the novel portrays the professional and personal crisis of its protagonist Paul Grünzweig, the fictional alter ego of the author Peter Henisch. Grünzweig's crisis is clearly connected to the events of the sixties which, in the recollections of the protagonist, appear as missed opportunities for a truly new way of life.

Although *Der Mai ist vorbei* focuses on the subjective crises of its protagonist, the novel aims to reveal how these personal crises exemplify a broader societal crisis. This intention is clearly stated in a conversation between the protagonist, author and journalist Paul Grünzweig, and his friend and fellow writer Gabriele. Grünzweig answers Gabriele's inquiry concerning the progress of his novel as follows:

> You know, I have the feeling I'm in a severe crisis. Or maybe it's not just that I am but we all are, and one is mirrored in the other. There is an uncanny discrepancy between what we think and what we do. The schizophrenia from which our time suffers is also my own . . . Maybe that's always the case when something old ends and something new is coming. Or when something new wants to begin but the old still carries too much weight. And this conflict gets played out within us as well as around us. If I could portray that then I could finish the novel. (121-22)

This exchange, which by no coincidence takes place at the exact center of the novel,[6] points to the main objective of the work: to show that individual and collective history are inextricably bound. Moreover, Grünzweig's response identifies what the protagonist/author believes to be the central reason for the perceived private and public crisis: namely, the conflict between old and new ideas. The individual and the collective, unable to either completely abandon the old or fully embrace the new, experience a crisis of identity which Henisch has defined in an earlier work as schizophrenia: "Schizophrenia is a state of mind which, in my opinion, corresponds most completely to our social existence. With one half of our personality still in the connections we want to abandon, we find ourselves standing with the other half in new and unfamiliar ones."[7] This individual and collective schizophrenic state of mind stands as the central theme of *Der Mai ist vorbei*, manifesting itself in both the form and content of the novel.

Henisch's own experiences in the student movement of the sixties, a movement intent on propagating new forms of existence based upon the central premise that the private is essentially political, serve the author as a vehicle to illustrate both his belief in the interrelatedness of individual and collective history and the inherent conflict between the old and the new in times of social upheaval.[8] The retrospective evaluation of the events and ideas of the sixties from the perspective of the so-called "Tendenzwende"[9] of the seventies serves as a means to identify the subjective and objective conditions which, in turn, not only led to the protagonist's present crisis but are also preventing the constitution of a new, meaningful identity. In order to make the exemplary nature of his subjective experience visible, Henisch employs a double narrative: a third-person narrative featuring the fictional character Paul Grünzweig, whose experiences are almost identical with those of the author; and a first-person narrative featuring the author Peter Henisch.[10] The impetus behind this double narrative is presented at the beginning of the novel as an aesthetic choice:

> "What can I tell you?" I asked, "I don't know much myself. Only that the novel is about a more or less loser of a student, writer, and journalist named Paul Grünzweig who is supposed to write an article about the year '68 but actually does not want to. And that at

the same time I worry about writing exclusively in the third person because it goes against my grain to simply write a novel creating illusions. But I am also dissatisfied with a mere autobiography." (17-18)

The autobiographical narrator's struggle with the appropriate form for his novel corresponds to Henisch's attempt to find a new literary realism that allows for an exemplary representation of seemingly subjective problems.[11] Autobiographical writing for Henisch must go beyond a mere preoccupation with the self to portray the conflict between individual and society. Henisch proceeds from his subjective experiences, but he tries to reveal their relationship to broader social conditions. In *Der Mai ist vorbei*, the third-person narrative represents Grünzweig's past and present experiences, while the first-person narrator comments and reflects upon them, thereby illuminating their social context.

The double narrative not only serves as a means to show the connections between individual and collective experience but also as an expression of the narrator's crisis. By attributing his personal experiences and desires to his fictitious alter ego, the autobiographical narrator hopes to be able to reflect upon them objectively and thus find a way out of his crisis: "I believed I would be able to objectify a certain part of my personality. I remove it from myself and put myself in opposition to it. I give it a name and get rid of it" (164). As we will see, however, instead of providing a way out, this experiment only functions to foreground the contradictions within the autobiographical narrator. The narrative structure itself thus reflects the very schizophrenia that the novel identifies as the central problem of the age.

The notion of schizophrenia as the protagonist's crisis of identity is thematically introduced at the very beginning of the novel through a recurring dream that takes Paul Grünzweig back to his school days. He not only arrives too late at school but is unable to find his class, i.e., the appropriate group of pupils. The heavy symbolism of this dream points to the protagonist's status as an outsider and also to his lack of identificatory possibilities. The word "class" in its sociological sense evokes the broader context of the protagonist's problem: he cannot find his proper place in society and thus feels isolated and alone. Grünzweig expresses this feeling again in his conversation with Gabriele at the center of the novel. Pointing out two different tables at the restaurant, one occupied by a stiff group of businessmen in pin-striped suits, the other by a boisterous group of workers in overalls, Grünzweig states his conviction that he would not be accepted by either group. The fact that Gabriele shares this feeling of isolation underscores the broader social implications of this seemingly individual problem.[12]

Both scenes present strong evidence that Grünzweig's identity crisis is clearly connected to the past, more precisely, to the sixties, which are metaphorically represented in the novel as a recurring toothache. Grünzweig answers Gabriele's question about how much he really was affected by the events of the sixties as follows: "'Obviously I was,' Paul said, 'and more so than I would like. It feels as if I had bitten down on a bad tooth which I wanted to forget.' (He felt for his missing filling with his tongue.) 'Now I am overly conscious of it and it hurts'" (122). This conversation throws light on the function of Grünzweig's toothache at the beginning of the novel. His act of numbing with alcohol the severe toothache caused by a lost filling is retrospectively invested with symbolic meaning. He is not only suffering from a bad tooth but also from his repressed memories. This suffering, in turn, points to the obvious solution to Grünzweig's problem: not repression but constructive re-evaluation of the obviously painful past would help him overcome his crisis.

The opportunity for such a re-evaluation presents itself to Grünzweig in two ways. First, he reluctantly accepts a conservative editor's commission to write a retrospective article about the protest movement of the sixties: "What he had in mind were ten nice legal-sized pages spanning an elegant arch from the idealistic beginnings of the student movement to its terrorist abominations" (12). While conducting indifferent research for his article at the university library, he meets his former tutorial student and new love interest Julia. Julia, a journalist herself, wants to hear about Grünzweig's personal

The Collective Nature of Subjective Crisis 151

experiences during the sixties: "So, tell me about your experiment with a commune" (177). Both of these opportunities to talk about the past influence the nature of Grünzweig's recollections and memories. Trying to write the article directs him to the public events, the conversation with Julia to more private ones.

Altogether, Grünzweig's memories of the sixties are less bound up with the political aspects of the period than with his subjective feelings and experiences. Trying to recall specific political events such as the attempted assassination of Rudi Dutschke, the leader of the German student movement, or the large demonstrations in Paris, Grünzweig discovers that such public events are invariably linked in his memory to private actions: the attempt on Dutschke's life coincides with his decision to get married, and the Paris demonstrations with a vacation with his wife.[13] On the one hand, this response can be seen as another demonstration of the close relationship between the private and the political; on the other hand, it reflects to a certain extent the objective reality of the student movement in Austria which was infinitely less politically motivated than the movement in other countries.

In comparison to Germany, France, or the United States, the political protests of 1968 in Austria seem relatively tame. The demonstrations against the Shah of Iran on February 10 and against the war in Vietnam on February 13 led to altercations with the police; on February 22, demonstrators protesting the Viennese Opera Ball caused a disturbance; in April, students took to the street after the attempted assassination of Rudi Dutschke. In addition, a few "teach-ins" were staged at the university and the younger, more radical members of the Socialist Party revolted against the old guard.[14] In recalling this time in the draft of his article, Grünzweig relates the lack of political activism in Austria to the prevailing sociopolitical climate, citing in particular the lack of a clearly defined public opponent:

The Americans had their war in Vietnam, the Germans their mendacious Springer Press, the French their authoritarian Gaullism. You could oppose that. It was

> *possible to protest against that. In a pinch you could fight against it. In other countries the social contrasts were obvious. Therefore, it was easier to make a fist. They weren't just contradictions in your head.... We in Austria, lulled to sleep by politics designed to balance different interests, to level opposition, to blur contradictions, and which moreover worked... what possibilities did we have...?* (162-63)

Grünzweig holds the political system of postwar Austria, and particularly the so-called "Sozialpartnerschaft" (social partnership)—with its objective of always finding a middle way and never fully committing to one side or the other—responsible for the lack of political activism in Austria. The indecisiveness on the political, that is, public level mirrors the individual indecisiveness of the protagonist. The marginal role of the Austrian student movement corresponds to the even smaller role Grünzweig played in it. His contention that, as far as the student movement was concerned, the students of Austria were spectators rather than actors is especially true when applied to himself. Paul Grünzweig is indeed the best example of this collective passivity. He participated even less than some of his friends and colleagues:

> Even before, he had very seldom taken the time to participate in demonstrations. To be sure, he presented himself as vaguely active. Without a doubt he would have described himself as leftist, and he wrote poems that strove for solidarity with the left. But truly, he always felt he was sitting in his room while things were happening outside which he could not influence. He did not like to summon the energy to leave the room and take to the street. (46)

Grünzweig's personal history (as well as that of his creator) presents an explanation for his reluctance to join in with the demonstrators. His father's fascination with the uniforms of the Nazi regime has left him with a distaste for any organized movement.[15] Henisch again connects individual and collective history by referring to Austria's complicity in the Nazi dictatorship: "This abundance of history between the Burg Gate and Michaela Gate, between the Volksgarten and Burggarten oppressed him! Again and again he felt a certain apprehension when crossing the Heldenplatz. It was difficult to breathe" (153). The beautiful Viennese cityscape reminds Grünzweig of Austria's involvement with the totalitarian regime and embodies for him the need to reject anything that threatens to co-opt individuality:

> This generation and that one: Heldenplatz and Woodstock. Hitler, the first pop star, as some rock singer recently had said in an interview. What was happening here? They too had celebrated their mystical festival and had longed for an unbelievable spring, they too were a giant tribe. It was just that the sons had yelled NO instead of YES like their fathers, that was the difference and would hopefully remain so. (153)

But while Paul himself was once satisfied with simply rejecting the beliefs and way of life of his parents' generation, he now questions the validity of just saying no.

While the rejection of the parent generation—to a large extent because of its guilty and largely unacknowledged participation in the Nazi regime—was an important component of the Austrian protest movement, it was not the major one. According to Grünzweig, the absence of a clear political agenda in Austria reduced the movement of the sixties to a mere generational conflict. It thus amounted in large part to a desire of the younger generation to live life differently than their parents: "We did not want to relive the life that our parents modeled for us, neither their war nor their peace" (162). But the desire of the young Austrians to establish a different form of existence that explicitly challenged the *status quo* does, in fact, have significant political implications, especially when seen in the context of the central demand of the student movement to abolish the division between the private and public spheres. This is also true of the experience that had the greatest impact on Grünzweig's life: his ill-fated attempt to form a commune with some friends and acquaintances. Paul Grünzweig and his friends are inspired not only by the sixty-eighters' belief in the inherently political nature of the private but also by the many alternative newspapers which praised communal living arrangements as a way to oppose the traditional forms of existence sanctioned by a decaying society: "And what was the primary cell of this decaying society? The family unit. And what should be considered as the alternative? A commune! Daily life would be easier and cheaper; it would dissolve restrictive bourgeois privacy, leading to an overall politicization in the sense of consciousness raising" (197). Grünzweig's account of his experience with communal living, however, reveals the political naiveté of the commune's initiators who mistook unconventional private behavior for political activism. It becomes very clear that the lofty political motives for forming a commune went hand in hand with very practical private reasons for each of the communards. Paul Grünzweig feels overwhelmed by his needy former schoolmate Schubert and looks to share the burden. In addition, he is attracted to Bärbel, the wife of his friend and colleague Willy. For their part, Bärbel and Willy seek to share child-rearing responsibilities for their newborn. Harry and Ed, the two Americans, are in need of housing. In addition, sparks of attraction fly between Harry and Silvi, Paul's wife. Schubert, meanwhile, forced by circumstances and his mother to do work that proves detrimental to his ambition of becoming a musician, looks to his friends for help. Given these hidden agendas, the failure of the commune comes as no surprise. Despite the irony that permeates the narration of the conflicts and tribulations of life in the commune, the real pain they caused is clearly detectable.

Henisch once again employs the dichotomy of the old and the new to characterize the commune and to foreshadow its failure. The communal living experience is to take place in the former apartment of Willy's parents. It is not only filled with old furniture, but it also houses Willy's grandmother. Grünzweig interprets the symbolism of this situation: "So we had to make ourselves at home with our new ideas in existing conditions" (187). This non-integrated side-by-side of the old and the new also characterizes the members of the commune, who want to try a new way of living but are not able to relinquish their old habits and beliefs. The male members of the commune cling blindly to traditional gender roles. Incompatible eating habits cause unsurmountable problems and lead to absurd statements like "Napkins are reactionary" (196). Henisch ironically foregrounds the discrepancy between lofty ideals and prosaic reality: "It was a matter, he [Paul] wrote, of recognizing the appearance of the new wherever it showed itself as an opportunity. At that instant little Michael began to stink and Silvi and Bärbel changed him in teamwork. But Paul, who was a bit nauseated by the yellow, mushy baby stool, put *The Principle of Hope* away again" (195). Paul is unable to recognize the new—represented here by the infant—much less see it as an opportunity. He instead experiences it as an unwelcome interruption.

Another reason for the failure of the communal experience is the inability of the couples to reconcile the discrepancy between their respective feelings of propriety toward their partners and the new call for giving up such demands. Since such feelings are deemed reactionary, they cannot be openly admitted. Thus, Paul and Willy sublimate their jealousy and engage in philosophical and political battles or they use a game of table tennis to get the better of their opponent. Neither of them recognizes that, by trying to best their rival either intellectually or physically, they are only acting out stereotypical male behavior. Repressed jealousy leads both Willy and Silvi to irrational, almost suicidal, behavior. Excluded from these sexual and emotional entanglements, Schubert feels even more isolated than before. The end is thus foreseeable: the commune is dissolved; former friends turn into bitter enemies. It is not difficult to recognize the exemplary nature of this failed experiment. Because the members of the commune cannot overcome their old beliefs and habits, they fail to find a common ground for individual (private) and collective (public) interests. Grünzweig's unsuccessful attempt to explain this unattained objective to his mother suggests both the difficulties of putting it into practice and his own political naiveté: "The type of socialism he had in mind would be a state of being that would give this existence a different quality (in what way?). In that each individual would live according to his or her true needs while negotiating these needs with those of the general public (how?)" (31). The impossibility of this goal, indicated throughout the novel, echoes Peter Henisch's personal convictions as expressed in the fifth part of his "Endless Interview" in *Zwischen allen Sesseln* (1982, Between All the Stools):

> *I actually believed that I would be able to survive in the cultural market with my ideals, i.e., to be successful and find aesthetic recognition for my ideals, on the one hand, and not get demoralized, that is, not gradually get changed beyond recognition, on the other. But this is very similar to marriage. I mean, you want to have one when, in fact, you reject the system. I believed that we would be able to do it, to live in a petit-bourgeois marriage, on the one hand, and not fall victim to its inherent gender-specific patterns, on the other. But I was wrong. The contradictions cannot be reconciled.*[16]

In the novel, both the fictitious Grünzweig and the autobiographical first-person narrator experience the same problems. They suffer from the compromises demanded of them in their marriages and their careers. In his "Endless Interview" Henisch draws parallels between subjective experience and socio-political reality: *"there is by the way a connection between democracy and reformed marriage. I have written that in May [Is Over], but it cannot be said often enough. You cannot, on the one hand, brown-nose industry and, on the other hand, pass reforms that would like to be revolutionary. That is not possible. And it doesn't work either."*[17] However, despite his obvious disappointment with the protest movement's failure to effect a true change of both subjective and objective conditions, Henisch emphasizes the positive aspects of its objectives. Looking back at the experiences of the sixties, the autobiographical narrator Peter states: "it's true, the situation was absurd. It couldn't have worked, and still there was something right about it. I mean, the attempt to cross boundaries that constrict us, inside and out. We tried it and others tried it. The fact that we didn't succeed doesn't prove anything" (225).

If Henisch does not criticize his protagonists for failing to create better and freer ways of living, he criticizes them for abandoning the attempt to do so. When Grünzweig returns to the university in search of material for his article, Henisch uses his visit to depict ironically some of the results of the "Tendenzwende"—for example, the opportunistic adaptation of the movement's former members to the political *status quo*. At the university, Grünzweig almost fails to recognize his former colleague Schestak: "Finally he understood: Schestak's curls, which formerly had reached his shoulders, had been cut. And the loose-fitting corduroy suit which he had always worn had been exchanged for an unobtrusive suit of light brown linen" (26). Schestak had not only changed his look but he also accepted a position as an assistant professor under the supervision of one of the most conservative professors in the philosophy department. Schestak responds to Grünzweig's obvious astonishment with the retort that times have changed. Schestak's changed appearance and his defense of the conservative Professor Killian leave no room for the illusionary belief that the former protester is attempting to reform the institution from within. Schestak has simply arranged himself on the side of the power.

Another phenomenon of the "Tendenzwende" is the splintering and infighting among the new generation of the political left. Grünzweig is handed flyers by "two strikingly pale young men with metal-rimmed glasses and seal haircuts" (25). The flyers are produced by two leftist groups trying to discredit each other: "Both used the same expressions in order to prove that they (contrary to the others) were the true left" (28). The fact that both ideas and proponents are practically interchangeable recalls the "deficiency of identity" Henisch sees as characteristic of the seventies. The novel clearly connects the opportunistic conformism of the old left and the schizophrenic behavior of the new generation. The old left has lost its identity and thus cannot serve as a positive model for the younger generation. Instead of deriving an identity from political objectives, they lose themselves in formalistic battles. Moreover, while the left is growing increasingly impotent, new right-wing political organizations crop up. The renewed interest of young people in right-wing extremism in particular underscores the failure of the left. Accordingly, the heroic image of the defeated but righteous left can only be created with irony: "In the street he met the red tomcat. He was big and strong and disheveled from fighting. An opponent had most likely bitten off the end of his tail, but he carried the rest of it with unrelenting pride. 'I would like to be like you,' Paul said and stroked his head" (170). The "red" cat, with its unremitting will to fight and its obvious pride in its battle scars (even if they indicate losses), demonstrates the impotence of the "red" party which it satirically represents. However, while the red cat has not given up its fights and thus can still serve as a positive role model, the left has arranged itself with the prevailing power structure.

The novel touches at least indirectly on another reaction to the failed protest movement: left-wing terrorism. However, Henisch focuses more on the hysterical reaction of the public which allowed the police to suspend individual rights. Following a neighbor's report about the coming and going of "suspicious elements," Paul receives a visit from two policemen who react suspiciously not only to Paul's reading material (Genet, Sartre, Böll) but also to the fact that the owner of the apartment, Paul's friend Fritz Steinwendner, is traveling in South America. When Paul recommends that they should investigate the new right-wing organization at the university, suggesting that this would be more effective in securing Austria's democracy and freedom, the police show little interest. Henisch thus points to the old double standard vis-à-vis political extremism.

Seen from Paul's perspective, the political reality of the seventies appears truly alienating. The poem preceding the first part of the novel calls the period a new "Biedermayer,"[18] thus linking it to the historical period of political restoration and conservatism following the "Wars of Independence" against Napoleon. While the political and social realities of the 1970s are far removed from those of the mid-nineteenth century, the comparison is valid to a certain extent. In the mid-1800s as well, disappointment over unfulfilled promises of democratization and political rights led to disillusionment and resignation among many intellectuals. The latter response is especially characteristic of Paul Grünzweig: "Paul saw very clearly that he himself personified resignation excellently. (That he admitted that fact, however, was already part of his resignation)" (23). The reason for his resignation may be that he is not able to believe that he really can change existing conditions. And as his lack of involvement in the student movement indicates, he may never have really believed in the possibility to do so. Still more problematic is Grünzweig's unwillingness to take a stand. His refusal to get involved is not limited to large public demonstrations but also carries over into his private actions. There are several instances in which he fails to interfere when weaker members of society are the victims of violence. The brutal beating of a foreign worker by the Austrian police only evokes in him the desire to evade the spectacle, and he does nothing to break up a very one-sided fight between three drunks in a bar. Grünzweig and his friend are aware of their guilt: "'And even if they'd killed him,' Paul said, 'we still would have watched. We'd have sat there and our unapplied muscles would have made micro-movements like during a fight at the movies. And if they come one day and beat us up, what will we do?' 'Yes,' Nick said, 'I know.' But that wasn't an answer" (157). Such passivity in the face of an obvious injustice recalls the earlier failures of passive intellectuals, thus connecting Grünzweig and the members of his generation to the past. This link can also be seen in the context of Henisch's criticism that the Austrian political system promotes passivity in its citizens. On account of his passivity and in spite of his self-criticism, Grünzweig is not conceived of as an ideal protagonist who invites imitation.

 Nevertheless, Grünzweig has taken little steps to overcome his resignation. He has made the painful move of leaving his wife and child, thus breaking out of his private misery. The disorderly chaos of his new existence (no clean shirts, unpaid bills, messy apartment) indicates that his first step towards liberation constitutes more of a negation of his old life than true progress. However, the end of the novel suggests the emergence of new possibilities for Grünzweig. Julia takes him to the countryside where she and her friends are experimenting with a different type of communal experience. In its unconventionality and commitment to spontaneity, this living experiment is reminiscent of those of the sixties. It appeals to Grünzweig because it offers a new form of communal living, one that provides for the possibility of retaining one's individuality while also claiming to promote a new collective political consciousness. The people living together pursue their individual political or social causes. They also do not completely conform to the traditional mode of heterosexuality, as one of the couples is homosexual. Their invitation to Grünzweig to stay is made in a spirit of tolerance and openness. He can stay if he wants to and work out his problems on his own terms: "You could talk about them if you feel like it, and if you don't feel like it you could maybe think about them and lose them somewhere in the forest if they don't seem important to you anymore" (251). In light of this new opportunity, Grünzweig feels both nostalgic and revitalized: "It seemed to Paul as if he had been here before, but that was a very long time ago, and so he remembered it only vaguely like an old dream. In a pleasant way he felt that he had five senses, perhaps even more. A motif from *The Four Seasons* occurred to him and went repeatedly through his head. It came from 'Spring'" (251-52).[19]

While Grünzweig seems to be granted the opportunity of a new beginning which might help him to overcome his identity crisis—he may have found a group in which he will be accepted and which he likewise can accept—this is not the case for the autobiographical narrator Peter. In the course of the novel it becomes evident that Peter and Paul are not identical, but rather two possible representations of one person. They may share a past, but they do not share the present. This is already foreshadowed when Peter explains to his wife his problems with finding the appropriate narrative voice for his novel:

"Aha," says Sonja, " So you're hiding behind Paul."
"On one hand," I say, "But then again, on the other hand I am not. It may be that Paul resembles me more than I myself. And that I grow more like him than I would care to." (18)

This response suggests that the fictitious protagonist reveals the true "Peter," especially in his desire to escape an orderly, conventional life and its necessary compromises. Since Grünzweig has taken this step he is no longer identical with Peter, as the autobiographical narrator establishes in the second chapter of the first segment of the novel: "This is about Paul, about Grünzweig, and not about me" (15). The difference between them is reflected in their respective environments. The cracked ceiling and general disorder of Paul Grünzweig's living quarters and his irregular lifestyle contrast sharply with Peter's well-ordered existence: he gets up early, his ceiling has no cracks but is clean and white, as is the convenient and efficient furniture of his apartment. Peter emphasizes, however, that it is not "his order," but rather that of his wife Sonja. While Peter and Sonja struggle to make their marriage work despite their frustrations and differing needs, Grünzweig has left his wife and child after a painful fight, one not unlike those Peter and Sonja experience time and again. Peter rebels against the imposed conventionality of his life in small ways (e.g., burning the milk every morning), but unlike Paul he is not able or willing to take the final step, in large part because of his daughter. However, Peter's desire to be Grünzweig grows stronger in the course of the novel, a desire perceived to be a consequence of writing or, at least, as a consequence of his particular way of writing:

At a certain point in time when I am writing a novel, I start living in and from it. . . .
This unfortunate desire, not only to imitate life by writing but also to model life for writing, or at least to be on a par with it. You cannot constantly play with consciousness without changing reality. (163)

Der Mai ist vorbei fulfills this "unfortunate desire" only partially: Paul is able to change his reality, but not Peter. While Paul senses "a new freedom" (251) in the country idyll, Peter returns to his restricted environment: "WALKING ON THE LAWN PROHIBITED / BIKING AND PLAYING SOCCER PROHIBITED / MAKING NOISE AND MUSIC PROHIBITED . . . Now they have even put the garbage cans behind bars so no unauthorized person can dump his dirt with us: FOR RESIDENT GARBAGE ONLY" (252). Peter experiences an increased alienation which even the rather harmonious evening with his wife and daughter cannot change. It is Sonja who articulates their inherent problem: a system that "is good for the reproduction of existing conditions and that does not leave room for beauty" (254). Although Sonja is talking about her particular experiences as a schoolteacher, parallels to the larger social reality depicted in the novel are evident.

The double ending indicates that Peter has not been able to overcome the schizophrenic state of his existence. He is still split between the wish to abandon the norms and expectations of society, on the one hand, and the realization that this is not entirely possible, on the other. The novel does not provide any solution or easy answers to the protagonist's dilemma. Moreover, its schizophrenic ending forces the reader to reflect on these unresolved issues and thus examine the contradictions within his or her own societal identity. This is not to say, however, that the novel ends on a purely negative note. It is true that Peter's reality, which stands at the end of the novel, seems to overshadow the positive ending of Grünzweig's story. Despite its utopian nature, however, the desirability of Grünzweig's end cannot be denied, a desirability that is even more evident when compared to the ending of Peter's story. Articulating the possibility of a better and more satisfying way of life is, according to Peter Henisch, one of the most important functions of literature, even if such a function may seem unrealistic: *"because n o t h i n g is p o s s i b l e anymore if you repeal fantasy."*[20] *Der Mai ist vorbei* thus contributes in two important ways to Henisch's struggle to activate the communicative potential of literature: it represents the interrelationship between individual problems and their social contexts while also offering at least the vision of a better way of life.

Notes

1. Peter Henisch, *Der Mai ist vorbei* (Frankfurt/M: Fischer, 1978) 235.
2. These authors and texts include: Paul Peter Zahl, *Von einem der auszog, Geld zu verdienen* (1970); Gerd Fuchs, *Beringer und die lange Wut* (1973); Peter Schneider, *Lenz: Eine Erzählung von 1968 und danach* (1973); Roland Lang, *Ein Hai in der Suppe oder das Glück des Philipp Ronge* (1974); Uwe Timm, *Ein heißer Sommer* (1974); Nicolas Born, *Die erdabgewandte Seite der Geschichte* (1976); and Elisabeth Plessen, *Mitteilungen an den Adel* (1976).
3. For example, in the works of Fuchs, Lang, Plessen, Timm, and Zahl.
4. For example, Born and Schneider.
5. The novel attracted little attention in either Austria or Germany. Delays in publication and indifferent marketing due to personnel changes at Henisch's former publishing house S. Fischer were at least partially responsible for this reception. For additional information on the publishing history of the novel, see Eva Schobel, *Peter Henisch: Eine Monographie*, diss., U Vienna, 1987 (Vienna: Verband der wissenschaftlichen Gesellschaften Österreichs, 1988) 428-30.

Thirteen years after the publication of *Der Mai ist vorbei*, *Morrisons Versteck* (Morrison's Hideout), Henisch's second literary treatment of the social and cultural implications of the sixties, appeared. By reconstructing the life of Jim Morrison, lead singer of the legendary rock band The Doors, Henisch explores the broader philosophical and cultural basis of the international rebellion against the political, social, and cultural *status quo*.

6. The novel is divided into four parts, each covering one day. The first part consists of eight numbered chapters, the second of sixteen, the third of five, and the last part of two, amounting to thirty-one chapters altogether. The conversation between Grünzweig and his writer friend takes place in the eighth chapter of the second part. It is the sixteenth chapter of the novel, preceded and followed by fifteen chapters each.

7. Henisch, *Vom Baronkarl: Peripheriegeschichten und andere Prosa* (Frankfurt/M: Fischer, 1972) 64.

8. The Austrian reviewers focused mainly on the autobiographical content of the novel. The reviewers were primarily interested in identifying the real-life counterparts of the novel's protagonists. It was felt that Henisch had taken the popular conviction of the sixties that everything private was also public too far. Eva Schobel discusses in detail the autobiographical background of this novel (*Peter Henisch* 249-74). An identification of the persons behind the literary figures can also be found in Joseph P. Strelka, "Eine Phänomenologie des Mitmachens: Zur frühen autobiographischen Erzählprosa von Peter Henisch," *Modern Austrian Literature* 13.1 (1980): 149-61, here 153.

9. "Tendenzwende," literally meaning "turn of tendency," denotes the return of a more conservative socio-political and cultural climate after the turbulent events of the sixties.

10. This type of narrative structure is very characteristic of Peter Henisch's work. It can also be found, for instance, in *Die kleine Figur meines Vaters* (1975) as well as in later works such as *Hoffmanns Erzählungen: Aufzeichnungen eines verwirrten Germanisten* (1983) and *Morrisons Versteck* (1991).

11. Henisch discusses his conception of literary realism in a conversation with Victor Suchy conducted and taped on 20 July 1971. The audiotape is available at the Dokumentationsstelle für neuere österreichische Literatur in Vienna.

12. Later in the novel, a professor at the university attributes the feeling of isolation from society, of being an outsider, to the bourgeois artist in particular (131-32).

13. Similarly, Grünzweig's involvement with the Socialist

Party was motivated by his desire to meet women. Later, the meetings and actions of the Party serve as a pretext for his meetings with Silvi, who subsequently becomes his wife. The political ideas he acquires during these meetings seem more of a side effect than his main purpose. This contradicts Joseph Strelka's assertion that many of the younger generation had erotic relations in connection with or under the domination of political ideas ("Eine Phänomenologie des Mitmachens" 155-56). In Henisch's text, the private clearly dominates the political.

14. See Fritz Keller, *Mai 68—eine heiße Viertelstunde* (Vienna: Juvius, 1983) 80 and 146-47.

15. See Henisch, *Die kleine Figur meines Vaters* (Frankfurt/M: Fischer, 1975).

16. Henisch, *Zwischen allen Sesseln: Geschichten, Gedichte, Entwürfe, Notizen, Statements 1965-1982* (Vienna: Hannibal, 1982) 117.

17. Henisch, *Zwischen allen Sesseln* 117. The reference to the novel concerns an exchange between Peter and his wife. While reading the newspaper published by the Social Democratic Party, Peter asks his wife if she has considered the connection between reformed marriage and Social Democracy. She agrees to the justification of his theory (226).

18. "children the times are getting strange / we're living in Biedermayer again / and know it / and do not want to know it / and don't know it" (8). Henisch uses a spelling different from that of the historical Biedermeier period. Schobel assumes Henisch wanted to identify it satirically as the time of Mr. and Mrs. Mayer, the stereotypical representatives of the lower-middle class (*Peter Henisch* 396). In the context of the poem, "Biedermayer" also means a return to conservatism, to traditional gender roles, and to traditional forms of living—in short, a return to cultural conservatism.

19. When Grünzweig had previously listened to Vivaldi's *Four Seasons* he always mistook the movement of "Summer" for "Fall," indicating that the "spring of '68" came to a premature end. Now this pessimism is replaced by the hope of a new spring.

20. Henisch, *Zwischen allen Sesseln* 155.

Literary Dialogues and Dialogic Literature: Peter Henisch's *Vom Wunsch, Indianer zu werden*

ANTJE HARNISCH

> He who imagines is alive.
> —Peter Henisch[1]

> You're writing a biography? Morgenrot said. No!
> A novel? No, a novel even less so!
> Can one after all? Can one still today? Can one once again today?
> Write something like that when one is not totally naive?[2]

One can, but not in the traditional way, would probably be the answer—and Peter Henisch's *Morrisons Versteck* (1991, Morrison's Hideout) from which this quote is taken, as well as *Vom Wunsch, Indianer zu werden: Wie Franz Kafka Karl May traf und trotzdem nicht in Amerika landete* (1994, Wishing to

Be an Indian: How Franz Kafka Met Karl May But Still Didn't End Up in America) attest to this. Together with two other novels by the same author, *Hoffmanns Erzählungen: Aufzeichnungen eines verwirrten Germanisten* (1983, Tales of Hoffmann: Notes of a Confused Germanist) and *Steins Paranoia* (1988; *Stone's Paranoia*, 2000), these texts display similarities with biographical novels or fictional biographies of the last decades, such as Christa Wolf's *Kein Ort: Nirgends* (1979; *No Place on Earth*, 1982), Peter Härtling's *Hölderlin* (1976) or Dieter Kühn's *Ich Wolkenstein* (1977, I Wolkenstein). This kind of biographical writing problematizes traditional genres and plays with the boundaries between fact and fiction,[3] a form of play that culminates in Wolfgang Hildesheimer's *Marbot* (1981; *Marbot*, 1983), a text that calls itself biography and presents itself as a biography, but which is fiction from beginning to end. What all these biographical endeavors have in common is the attempt of the narrator—whether identified as the author or not—to get closer to a protagonist and his or her time, to understand and communicate with an Other who is removed in time and place in order to learn something about the present and the self in the process. Thus, writing biography—or pseudo-biography—is dialogic from the outset.

The protagonists in this kind of biographical writing function both as figures with whom the narrator identifies and as figures from whom he distances himself. Henisch emphasizes the former when he calls his protagonists "literary identification figures," who include historical persons such as E.T.A. Hoffmann (1776-1822), Jim Morrison (1943-71), Franz Kafka (1883-1924), and Karl May (1842-1912), as well as fictional characters such as Max Stein.[4] Henisch goes on to explain that he shares with his "identification figures" the position of the outsider. In the case of Kafka and May, we can add the occupation and fascination with the New World. America has had an impact on the imagination of these two—otherwise so different—authors, just as this great imagined Other has exerted its influence on Henisch, as evidenced, for instance, in *Morrisons Versteck*. A further link between Kafka, May, and Henisch lies in their problematic relationship to their respective fathers, which *Vom Wunsch, Indianer zu werden* indicates regarding May and Kafka (122, 134) and *Die kleine Figur meines Vaters* (1987; *Negatives of My Father*, 1990) treats extensively regarding Henisch himself. Most importantly, however, Henisch identifies with Kafka and May—just as with Hoffmann and Morrison—as colleagues, and his text is above all a dialogue with other writers. Such a dialogue, of course, is typical of biographical fiction written by someone who writes himself: most of the biographies written by contemporary authors deal with writers and thus attempt to communicate with other artists, contemporary or past, and thereby learn something for the present or future. This also holds true for *Vom Wunsch, Indianer zu werden*, a text in which literature is not only the main topic of conversation between the two protagonists, but in which such conversations serve as a metacommentary on writing fiction, and not just any type of fiction, but fiction that is serious while, at the same time, appealing to a larger public.

Vom Wunsch, Indianer zu werden takes the dialogic principle that informs all biography to a new level. At least on the surface, the text appears to be less of a dialogue between author and protagonist than a dialogue between two (and at times three) protagonists. Like Christa Wolf's *Kein Ort: Nirgends*, Henisch's text depicts an encounter between two well-known authors. But unlike Wolf's text, it is not a meeting of kindred spirits. While Heinrich von Kleist (1777-1811) and Caroline von Günderrode (1780-1806) share an alienation from their environment and its prevailing artistic concerns, it is hard to imagine writers—and possibly individuals—more different than Karl May and Franz Kafka. And Henisch's text does not try to conceal this. Its protagonists are presented as antipodes in every imaginable way: in terms of age, marital status, social background, and, most importantly, in their approach to writing. But these differences present no obstacles to the communication between the two authors. On the contrary, these differences prove productive in Henisch's text, a text, that is, that focuses mainly on dialogue: dialogue between characters; dialogue between narrator and characters; dialogue between author and readers; and finally, but not least importantly, dialogue between colleagues. *Vom Wunsch, Indianer zu werden* is "constructed . . . as a great dialogue,"[5] with dialogue informing both its content and its structure. Henisch's text thus evokes a Bakhtinian universe of voices. "He said," "she said" can be found on virtually every page; direct and reported speech alternate with interior monologues. In addition to conversational exchanges between the protagonists, the thoughts of the characters are rendered in a quasi-dialogic mode. One of the protagonists, May, addresses them to Klara, who is a sympathetic audience and partner in conversation. Klara, the writer's second wife, is also the better wife because she is a better listener and reader; she is thus not only the perfect muse but also the, less appropriately feminine, perfect critic. "If she had been a man, she might have become his Eckermann" (44), his biographer, that is, and, perhaps more importantly, his conversational partner as well as supportive reader and critic. Kafka, however, is not as lucky as May. He does not have a supportive audience at his disposal twenty-four hours a day, but he does have a conversational partner with whom he communicates about his experiences and his writing, his wishes and his fears. Whenever Kafka is not talking to the Mays, we see him writing letters to Max, i.e., Max Brod (1884-1968), Kafka's Eckermann and yet another version of the partner in dialogue, the supportive reader and critic.

The literary representation of the dialogic mode culminates in *Vom Wunsch, Indianer zu werden* in an episode depicting a séance, a meeting in which the protagonists communicate with people who are either dead or absent. Depending on the medium—and again Klara proves herself more talented than May's first wife—the most diverse spirits can be summoned. In the past, Klara has managed to call up Ludwig von Bayern, George Sand and Chopin, the brothers Grimm, and Friedrich Schiller (68). Even though the spirits summoned usually belong to dead people, "every once in a while, people still alive make contact. For instance, when they are very far away and want to say something important or when they don't have any other means to get in touch" (91). May, however, is less interested in either dead or absent people; he wants to communicate with fictional characters, with characters from his novels. "You invent a figure. And then— whether you believe it or not—this figure makes an appearance during a séance" (69). Accordingly, May's fictional characters seem to exist strangely autonomously from the consciousness of their creator—"the figures that I have made up and still make up all lived or still live and were or are my friends" (69). Hence, Kafka comments in a letter to Brod how the "existence of the figures . . . that appear in [May's] books is a real or a somehow . . . sub-, extra-, intra-, or surreal one" (102). May's ideas, as presented here by Henisch, are curiously reminiscent of Bakhtin's description of the relationship between the author and his characters: once created, the characters seem to exist, at least to a certain extent, autonomously from their creator.[6]

As a dialogue with voices from the past, the séance is, moreover, the perfect metaphor for Henisch's text itself. *Vom Wunsch, Indianer zu werden* does not only represent dialogue, but is itself a dialogue, a dialogue with dead authors who are summoned by the text just like dead and absent people are summoned by the characters during the séance. *Vom Wunsch, Indianer zu werden* is a collage of textual voices that are juxtaposed and thus brought into dialogue with each other as well as with the author's own writing. The author-narrator is also a participant in the dialogue of and with his characters, and his text is a participant in the larger dialogue between texts. *Vom Wunsch, Indianer zu werden* includes quotes from and allusions to texts by both May and Kafka as well as other authors. Whether the intertextuality thus created is properly designated as parody or pastiche, as quotation or satire, cannot always be easily decided. When the text alludes to or quotes Karl May, parody seems to be the prevalent mode; when Kafka is evoked, the text might not be quite as openly parodic, but the reader senses an ironic distance here as well.[7]

Karl May, of course, is an easy target for parody, and this is thus not the first time that he has become the object of ridicule. May's exaggerations and the recurrence of clichés and topoi in his texts have invited many parodies, parodies that usually focus on sudden captures and miraculous escapes.[8] In

Literary Dialogues and Dialogic Literature 171

Vom Wunsch, Indianer zu werden, too, the amazing powers of May's protagonist Old Shatterhand are ironically alluded to more than once. *Vom Wunsch, Indianer zu werden* includes an episode from *Winnetou IV* (1910), in which Old Shatterhand, now literally an old man, proves not only to his enemies that he is still able to tame wild horses. Refracted through the perspective of Kafka, Henisch's text comments on the incongruity: May struggles when he climbs stairs, and his shattering hand is marked by age spots (31). However, it proves to be "shattering" one more time when May hits Kafka to prevent him from jumping into the water in an attempt at suicide (128). When Kafka doesn't regain consciousness right away, Klara states that she "thought that everybody wakes up again after having been hit by Old Shatterhand," to which her husband responds that this might be true "in principle," but not necessarily in the case of "someone with such a weak disposition" (129). Of course, Kafka does wake up again, and Henisch's text thus ironically affirms the fact that Old Shatterhand miraculously never kills his enemies.

If this were all, Henisch's text would just be the most recent installment in a series of clever parodies. But this is not all there is to Henisch's version of Karl May. *Vom Wunsch, Indianer zu werden* mostly refers to the least known and, not surprisingly, least popular Winnetou volume: *Winnetou IV* or *Winnetous Erben* (1910, Winnetou's Heirs). Since this is the volume that deals most explicitly with questions of literary production and reception, Henisch is able to focus less on May the adventure writer and more on May the modern author, an author who produces fiction to make a living and whose fiction, at least to a certain extent, resembles self-reflexive metafiction. In *Winnetous Erben*, the villains do not only chase after gold, but also after the rights to the previous Winnetou volumes. While this may sound like satire, it is in fact meant seriously by May. Thus, Henisch can let the author speak for himself, repeating with ironic distance and only interrupting him with interjections such as "So this is how it goes!" or "Lo and behold!" in order to indicate how ludicrous May's story really is. May's narrative is further ironized by comments of the narrator, such as the following: "And then, my dear audience, one will ride! Not immediately in a way that the stirrup, the saddle, the horse, and the surroundings are disappearing, but certainly impressively" (155). And thus the parody of May turns into a parody of Kafka, or rather, both are skillfully intertwined. Kafka's perspective seems to be privileged over May's as the more thoughtful and sophisticated one. However, it, too, is parodied throughout Henisch's narrative. Kafka, one of the great pillars of German-language literature, is ironized in Henisch's play with tradition, most explicitly and extensively in the conversations dealing with his text "Wunsch, Indianer zu werden" (Wishing to Be an Indian).[9] This prose poem, which Kafka recites as a response to May talking about America and the Indians, abstracts from the real-life experience of horseback riding and relates something that May later quite appropriately calls the "essential ride, a ride in which everything accidental becomes superfluous" (106). In an ironic twist, Henisch attributes the text to an author "inspired by Karl May" (29). Moreover, he lets the author himself comment—in letters to Brod—that the negation of everything superfluous is not only "untenable" (103), but also that "the idea of riding without a horse" is rather "ridiculous" (107). Attributing these comments to Kafka, Henisch thus underscores a difference between the two authors: Kafka—according to Henisch—is self-reflexive; he displays an ironic distance to himself and his work. This becomes apparent again when Henisch lets his protagonist Kafka describe the beginning of his novel *Amerika* (1927; *Amerika*, 1946) as "pulp fiction" (111) or "newspaper reading for rainy mornings" (113). Passages from this text by Kafka, repeated verbatim in *Vom Wunsch, Indianer zu werden*, are here attributed to the collaboration between the two authors, to a playful project to pass the time. Thus newly contextualized, Kafka's text does indeed seem to share traits with the more lowbrow literature represented here by May. This is further underlined by the fact that Delamarche and Robinson, the adversaries of Kafka's protagonist, not only appear here as the doppelgänger of Old Shatterhand's opponents, the brothers Enters (152), but their inclusion into Kafka's text is also attributed to a suggestion by May.

Quoting and playing with tradition, *Vom Wunsch, Indianer zu werden* is both homage and criticism. "*I gladly acknowledge these grandfathers*," Henisch once remarked concerning the influence of Heine and the Romantics.[10] If Heine belongs to the generation of Henisch's grandfathers, then May and Kafka—even though May could be Kafka's father—would be more properly designated as father figures to the contemporary author. And as we all know from Henisch's *Die kleine Figur meines Vaters* and from allusions to both May's and Kafka's father in *Vom Wunsch, Indianer zu werden*, the relationship of son to father is not quite as unproblematic as that of grandson to grandfather. When thinking of psychoanalytic models and Harold Bloom's adaptation of them to the analysis of literary influence, "patriarchal influence" and "Oedipal rejection" are father-son dynamics that come to mind.[11] Going back to Bakhtin, however, one can envision a different model, a model that would replace Oedipal rejection with "inclusion" into a "community of voices" in dialogue, a community into which one's predecessors could be integrated.[12] This appears to be a far more appropriate model for describing what is happening in *Vom Wunsch, Indianer zu werden*.

Some critics have argued that postmodern intertextuality—and I would claim that this is what we find in *Vom Wunsch, Indianer zu werden*—evokes the past nostalgically, reducing it to a museum of bits and pieces that are ever present and have lost their sense of historical belonging.[13] My sense is that Henisch is trying to avoid that trap, whether successfully or not. For it is precisely through the dialogue with tradition that Henisch tries to deal with issues that are relevant to the present and the future. "The present is the transition of the past into the future," the author emphatically proclaimed in a speech dealing with Austria's past and future.[14] Within this temporal continuum, contemporary literature connects with the past, "reworking, reaccentuating, and reinterpreting the voices of . . . prior writers"[15] in order to provide a springboard into the future. Even though Henisch's text is playful, its play with tradition is neither pure nor random, but serves a clear purpose: it negotiates notions of authorship and readership and it propagates dialogue as the—not only—discursive mode for the future.

Through its dialogue with tradition, the text negotiates concepts of authorship on the level of both content and form.[16] And in this context as well, Kafka and May function as antipodes. While Kafka is the poet ("Dichter") for whom writing is existential, May is the professional writer ("Schriftsteller") for whom writing is a means of making a living and of leaving the narrow confines of his lower-class background. Kafka appears as the quintessential modernist artist who is alienated from his surroundings; he appears as a neo-Romantic genius whose peculiarity ("Eigentümlichkeit") is not understood and who suffers from the petty demands of a bourgeois life, of family and profession, i.e., his prison. Compared to May's prison, of course, this is a rather figurative entrapment, a prison of the mind. Kafka is highly sensitive (40) and suffers from existential angst and psychosomatic ailments as well as from moribund thoughts and suicidal tendencies (127). Writing for him is an unhealthy addiction which, again reminiscent of the Romantics, is an activity undertaken at night. His current crisis—"I can no longer write. My whole body warns me about every word . . . the sentences are falling to pieces" (106)—reminds us of another late-Romantic modernist, Hugo von Hofmannsthal (1874-1929) and his famous Lord Chandos (1902).

While Kafka evokes Romantic notions of individuality and originality, May stands for the mass-produced product of popular culture, for copies and even plagiarism. But then Henisch's text itself suggests that notions such as originality and authorial ownership are Romantic constructs. Evoking Roland Barthes and his famous proclamation of the death of the author, *Vom Wunsch, Indianer zu werden* seems to view the author as someone who brings together quotations from and references to other texts. The author's "only power is to mix writings, to counter the ones with the others," according to Barthes.[17] For Henisch as well as for Barthes, the appropriate image for the disappearance of the author can be found in the disassociation of the writing from an authorial consciousness in the act of automatic writing, a process that

Barthes associates with the Surrealists[18] and Henisch connects with the reception of spirit communications during the séance. As May explains to Kafka, Klara's "hand writes what the spirits tell her. Professionals call it automatic writing" (92). Alluding to *Winnetous Erben* again, the spirit communications thus received entail sketchy directions to May-Shatterhand from his fictional characters to take a trip to America in order to deal with issues surrounding a monument to Winnetou. Thus, in contrast to Barthes, Henisch presents the concept of automatic writing ironically. The fact that Kafka cannot read the product of the automatic writing and eventually falls asleep during May's lengthy elaboration constitutes a further ironic twist (93-95).

For Henisch, the author is not dead, but neither is he the dominant voice that serves as the origin of meaning and bestows unity upon the text. Henisch's author seems to be one voice among many, and one that is not privileged over any of the others. This, too, is reminiscent of Bakhtin and his notion of an author whose point of view is one among many, an author who is in dialogue with the other voices in the text.[19] At least this is what the text's representation of writing as collective endeavor suggests. The collaboration is May's idea; he persuades a reluctant Kafka, who is suffering from writer's block, to participate. Kafka only agrees to cooperate to please the old man, but he finds to his surprise that his "addictive imagination" is invigorated by the playful exercise. Through questions and suggestions, May prompts his colleague into writing what turns out to be the beginning of the novel *Amerika*, a text that has remained a fragment. The episode thus represents the workings of the dialogic imagination in the act of writing, not quite the way Bakhtin might have imagined it, but nevertheless in such a way as to successfully challenge the "prevalent post-romantic concept of a single, originary writer."[20]

At the end of *Vom Wunsch, Indianer zu werden*, however, we do not find dialogic collaboration but rather only the lonely desk. Communication has stopped. The happy ending of another meeting and the continuation of the literary collaboration have been relegated to Kafka's dream, to the realm of wishful thinking. For the "real" May refuses to speak to Kafka, and the reader is left to speculate why the dialogue has come to an end. The motivation offered by the narrative itself is not too convincing: May is jealous of Kafka, suspecting that he and May's wife Klara shared more than just intimate conversation. Perhaps Henisch did not want to draw a picture that is too optimistic regarding the collaboration between two authors, and maybe May's jealousy has more to do with professional than with private matters. And maybe the solitary desk is the more appropriate place for the writer, at least under current conditions.

Kafka's desk is also a lonely desk, for he did not write with a reader in mind. Writing for Kafka was less the communication of an author with a reader than the communication of an author with himself. At least this is what has been inferred from the fact that he had instructed his friend Brod to destroy all of his writings upon his death. Henisch's interpretation is slightly different: *Vom Wunsch, Indianer zu werden* suggests that Kafka did consider the reader and the effects a text has or should have on an audience, but Kafka wanted his texts to have a different effect on the reader than May. In a very early conversation with May, before Kafka knew the identity of his new acquaintance, Kafka reveals his preference for a literature that causes the reader pain—"A book should be the ax for the frozen sea in us" (32)—over literature that makes the reader feel good, e.g., May's escapist America adventures to which Kafka explicitly refers in this context (31).

May's case is less ambivalent. In contrast to Kafka, May clearly wanted to communicate with his readers. On the one hand, he needed a readership to make a living; on the other hand, he was trained and actually worked as a teacher. This didactic impulse manifests itself in his writings: May wanted to educate his audience and change the world through his books. Thus, it comes as no surprise that he is presented as an avid reader and admirer of Lessing (1729-81) and Schiller (1759-1805), authors also concerned with the moral and aesthetic education of their audiences. Like his classical predecessors, May had a vision—this becomes very obvious in *Winnetous*

Erben, for instance—that he wanted to share with the readers of his books and the audiences at his public lectures. He is proud that "teachers and bishops have recommended his books" and that "more than a million readers have divulged his stories" (142).

May's popular appeal can be traced back to his rather unique relationship to fiction and reality. May, according to Henisch's protagonist Kafka, "doesn't want to or can't distinguish between literature and reality" (116). May's books are his life; they confirm it, and they are more real than reality. "The characters that I have created are all alive and were or have been my friends. Or my enemies . . . " (69).[21] In the same vein, his books authenticate his supposed travels. "The first time I traveled to the United States in 1864 or '65, the second time in 1869. You can read about it in my books" (49), Henisch's May recollects having responded in an interview. When May then re-enacts the travels described in his texts to prove "those gentlemen" wrong "who had doubted the truth of what the travel writer Karl May had written" (76), he further ignores the border between fiction and reality. May's life itself is fictionalized when he calls his house "Villa Shatterhand" (80), dresses up as "Westmann" armed with Winnetou's rifle (85), and braids Klara's hair Indian-style, an act that constituted the couple's "favorite foreplay" for many years (45). It is this fantastic mixture of fiction and reality that explains May's talent to attract and seduce his readers.

While Henisch, on the one hand, admires May for this gift, he also seems to accuse him of deceiving his readers. And he is not the first to do so. As we can read in *Vom Wunsch, Indianer zu werden,* May's contemporary adversaries compared the author's identification with his fictional characters to earlier incidents of confidence tricks and accused him of deceit. Young May had pretended to be "ophthalmologist Dr. Heilig," "seminary teacher Lohse," "music engraver Hermes," and "plainclothes police lieutenant von Wolframsdorf" (138) in order to counterfeit people out of their money. Playing with fiction and reality in this way has very concrete consequences, including the imprisonment May alludes to in Henisch's text. "In theory or in the imagination it is easy to come up with such stories, but in practical reality they always go wrong sooner or later" (65), May explains to Kafka. Henisch is intrigued with this aspect of May's life and work, as evidenced by the large role these stories play in *Vom Wunsch, Indianer zu werden*. Like May, Henisch believes in the powers of the imagination. Henisch is interested in unveiling the potentials of collective and individual histories, and this can only happen by means of the imagination and in the realm of the imaginary, i.e., fiction. "Empower the imagination" served as an important slogan in 1968,[22] and an active imagination still serves as a vital sign in *Vom Wunsch, Indianer zu werden*. Indeed, what Kafka and May have in common is an "addictive imagination" (113), and only the imagination makes it possible to reveal reality's potential. "It's the possibility after all, the possibility" (10), we read early in the text, and this notion stands as the programmatic statement of the text itself. Those who see themselves as pragmatic or realistic, and whom Henisch calls "the administrators of reality,"[23] might belittle such an endeavor as "escapism" or "fantasy," while the narrator and, most probably, the author of *Morrisons Versteck* would call it "realism,"[24] a realism that stresses reality's potentiality. Henisch thus acknowledges May's influence, but again there is repetition with a difference. For even though Henisch plays with reality's potentialities, he never conceals from his readers that this is indeed a play with possibilities. Unlike May, Henisch puts his cards on the table: self-reflexive comments of the narrator and the extensive use of the subjunctive reveal to the reader from the very outset of the text that this is fiction—fiction, however, that plays with the possibilities inherent in reality itself. The same holds true for Henisch's practice of borrowing from other authors. Like May, Henisch borrows without acknowledging the borrowings; he does not provide us with either bibliographic references or quotation marks. (The only annotation we find in *Vom Wunsch, Indianer zu werden* appears on the very first page, where Henisch quotes a postcard that Kafka sent to Brod in 1908.) Using very similar strategies, Karl May was accused of plagiarism a hundred years ago. But in contrast to May, Henisch's text is not driven by a desire to conceal the fact that he is borrowing from other sources; rather, the reader is asked to become active, to become a collaborator in detecting quotes and allusions, parody and pastiche.[25]

While Henisch's sympathies clearly lie more with the angst-driven Kafka and his lonely desk than with the writer of popular fiction, there are nevertheless aspects of May's authorship that Henisch finds well worth considering. Like May, Henisch is very interested in reaching an audience. He does not want to "*leave the literature that people actually read to the [Johannes Mario] Simmels and [Heinz G.] Konsaliks without a fight.*"[26] He wants to be accessible—like May—and entertaining; he wants "to appeal" to an audience.[27] He attempts to mediate between what Kafka and May stand for, between a serious but abstract and thus inaccessible modernism—high—and a somewhat naive but popular and populist realism—low. While *Morrisons Versteck* tries to accomplish such mediation in one figure, namely, Jim Morrison, in *Vom Wunsch, Indianer zu werden* Henisch splits the attempt into two figures who, in the course of the narrative, illuminate the issue from two different perspectives in order finally to compose a text together and thus possibly create a paradigm of successful mediation. Presenting two figures in dialogue allows Henisch to dramatize the contradiction more effectively and perhaps also to indicate that the envisioned third, the successful mediation, is not a dialectical synthesis.[28]

Dialogue is thus not only a thematic and structural element within the text, but also extends beyond the text to include the reader. Henisch wants his text to be a vehicle of communication with a reader; this is what the emphasis on dialogue in *Vom Wunsch, Indianer zu werden* ultimately points to. Henisch wants his reader to be a true collaborator, an active participant and not a passive consumer. Passive consumerism—so prevalent among the recipients of today's popular culture—is precisely the attitude against which Henisch's intertextual collage works. Like any other intertextual collage, Henisch's text needs an active reader, a reader who looks for quotes and allusions, who figures out their sources and their meanings in new contexts. Without a reader, intertextuality is a mute phenomenon. The intertextual collage that Henisch creates, however, not only demands an active reader, but also a knowledgeable reader. Thus, I am not sure whether the dialogue Henisch envisions is actually taking place, or put differently: exactly what kind of a reader does this text really appeal to? *Vom Wunsch, Indianer zu werden* is not only a "masterpiece of satirical reflection on literature," but also a good read, "a story that is entertaining and full of suspense," according to a review in the *Süddeutsche Zeitung*. It is certainly no coincidence that the latter part of the quote has been printed on the back cover of the paperback edition and that the former appears on the first page, i.e., only after we have opened the book. While literary satire does not necessarily appeal to a larger public, a good read does. As should be obvious by now, *Vom Wunsch, Indianer zu werden* is in fact literary satire—whether it is pure satire *per se* is debatable, but a discussion of the definition of satire goes beyond the scope of this analysis. But whether it is also "entertaining and full of suspense" is an altogether different question. One wonders what kind of a reader would find *Vom Wunsch, Indianer zu werden* "entertaining and full of suspense"; most likely not the kind who reads Simmel and Konsalik. In order to be really popular, like Umberto Eco's *The Name of the Rose* (1983) or Patrick Süskind's *Das Parfum* (1985; *Perfume*, 1986), for instance, self-reflexive metafiction would have to be embedded in a story that would engage a reader who otherwise would not be particularly interested in the production and reception of literature in such a way that he or she would want to read on. Whether this is the case with *Vom Wunsch, Indianer zu werden* is doubtful. There is narration, to be sure, but the story that is narrated is rudimentary at best. Three characters meet on the passage to America; they eat and drink, wander about on a boat, write, and summon ghosts. It is obvious that Henisch intended to write a book that is not only entertaining to a reader who is versed in literary tradition and thus able to recognize every quote, but also to a reader who perhaps has read May but certainly not Kafka. However, it is questionable whether *Vom Wunsch, Indianer zu werden* is indeed pleasurable for those who do not carry around substantial cultural capital. It is more likely that the obvious plethora of quotes

Literary Dialogues and Dialogic Literature 181

and allusions scares off those used to lighter fare. "Can the producer of parody today assume enough of a cultural background on the part of the audience to make parody anything but a limited . . . or elitist literary genre today?" Linda Hutcheon wonders[29]—as do we.

Henisch's emphasis on language and literature as communication—as dialogue—implies an attack on monologizing discourse, a discourse that bans ambiguity, flux, and variety. He thus again evokes Bakhtin. Bakhtin's attack on monologizing language was directed at Stalinist authoritarianism and the cultural politics it produced. In the case of Henisch, the object of the attack cannot be as clearly defined. It is the monologizing voice of the author just as much as it is a monologizing discourse that privileges high over popular culture. It is also a monologic notion of individuality and history, as well as centralized, totalizing hierarchies and discourses that assume to proclaim the truth. More specifically, it might also be the post-World War II social partnership ("Sozialpartnerschaft") that Robert Menasse has aptly described as a particularly Austrian way of (not) dealing with conflict in the realms of politics and aesthetics.[30] In the political arena, the Austrian social partnership has served to harmonize domestic conflicts that are otherwise typical of class societies, and a social partnership in the aesthetic realm has functioned to deflect conflicts between different generations of writers or different conceptions of literature. The Austrian literary scene has been characterized as a "multiplicity of monologues."[31] Henisch's emphatic insistence on dialogue seeks to reconfigure this particularly Austrian kind of monologic literary landscape.

Notes

1. Peter Henisch, *Vom Wunsch, Indianer zu werden: Wie Franz Kafka Karl May traf und trotzdem nicht in Amerika landete* (1994; Salzburg and Vienna: Residenz; Frankfurt/M: Fischer Taschenbuch, 1996). All references to this text are based on the paperback edition.
2. Henisch, *Morrisons Versteck* (Salzburg and Vienna: Residenz, 1991) 6.
3. In bookstores, conventional biography that celebrates the unique, authentic self is still the dominant form of the genre, particularly in its popular manifestations. Jürgen Schläger ("Biography: Cult as Culture," *The Art of Literary Biography,* ed. John Batchelor [Oxford: Clarendon, 1995] 57-71) is thus not the only one who describes the genre as conservative; for in the context of a postmodern culture attacking the individual, biography has tended to be defensive, not subversive. In contrast to England, however, where, according to Schläger, the genre has proven immune to the trends of the times, biography in German-speaking cultures has become problematic.
4. Henisch, "Warum ich nicht will, daß Österreich untergeht," *Reden an Österreich: Schriftsteller ergreifen das Wort*, ed. Jochen Jung (Salzburg and Vienna: Residenz, 1988) 90.
5. Mikhail Bakhtin, *Problems of Dostoevsky's Poetics*, ed. and trans. Caryl Emerson (Minneapolis: U of Minnesota P, 1984) 72.
6. See Bakhtin, *Problems of Dostoevsky's Poetics* 47-77.
7. For a definition of parody that is broader than the one commonly used, see Linda Hutcheon, *A Theory of Parody: The Teachings of Twentieth-Century Art Forms* (New York and London: Methuen, 1985) 30-49. She defines parody as "repetition with critical difference."
8. See Rudolf Schweikert, "Karl Mays literarische Wirkung: Ein Rundgang mit 10 Stationen," *Karl May*, ed. Heinz Ludwig Arnold (Munich: edition text + kritik, 1987) 244-68.
9. "Wunsch, Indianer zu werden" first appeared in Franz Kafka, *Betrachtung* (Leipzig: Rowohlt, 1913).
10. Henisch, *Zwischen allen Sesseln: Geschichten,*

Gedichte, Entwürfe, Notizen, Statements 1965-1982 (Vienna: Hannibal, 1982) 9.

11. See Michael Macovski, "Textual Voices, Vocative Texts: Dialogue, Linguistics, and Critical Discourse," *Dialogue and Critical Discourse: Language, Culture, Critical Theory*, ed. Michael Macovski (New York and Oxford: Oxford UP, 1977) 3-26, here 5.

12. Macovski 5.

13. See, for instance, Frederic Jameson, *Postmodernism or the Cultural Logic of Late Capitalism* (Durham: Duke UP, 1991) 96.

14. Henisch, "Warum ich nicht will, daß Österreich untergeht" 94.

15. Macovski 11.

16. For the relationship between parody and authorship, see Hutcheon 4-5 and Macovski 4.

17. See Roland Barthes, "The Death of the Author," *Image, Music, Text*, ed. and trans. Stephen Heath (New York: Hill and Wang, 1977) 142-48, here 146.

18. Barthes 144.

19. See Bakhtin, *Problems of Dostoevsky's Poetics* 285.

20. Macovski 4.

21. This notion evokes Bakhtin's analysis of Dostoevsky, in which he has described the relationship between an author and his characters as follows: "the author . . . creates . . . living beings who are independent of himself and with whom he is on equal terms" (*Problems of Dostoevsky's Poetics* 284).

22. Henisch, *Zwischen allen Sesseln* 155.

23. Henisch, "Warum ich nicht will, daß Österreich untergeht" 81.

24. Henisch, *Morrisons Versteck* 70.

25. For a discussion of the difference between parody and plagiarism, see Hutcheon 38.

26. Henisch, *Zwischen allen Sesseln* 227.

27. Henisch, *Zwischen allen Sesseln* 31.

28. Again, this is reminiscent of Bahktin's analysis of Dostoevsky: "Out of every contradiction within a single person, Dostoevsky tries to create two persons, in order to dramatize the contradiction and develop it extensively" ("Dosto-

evsky's Polyphonic Novel: A Plurality of Consciousnesses," *The Bakhtin Reader: Selected Writings of Bakhtin, Medvedev and Voloshinov*, ed. Pam Morris [London/New York/Melbourne/Auckland: Edward Arnold, 1994] 88-96, here 91).
29. Hutcheon 88.
30. See Robert Menasse, *Die sozialpartnerschaftliche Ästhetik: Essays zum österreichischen Geist* (Vienna: Sonderzahl, 1990).
31. Menasse 63.

The Politics of Quotation in Henisch's Poetics

ARND BOHM

In comparison with his prose works, Peter Henisch's poetry has been relatively neglected.[1] But the limited reception is not an accurate index of production, given that Henisch has published six books consisting exclusively or largely of poetry: *wiener fleisch & blut* (1975, viennese flesh & blood); *mir selbst auf der spur / hiob: gedichte* (1977, on my own track / job: poems); *Zwischeneiszeit* (1979, Interim Ice Age); *Zwischen allen Sesseln: Geschichten, Gedichte, Entwürfe, Notizen, Statements 1965-1982* (1982, Between All the Stools: Stories, Poems, Drafts, Notes, Declarations 1965-1982); *Hamlet, Hiob, Heine: Gedichte* (1989, Hamlet, Job, Heine: Poems); and *Black Peter's Songbook* (2001). Individual poems have appeared in a wide variety of publications.[2] Nevertheless, Henisch seems to have been classified as a prose writer rather than to have been accorded much respect for his contributions as a poet. There are various reasons for this, not least the general disdain for poetry these days, and a particular resistance to verses that are political or socially critical. But I suspect the real difficulty Henisch presents is indicated, unwittingly, by Christoph Parry, who notes the accessibility of the poems in *Hamlet, Hiob, Heine*: "Often conceived as song lyrics, the poems aim at being lucid and understandable. In some of the older poems the technique of 'concrete poetry' is ironically alienated. But the poems always have a 'meaning' even outside the structures of language."[3] Paradoxically, poetry which is *easy* to read, as opposed to the difficult, hermetic verse of a Paul Celan (1920-70) or Friederike Mayröcker (1924-), for instance, falls victim to the enshrined aesthetics of modernism, where the demands made upon readers by the texts were measures of "greatness," of "originality." The less accessible the poem, the more likely it was to achieve canonical status.[4]

Henisch's disagreement with the programmatic withholding of meaning from audiences came to a head with the founding of the literary journal *wespennest* (wasp's nest) by Henisch and Helmut Zenker in 1969, proclaimed by the subtitle to be a "Journal for Usable Texts."[5] The criterion of utility was a rebuttal to the literature for the elite audience still loyal to the modernist ideal of a pure literature: "It is supposed to be a journal for usable texts. Not literature for literati, not a literary periodical for the readers of literary periodicals."[6] The provocation of an aesthetic program calling for the usefulness and accessibility of literary and artistic production can only be grasped within the context of the increasing subordination of art to the interests of business.

Although it is difficult to realize how even our common language may yet be fully privatized, it would be futile to hope that capitalism should not attempt to extend its hold over this domain of human life as well as everywhere else. Not satisfied with claiming to own names such as "Harvey" and "Wendy" and words such as "olympic" or "roots," more and more business corporations are now registering phrases and entire sentences, such as "It's what's next" or "Where do you want to go today?"[7] Although we are told that such appropriations are restricted to specific products and environments, the bearers of names such as "McDonald" are discovering that even if they have identified themselves with that name for generations, they may not have the legal right to use the name any longer and may even be the targets of lawsuits. There is no reason to suppose that Bill Gates will not begin to charge a fee from anyone who innocently asks "Where do you want to go today?" as soon as a means is developed for tracing and confirming the incidents.

Ironically, this pressure from the private sphere upon public, collective ownership of language has arisen in tandem with something generally considered by poets and writers to have been good, namely, the introduction of copyright. The concept of registering a literary text and subsequently all creative works for the protection of writers, artists, musicians, and filmmakers has made it possible for the producers to collect some of the profit from their labor.[8] The profound implications of copyright for the organization and distribution of knowledge is only apparent when the present conditions governing "fair use" of quoted materials are contrasted against the system that had predominated before. When the only lasting reward was fame, it was a distinction to have one's works widely and often quoted, until they became "commonplaces."[9] Great philosophers, jurists, poets, and statesmen often lived on in memory through some pithy observation or penetrating aphorism. The value of a memorable utterance increased the more it came into circulation, so that the restrictions of copyright would have seemed counterproductive. The ability to recognize such utterances, the commonplaces of the collective memory, was an essential skill for anyone aspiring to wield authority among the authorities.[10]

Against this necessarily sketchy background, Henisch's use of quotations, allusions, and intertexts in his poetry can be seen as operating on two fronts. These are, as will become evident, not discrete arenas. On one side, Henisch has participated in the radical attempt since the 1960s at subverting the capitalist economic order by means of an alternative economy, one based on communal ownership and sharing. For that alternative economy, copyright was only one instance of the constraints imposed by a legal system designed to defend private property. The charge of plagiarism leveled against those who quoted without permission was therefore taken to be ideologically motivated. Conversely, those undertaking extensive appropriation had to be mindful of the risk that such a charge might be brought. Although not quite as extreme as Kathy Acker, Henisch does violate the boundaries which are supposed to be maintained between different authors and their respective texts, as when he quotes a large chunk from a story by Ingeborg Bachmann (1926-73) into a text.[11] From the other side, Henisch has supported those who were determined to establish an alternative collective memory by replacing traditional commonplaces with slogans and phrases essential to the self-understanding and maintenance of an oppositional movement. An important role model here was Bertolt Brecht (1898-1956), who coined many slogans that did become common coin for the oppositional culture. Another, less noticed, was Celan, who had an uncanny ear for striking sentences and who knew how to invoke the revolutionary commonplaces.[12] The instauration of new commonplaces implied the displacement, the enforced forgetting, of older clichés and unquestioned slogans. Because quoting becomes desirable and laudable for Henisch's aims, the poetry is free to give various open signals to alert readers when quoting occurs. We no longer have to rely solely upon erudition in order to be able to detect when an allusion is being made. The cycle "Andere Verhältnisse" (Other Relations) displays the variety of such indicators. Most obvious are the numerous quotative verbs, which frame utterances as direct speech even without conventional punctuation:

Cool says Mr. Karl to Marx[13] (*Zwischen allen Sesseln* 120)

(I reply) (*Zwischen allen Sesseln* 121)

What do parents matter to us I don't ask & educators in other rooms (*Zwischen allen Sesseln* 123)

Sleep with me you invite me (*Zwischen allen Sesseln* 125)

I love you she says (*Zwischen allen Sesseln* 126)

I look into the pillow & say SUPERGILETTE (*Zwischen allen Sesseln* 130)

Okay I say but how should I
not entangle myself

Fool (says the wise man)
it's not about you at all   (*Zwischen allen Sesseln* 134)

Such quotatives are used regularly and frequently in Henisch's poetry. As the last of these examples shows, the effect frequently is to suggest snippets of conversation, evocative of the dialogical function of language as it is used in communication. The quotations prevent the domination of monologues; they implicate others in a joint project of speaking.

Another typographic indicator is the use of capital letters, as in the example of SUPERGILETTE. These are more than optical signals, for they also mark a shift in register from private to public or anonymous voices:

my head full of piercing music WHOLE LOTTA
   LOVE (*Zwischen allen Sesseln* 129)

abovemyhead a sign with the inscription NO
   TRESPASSING
ON CONSTRUCTION SITE   (*Zwischen allen Sesseln* 132)

inscription CREDIT UNION THE FRIENDLY
   LAAERBERGERS[14]

TRESPASSING
FORBIDDEN
EXTREME DANGER   (*wiener fleisch & blut* 50)

CHILDREN NOT LIVING HERE
ARE ABSOLUTELY
FORBIDDEN
TO USE THE SLIDE

TO SLED & ROLLERSKATE (*wiener fleisch & blut* 74)

The impersonality of such instructions, usually couched in passives and imperatives, is difficult to convey in English, but they are omnipresent in German-speaking countries. In whose voice are they given? It is hard to know, and yet one is required to hear and obey. The extremity of such discourse is revealed by Henisch in the poem "Haben Sie Mut für die Bahamas" (Take a Dare on the Bahamas), which repeats station names: Florisdorf, Stockerau, Gänserndorf. Day after day, commuters obey the instructions, without questioning the routine or wondering about the discrepancy between it and the fantasy destination "Bahamas," also offered in an imperative. The insertion of foreign languages is yet another way to suggest quoted material:

Mir ist nach besaufen zumut
& später nach tanzen

Harry oh Harry
why did you come
from your damned America

to take my beloved with you
to another room   (*Zwischen allen Sesseln* 124)
[I feel like getting soused / & later like dancing // Harry oh Harry / why did you come / from your damned America // to take my beloved with you / to another room]

Henisch's attitude to plurilingualism is mixed, especially in regard to the pervasive influence of American English, which is both inevitable and a threat.[15] Other languages as well have had an impact on Austria since the end of World War II, something the following macaronic verse parodies:

MY BONNIE is over the ocean mister
Das Schifferl schwingt sich

daune vom Land das heißt
down flußabwärts ade
Nein wir sind keine
Geschwister Monsieur
aber wir können ein Lied
das geht so:
Sur le pont
d'Avignon
sitzt a große
Wanzen karascho[16]
[MY BONNIE is over the ocean mister / The little ship sails / down from the land which means / down downstream g'bye / No we are not / Siblings Mister / but we know a song / that goes like this: / Sur le pont / d'Avignon / sitsa big / bug korosho]

The snatches of song, which the children do not understand, have become detached from the context in which they could be meaningful and are now simply empty phrases. "Okay" is another telling example, given that it is a word without a definite etymology and yet has become a universal fill-word:

es ist alles
in ordnung leute
es ist alles
völlig okay[17]
[everything / is in order folks / everything / is totally okay]

The reception of "okay" belongs to the coca-colonization of Europe by American trademarks, such as "Budweiser Bier" (*Zwischen allen Sesseln* 125), "SUPERGILETTE," "McDonald's" (*Hamlet, Hiob, Heine* 8) and "Mickeymausheften" (Mickey Mouse comic books, *Hamlet, Hiob, Heine* 108). However, elements of American counter-culture are received and quoted in the original with approval, or at least without disapproval: "thirtiest birthday blues" (*wiener fleisch & blut* 41), "(solidarity for ever)"[18] (*mir selbst auf der spur* 46), "mein poetisches Ich *on the road*"[19] (my poetic self on the road, *Hamlet, Hiob, Heine* 102).

Surprisingly enough, Henisch makes only limited use of indirect discourse subjunctives for quoting. The major exception is "Manöver" (Maneuver), in which subjunctive forms of "to be" become the crux of the manipulated language:

> it was said that party blue lost significant amounts of territory
> it was said that party orange gained significant amounts of territory
> it was said that the ruthlessness of the action had been satisfactory
> it was said that the morale of the troops had been excellent. (*mir selbst auf der spur* 16)

From this poem, it would seem that for Henisch the use of this subjunctive is tainted by its association with the duplicitous and pompous jargon of governments and bureaucrats. Stylistically marked as a written rather than a spoken form,[20] the indirect discourse subjunctive here represents the artificial rhetoric of those who distance themselves from responsibility for their actions, escaping from the indicative world into the world of subjunctive reports.

Complementing quotations marked blatantly are the more traditional allusions requiring readers to be familiar with a shared library of texts. Indeed, it is quite interesting to observe just how extensively Henisch does rely upon such references, which are drawn from the German, English, American, and French literary canons, from standard works of the Left, from Scripture, from proverbs and folk sayings, and from popular culture. To some degree, there is a contradiction between such allusiveness and the intent to produce literature that would be easily accessible to readers, since those unfamiliar with the intertexts will not be able to participate fully in the literary game and will have only a partial understanding of the text. There is no denying that Henisch's academic training has made him susceptible to the play of intertextual networks. At the same time—the contradiction cannot be evaded—without such allusions the connections to the literary and intellectual heritage would be weakened. Just such a rupture with tradition is a flaw of the utterly abstract works of concrete poetry. There is an undercurrent of elitism in such exercises, because they exclude ordinary readers from the experience of invigoration by their cultural heritage. A counter-example was provided by Brecht, whose adaptations of and references to the entire scope of world literature served simultaneously to introduce that heritage to those struggling for change, enlarging their arsenal of ideas, and to critique the received interpretation of the canonical texts.

Many of Henisch's poems do gesture plainly at other texts. Presumably most readers will be able to situate and decode lines such as these from the "Hamlet" cycle:

Ophelia
is not there
His father
is dead
His mother
lies in her bed, without make-up

Where is Horatio?
Where is Claudius?
Polonius is hiding behind the curtain   (*Hamlet, Hiob, Heine* 63)

Usually, Henisch quotes from canonical texts with ironic twists, so that readers are compelled to reconsider the original. It would require a separate study to explicate Hamlet's function in these poems, beginning with the performing of performance—or, more to the point, with the failure to perform, with misquotation and falsely attributed quotations. Hamlet, we know, did not say what Henisch ascribes to him:

Lost in his telescope
Hamlet has
(he says)
become aware of the chance
for a new constellation   (*Hamlet, Hiob, Heine* 62)

Or did Hamlet perhaps say this or something like it after all? Inevitably, the intertextual link would send us back to the source, but the German history of Shakespeare—and *Hamlet* in particular—makes the source difficult to locate. Do we recur back to the English texts or rely on one of the translations competing for supremacy on the German stages? Furthermore, *Hamlet* is a drama in which quoting is by no means an innocent activity, from the opening anxiety about what the Ghost really said to Hamlet's injunction to the players to speak the speech as he has taught it to them,[21] that is, to become the instruments for his ventriloquism, uttering quotations.

Today no writer can assume with much confidence that the audience will recognize allusions to the Bible and the Judeo-Christian heritage. Henisch is quite aware of the problem:

> It is astonishing how few people in general today know the Bible, or rather which people in particular do not know it. To take that as a question of faith or lack of faith is in my opinion the view of dunderheads. Brecht, who probably is above the suspicion of having been a religious person, would, for example, be unthinkable without the Bible, and he referred to it quite decidedly.[22]

Despite his reservations, or because of them, Henisch often alludes to Scripture. The "Job" poems could hardly operate without the intertexts, which are once again drawn in via quotation so as to challenge complacent readers:

> Unto Caesar
> what is Caesar's
> God
> what is God's?
> Cheap
> trick!
>
> To him who has

more
shall be given
from him who doesn't have
more shall be
taken
that
is the truth.²³ (*Hamlet, Hiob, Heine* 71)

Such allusions can only make for an effective argument if the audience is still sufficiently familiar with the Bible to be able to recognize the sources. The Job poems are testimony to Henisch's intensive concern with the gap between the claim of his society to be Christian and the gradual forgetting of the basic tenets of the faith. The social teachings of the Gospels are largely ignored in the world:

Peace to the huts
War to the palaces
who could
ordain that²⁴ (*Hamlet, Hiob, Heine* 81)

The third cluster of poems in *Hamlet, Hiob, Heine* exposes Henisch's affinity with Heinrich Heine (1797-1856), who also used satire and parody to critique the hypocrisy of society. The key intertext is Heine's *Deutschland: Ein Wintermärchen* (1844; *Germany, A Winter Tale*, 1861). Henisch too imagines returning to a country that should be his own but turns out to be a space of alienation:

scarcely
         across the border
the people seem old
and have forgotten how
to talk with each other
in this language
which is also mine
everyone looks at
no one else (*Hamlet, Hiob, Heine* 140)

Henisch sympathizes with Heine's irritation with the naive late-Romantic sentimentality of the petite bourgeoisie. The attachment to nature and a landscape made up of forests and meadows is subverted by the reality of industrialization, urbanization, and pollution. "Geflohen nach Norden" (Fleeing North) lists all the waste products and toxic chemicals that are dumped into the environment (*Hamlet, Hiob, Heine* 144-45). The technique is very much in the tradition of Heine's use of mundane details in lyric poetry so as to destroy the false illusions of the imaginary realm.

The final word on Heine is delivered by "LETZTE NACHLESE ZUM BUCH DER LIEDER" (Final Gleanings from the *Book of Songs*) which consists mainly of a quotation from a letter by Friedrich von Gentz (1764-1832) to Rahel Varnhagen (1771-1833) (*Hamlet, Hiob, Heine* 150). The irony lies in the fact that von Gentz, as Metternich's "right-hand man," was instrumental in the suppression of opponents to the conservative government, and yet he writes his letter in language suffused with Romanticism. Although the governing elites were able to mimic the sentiments of the writers, they ultimately betrayed the revolutionary potential of art and opted for a state based upon censorship and military might. That outcome saddened Heine when it could no longer anger him, as it does Henisch, whose narrative voice harmonizes with Heine's melancholy:

> Well forget that I'm bathing
> I bathe for hours in these
> melancholic fresh
> waters   (*Hamlet, Hiob, Heine* 150)

The identification is reinforced by the feeling on the part of those who had vested high hopes in the student movement of the late 1960s that their defeat was a repetition of the defeat of the "Vormärz" (pre-March) struggles that came to an end in 1848.[25] Looking back, Henisch and his cohort could see how 1968 might be the beginning of another long "winter" after the springtime of revolution, a winter of the sort that had inspired Heine's *Wintermärchen*.

Contemporary poetry also appears in Henisch's verse,

often without explicit signals. The opening lines from Günter Eich's well-known "Inventur" ("Stocktaking") have been taken as a representative assessment during the "Stunde Null," the putative "zero hour" after World War II:

> This is my cap,
> this is my greatcoat,
> and here's my shaving kit
> in its linen bag.
>
> A can of meat:
> my plate, my mug,
> into its tin
> I've scratched my name.[26]

Although the recovery had in the interval made Europeans much wealthier as far as material goods were concerned, the first poem of "Licht- & Schattenbilder 2" (Slides and Silhouettes 2) presents a world no less impoverished:

> THAT IS my sheet of paper
> That is my typewriter
> That is my desk
> That is my room
> That is my window (*Hamlet, Hiob, Heine* 28)

If anything, the deletion of adjectives and of the possibility of inscribing the poet's name on an object describes a condition even more reduced to primal needs than in Eich's world. The poet is also a prisoner, confined now to the space of material production: he lives with his tools and is starkly confronted by the necessity of writing in order to earn a living.

Celan's impact is evident in Henisch's imagery and in direct evocations, especially in the Job poems. "Todesfuge" (1954; "Death Fugue," 1980) is echoed unmistakably:

> digging a grave and singing the while
> whose grave is that / it is mine, sir

digging a grave and not singing the while
whose grave is that / it is yours, sir   (*mir selbst auf der spur* 45-46)

The singsong rhythm and characteristic repetitions, the themes of music, death, and graves, all point to the presence of Celan's most famous poem in Henisch's text. It is heard again elsewhere:

                What lies
in the air
         The dead   (*Hamlet, Hiob, Heine* 99)

Measuring the full extent of Celan's significance for Henisch is an important project still to be completed, as is his reception of Holocaust themes overall. Worth noting is his awareness of Nelly Sachs (1891-1970), all too little known in German even today. The beautiful poem "Treffen sich 2" (When 2 Meet, *Hamlet, Hiob, Heine* 150) deals with the encounter between Celan and Sachs in Zurich on May 6, 1960, a meeting commemorated in the former's "Zürich, Zum Storchen" (Zurich, At the Sign of the Stork).[27]

Although Henisch resents the cultural hegemony of American coca-colonization, he is alert to the developments of twentieth-century American poetry. The ironies of the relationship are epitomized by "Der blaue Kaugummiautomat" (The Blue Chewing Gum Vending Machine). Already the mention of chewing gum evokes the ambivalence of Europeans to Americans, who are often caricatured on the basis of their strange habit of (loudly) chewing gum. And even without the dedication to William Carlos Williams, it would be easy to recognize which of his poems is meant:

So much depends
upon

a blue chewing gum
vending machine

Glazed by rain
water

beside a red
wall (*Hamlet, Hiob, Heine* 132)

The original, published in *Spring and All* (1923) as number "xxi" of the cycle, would be frequently anthologized as one of the quintessential texts of American modernism:

so much depends
upon

a red wheel
barrow

glazed with rain
water

beside the white
chickens[28]

As Roy Harvey Pearce has observed, the poem is remarkable for its "pathos and sentimentalism."[29] By shifting the setting out of the farmyard into a bare urban setting, Henisch strips away Williams's vestiges of nostalgia for an idyllic world and replaces it with icons of consumerism. Chewing gum and vending machines exemplify the new tastes and their mechanical distribution. The two poems do however exist in symbiosis, with Williams contributing the red and white and Henisch the red and blue so as to construct the red, white, and blue of the American national colors. But Henisch has not set out to negate Williams and the American influence, for the concision of the language and imagery is loyal to the original; some might say too much so. "Der blaue Kaugummiautomat" thus replicates the situation of Europe under American hegemony, acknowledging the attractiveness of the American ways to arouse and satisfy desire while wryly protesting that those desires are outmoded. Not least, the "red wall" stands as a reminder of the political realities in a then still divided Europe and as a subtle warning that the socialist alternative is quite tangible, vivid, and visible. The emphasis upon red, the symbol of socialist agitation, also reverberates back upon Williams's poem, making us hear the "red wheel barrow" anew as a tool of hard manual labor, a figure of Williams's own political sympathies which were often occluded by New Criticism.

The cultural politics of the Cold War induced a systemic amnesia by attempting to erase all traces of the left-wing heritage from the collective memory. It remained an obligation of engaged poets and writers to preserve the links to an alternative version of history, keeping the winter count. Thus the title of "Was tun kann uns Lenin helfen" (What to Do Can Lenin Help Us) refers to the title of Lenin's pamphlet *What Is To Be Done?*[30] And as though to teach readers basic historical facts, Henisch cites Marx with an additional biographical detail:

> are we nature?
> inquired karl marx
> born eighteeneighteen
> and died anyway
> (eighteeneightythree
> of an
> inflammation of the lungs)   (*mir selbst auf der spur*
> 33)

As with references to the Bible, such allusions open up the possibility, indeed the necessity, for readers either to recollect the relevant discourse or to undertake further research. Either way, the poem will have succeeded in actualizing a tradition that would otherwise be silenced. "Hommage à Neruda" (*mir selbst auf der spur* 54-55) preserves the memory of the Chilean poet and Communist leader Pablo Neruda (1904-73) by quoting lines from his work and supplementing them.[31]

Among the most powerful of Henisch's poems in this regard is "GOLGOTHA/INVENTARAUFNAHME" (Golgotha/Inventory). In a series of vignettes, he reviews the pantheon of revolutionaries, from Rosa Luxemburg (1871-1919) to Patrice Lumumba (1925-61). Some are famous, others less so, all were martyrs of political oppression. The commentaries in parentheses sound like quotations from police reports and official explanations:

> Further the skull
> of Giacomo Mateotti (quote: This person
> may not speak any more: end)
> The skull
> of Karl Münichreiter
> (on the basis of the crime
> of public
> use of violence
> delivered to the gallows
> with the bier
> stamped:
> Vienna
> in February '34) (*Hamlet, Hiob, Heine* 89)

The last in the sequence extends the series of repressions into the present. In the closing lines we hear the voice of the faceless citizens who may witness crimes being committed by the state, but who have learned to be indifferent and to respond only in the bland tones of official speakers. Despite the poet's effort to rouse their consciences, those citizens retreat from responsibility and shrug off the burdens of history.

The attack upon the emptiness of so much of ordinary speaking, the banal talk ("Gerede") that fills the space between thoughtful utterances, has been a major target for Austrian writers from Johann Nestroy (1801-62) to Karl Kraus (1874-1936). As Kraus did so often with devastating effect in *Die Fackel* (The Torch),[32] Henisch also uses quotations in order to expose the vapid phrases that circulate from mouth to mouth, the commonplaces of uncritical public opinion. Paradigmatic is the short poem "rollenspiel" (role playing):

> everyone (said the teacher)

> fulfills his role there
> where he has been put
>
> basically (said the teacher)
> no one is advantaged
> no one disadvantaged
>
> if you don't stop
> butting in constantly
>
> you will be (said the teacher)
> put in the corner   (*mir selbst auf der spur* 14)

Hiding behind his authority, the teacher parrots official rules, using clichés. The one moment when we hear something personal from him is at the breakthrough of a blunt threat, one no longer veiled by phrases learned by rote. In "Univ. Wien" (U Vienna) the hapless professors attempt to stem radical protests with the formulas of the seminar (*Zwischen allen Sesseln* 173). And another poem, too long to quote here, consists entirely of clichés put into the mouth of a newspaper editor (*Zwischen allen Sesseln* 148-49), reminding us that newspapers had been among Kraus's most deserving targets.

Henisch is unsparing when castigating the use of empty language to paper over the problems of the Nazi past. The major poem "heldenplatz" (heroes' square)[33] subjects fragments of public talk about that past to a child's questions. The grandmother's responses deflect away from hard truths:

> jew spit 'n yer shoe says another child & laughs
> that was my first conscious encounter with this word
>   what does jew mean
> you don't understand that yet don't squash the roses
>   otherwise they'll wilt   (*wiener fleisch & blut* 10)

The quick move to repress memories of the past by denying the questioner's authority and then immediately changing the topic is a tactic characteristic of such denials. Dead metaphors ("the war was a giant") further block critical examination of historical causality. And once again the closing lines bring the past home: it lives on in an ordinary brutality that suddenly breaks to the surface, as with the teacher in "rollenspiel." The true feelings behind the clichés are terrifying:

> look at those bums says a man with an umbrella
> what we need is compulsory work brigades again
> or—taking aim with his umbrella—execution commandos[34] (*wiener fleisch & blut* 11)

The examples could be multiplied; material for such analyses would be all too abundant. In "Erlernen der Bundeshymne" (Learning the National Anthem), the poem is constructed out of the everyday pronouncements with which people attempt to convince themselves and each other that the past was not all that bad:

> The business with the Nazis
> is exaggerated
> They should finally put an end
> to it we have many other things
> on our mind all our hands
> are full coping with the future   (*Hamlet, Hiob, Heine* 20)

Regrettably, such sentiments do represent widespread public opinion. Especially troubling is the attribution of the uncovering of history to some vague "them," as though the truth were being manufactured as part of a conspiracy against innocent people. The self-satisfied, smug conclusion dissolves all possibility of serious discussions about the past or the present.

However, it would be misleading to suggest that Henisch takes aim only at the conservatives or those on the right. He is equally critical of leftists who became convinced that the magic of slogans alone could bring about fundamental changes. Is it enough to sing in order to achieve revolution? Obviously not. The limits to the infantile fantasies about the power of poetry are traced by Henisch when he contrasts the language of rock music with the declarations of the state authorities:

> the yellow submarine
> with all friends on board
> has long since sunk
>
> and crashed
> is the lead zeppelin
> with its whole load of love
> fantasy
> into power?
> what is that supposed to mean?
>
> I
> am not resigning
> said the general   (*mir selbst auf der spur* 50)

"Yellow submarine" is an allusion to a popular song by The Beatles; Led Zeppelin was another famous rock music group; the slogan about fantasy and power was widely heard in the late 1960s. But none of those poetic utterances carry the force of the straightforward pronouncement of the general, who would eventually prevail.

Since Henisch continues to be an active writer, it would be presumptuous to conclude with an attempt at summation. What a scrutiny of quotations in his poetry does show is how important they are in his work and how sophisticated he has been in appropriating a wide spectrum of sources. The tension inherent in quotations is that they refer to the past while functioning in the present, but this is a productive condition, not merely one of reproduction. Put differently, quoting is a profoundly dialectical tactic. Caught between the source and an unknown destination, quotations conform to what Henisch has described as the schizophrenia of the contemporary condition: "With one half of our personality still in the connections that we want to abandon, we stand with the other half already in the unaccustomed new ones. Given such a crisis something archaic may break into a culture with its normative patterns."[35] In just that way, quoting discloses the future by resurrecting the past, and so becomes a bridge to the utopian space of possibilities.

Notes

1. See, for example, Anne Close Ulmer, "The Son as Survivor: Peter Henisch's *Die kleine Figur meines Vaters*," *The Germanic Review* 61.2 (1986): 57-64; Christoph Parry, "Peter Henisch," *Kritisches Lexikon zur deutschsprachigen Gegenwartsliteratur*, ed. Heinz Ludwig Arnold (Munich: edition text + kritik, update of 1991); Craig Decker, "Photographic Eye, Narrative I: Peter Henisch's *Die kleine Figur meines Vaters*," *Monatshefte* 83.2 (1991): 147-60; and Jennifer E. Michaels, "Is Stein Paranoid? Peter Henisch's Reflections on the Jewish Experience in Austria after the Presidential Election of 1986 in his Novel *Steins Paranoia*," *Modern Austrian Literature* 27.3/4 (1994): 107-25. The major exception is Eva Schobel's 1987 dissertation at the University of Vienna, published as *Peter Henisch: Eine Monographie* (Vienna: Verband der wissenschaftlichen Gesellschaften Österreichs, 1988), which deals with the entire œuvre available up to that time.
2. See the detailed bibliography in Schobel 611-27.
3. Parry 4.
4. On this process, which was also at work in German and French literary systems, see John Guillory, *Cultural Capital: The Problem of Literary Canon Formation* (Chicago and London: U of Chicago P, 1993) 168-75; and John Timberman Newcomb, *Wallace Stevens and Literary Canons* (Jackson and London: UP of Mississippi, 1992) 172-235. See also the observations at the opening of Herbert Krämer, "Nochmals zur Metaphorik von Celans *Todesfuge*," *Dikt og idé: Festskrift til Ole Koppang på syttiårsdagen, 18. Januar 1981*, ed. Sverre Dahl (Oslo: Germanistisches Institut of the University of Oslo, 1981) 248-55.
5. On the context, see Markus Paul, *Sprachartisten— Weltverbesserer: Bruchlinien in der österreichischen Literatur nach 1960* (Innsbruck: Institut für Germanistik, Universität Innsbruck, 1991) 197-211.
6. Quoted by Paul 4.
7. The former is now a registered trademark for Cadillac Seville; the latter for Microsoft.

8. For an excellent analysis of the connections between copyright and aesthetics, see Martha Woodmansee, *The Author, Art, and the Market: Rereading the History of Aesthetics* (New York: Columbia UP, 1994), with a good bibliography on the subject.

9. Entry points into the extensive bibliography are provided by Margreta de Grazia, "Sanctioning Voice: Quotation Marks, the Abolition of Torture, and the Fifth Amendment," *Cardozo Arts & Entertainment Law Journal* 10.2 (1991): 545-66; Ann Blair, "Humanist Methods in Natural Philosophy: The Commonplace Book," *Journal of the History of Ideas* 53 (1992): 541-51; Ann Moss, *Printed Commonplace-Books and the Structure of Renaissance Thought* (Oxford: Clarendon, 1996); Yves Vadé, "Citations dans le texte: Les Anciens, les Modernes et les autres," *Tradition und Modernität: Aspekte der Auseinandersetzung zwischen* Anciens *und* Modernes, ed. Volker Roloff (Düsseldorf: Reimar Hobbing, 1988) 13-26; Morton W. Bloomfield, "Quoting and Alluding: Shakespeare in the English Language," *Shakespeare: Aspects of Influence*, ed. G.B. Evans (Cambridge, MA and London: Harvard UP, 1976) 1-20; and Bettine Menke, "Das Nach-Leben im Zitat: Benjamins Gedächtnis der Texte," *Gedächtniskunst: Raum—Bild—Schrift: Studien zur Mnemotechnik*, eds. Anselm Haverkamp and Renate Lachmann (Frankfurt/M: Suhrkamp, 1991) 74-110.

10. On the mechanics of commonplaces in memory, see Mary J. Carruthers, *The Book of Memory: A Study of Memory in Medieval Culture* (Cambridge: Cambridge UP, 1990).

11. Peter Henisch, "AUSBRUCHSVERSUCH (Ein Fragment)," *Zwischen allen Sesseln: Geschichten, Gedichte, Entwürfe, Notizen, Statements 1965-1982* (Vienna: Hannibal, 1982) 80. The passage he uses is the opening of "Das dreißigste Jahr"; see Ingeborg Bachmann, *Das dreißigste Jahr: Erzählungen* (1961; Munich: dtv, 1966) 15. The allusion to Kathy Acker concerns the opening of her *Great Expectations* (New York: Grove Weidenfeld, 1982) 5.

12. For example, the quoted slogans "No pasarán" and "Friede den Hütten!" in his "In Eins" (Paul Celan, *Die Niemandsrose. Sprachgitter: Gedichte* [Frankfurt/M: Fischer,

1980] 62).
13. My translation here and throughout. The translations are intended to convey the meaning, without any pretense at conveying the poetic qualities of the original.
14. Henisch, *wiener fleisch & blut* (Vienna and Munich: Jugend und Volk, 1975) 39.
15. Untranslatable is the example he cites at one point: "Aber wenn man zum Beispiel, mir passierts ja auch ununterbrochen, wenn man sich gar nicht mehr überlegt, welches andere Wort es dafür gibt, und man sagt nur mehr: 'Das muß ich jetzt checken' oder so was, also dann wirds stereotyp und das halt ich für einen eindeutigen Niveauverlust" (*Zwischen allen Sesseln* 213).
16. Henisch, *Hamlet, Hiob, Heine: Gedichte* (Salzburg and Vienna: Residenz, 1989) 18-19.
17. Henisch, *mir selbst auf der spur / hiob: gedichte* (Baden bei Wien: Grasl, 1977) 11.
18. The refrain of "Solidarity Forever." According to the liner notes by Mark Greenberg to Pete Seeger, *If I Had a Hammer: Songs of Hope & Struggle* (Washington: Smithsonian Folkways, 1998), the song was written by Ralph Chaplin, originally to the tune of "Battle Hymn of the Republic." With new music and additional words by David Welsh, the song became widely known in the 1960s, especially through performances by Pete Seeger.
19. An allusion to Jack Kerouac's *On the Road* (1957), a founding text of the Beat movement.
20. On the stylistic implications of the indirect discourse subjunctive, see Harald Weinrich, *Textgrammatik der deutschen Sprache* (Mannheim: Dudenverlag, 1993) 261-66.
21. "Speak the speech I pray you as I pronounced it to you, trippingly on the tongue; but if you mouth it as many of our players do, I had as lief the town-crier spoke my lines" (William Shakespeare, *Hamlet, Prince of Denmark*, ed. Philip Edwards [Cambridge: Cambridge UP, 1985] 152).
22. Quoted in Schobel 277. On Brecht's use of the Bible, see Reinhold Grimm, "Luther's Bible in Brecht's Poetry," *Brecht Unbound: Presented at the International Bertolt Brecht Symposium, Held at the University of Delaware Feb-*

ruary 1992, eds. James K. Lyon and Hans-Peter Breuer (Newark, DE: U of Delaware P / London: Associated U Presses, 1995) 227-40.

23. "Render therefore unto Cæsar the things which are Cæsar's; and unto God the things that are God's" (Matt. 22.21).

24. The message is Biblical; the formulation is best-known since the 1960s from Georg Büchner's "Der Hessische Landbote" (Büchner, *Werke und Briefe*, eds. Werner R. Lehmann, Karl Pörnbacher, Gerhard Schaub, Hans-Joachim Simm and Edda Ziegler [Munich and Vienna: Carl Hanser, 1980] 210.) According to the notes, "The slogan 'Guerre aux châteaux! Paix aux chaumières,' frequently evoked during the French Revolution, which the French writer Nicolas Chamfort (1741-94) allegedly suggested as a motto for the soldiers of the revolutionary armies" (463).

25. For the historical background, see Wolfram Siemann, *Die deutsche Revolution von 1848/49* (Frankfurt/M: Suhrkamp, 1985; rpt. Darmstadt: Wissenschaftliche Buchgesellschaft, 1997). For overviews of the period in terms of literary history, see Peter Stein, *Epochenproblem "Vormärz" (1815-1848)* (Stuttgart: Metzler, 1974); Rainer Rosenberg, *Literaturverhältnisse im deutschen Vormärz* (Munich: Damnitz Verlag / Berlin: Akademie-Verlag, 1975); Eda Sagarra, *Tradition and Revolution: German Literature and Society 1830-1890* (New York: Basic Books, 1971) 126-86.

26. Originally published in *Abgelegene Gehöfte* (1948). Reprinted in *German Poetry 1910-1975*, ed. Michael Hamburger (New York: Urizen, 1976) 220; Hamburger's translation 221.

27. Celan, *Die Niemandsrose. Sprachgitter* 16. For the background, see Ruth Dinesen, "Paul Celan und Nelly Sachs," *Datum und Zitat bei Paul Celan: Akten des Internationalen Paul Celan-Colloquiums, Haifa 1986*, eds. Chaim Shoham and Bernd Witte (Bern and Frankfurt/M: Lang, 1985) 195-210.

28. William Carlos Williams, *The Collected Poems of William Carlos Williams: Volume I 1909-1939*, eds. A. Walton Litz and Christopher MacGowan (New York: New

Directions, 1991) 224.

29. Roy Harvey Pearce, *The Continuity of American Poetry* (Princeton: Princeton UP, 1965) 339.

30. V.I. Lenin, *Shto delat'?* (1902). The German "was tun" translates the Russian infinitival construction more closely than the English passive. On the historical significance of the tract, see the introduction by S.V. Utechin to Lenin, *What Is To Be Done?*, trans. S.V. Utechin and Patricia Utechin (Oxford: Clarendon, 1963) 1-36. Lenin's title alludes, in turn, to Nikolai Chernyshevsky's revolutionary novel *What Is To Be Done?*, written while he was imprisoned in 1862-63. See Victor Terras, *A History of Russian Literature* (New Haven and London: Yale UP, 1991) 334-35.

31. See Schobel 284-85.

32. See Karl Riha, "'Heiraten' in der 'Fackel': Zu einem Zeitungs-Zitat-Typus bei Karl Kraus," *Karl Kraus*, ed. Heinz Ludwig Arnold (Munich: text + kritik, 1975) 116-26.

33. It is difficult to sum up in English the complex allusions and ironies evoked by the mere mention of the "Heldenplatz." A large public square in Vienna, literally "Place of the Heroes" or "Heroes' Square," it is dominated by statues of great men in Austrian history. But it became a byword for the politics of the Nazi occupation because it was there that Hitler addressed a huge crowd on March 15, 1938. Since the crowd seems rather enthusiastic in photographs, the event came to represent the contradictions of Austrian responses to the *Anschluss*. See William E. Wright, "Introduction," *Austria, 1938-1988: Anschluss and Fifty Years*, ed. William E. Wright (Riverside, CA: Ariadne, 1995) 1-13, here 11; and the provocation of Thomas Bernhard's title, *Heldenplatz* (1988).

34. "Genickschuß," as the original reads, is execution by means of a shot to the back of the head, and was the standard method for killing prisoners used by the Gestapo.

35. Henisch, *Vom Baronkarl: Peripheriegeschichten und andere Prosa* (Frankfurt/M: Fischer, 1972) 64.

Intertextual Satire and the Affluent Society: Production, Consumption, and *Kommt eh der Komet*

CRAIG DECKER

> For many, Austrian literature might begin with Grillparzer or with Stifter; for me, it begins with Nestroy.
> —Peter Henisch[1]

In his 1988 essay "Warum ich nicht will, daß Österreich untergeht" (Why I Don't Want Austria to Sink), Peter Henisch addresses the relationship between culture and politics in contemporary Austria. Against the backdrop of the "Waldheim Affair," which functioned as a long-overdue catalyst for many to reexamine their understanding of Austrian culture and politics, Henisch begins his essay by pleading for the emergence of a collective historical consciousness. Such a consciousness, he appears to argue, could then serve as the precondition for reconstituting Austria as a *bona fide* "Kultur-

Intertextual Satire and the Affluent Society 211

nation" ("cultural nation"), one that would not only propagate socially critical works of art but also collectively value the intellectual abilities of those individuals who produce and consume them. Henisch's "alternative Austria" rests upon a refunctionalized notion of production and consumption. In order to render more concrete that which ideally could be, Henisch proceeds by evoking that which no longer is. Commenting upon the concerted socialist attempts to produce culture for the masses in the 1920s and 1930s, Henisch contends:

> Workers' culture—that, one hears and reads, was a great idea. In the meantime, the workers they had in mind back then no longer exist (which, in many respects, actually constitutes progress). But the working people of our Second Republic have been conceived of as consumers for so long and so resolutely that—no longer properly trusting their own productivity—they now only see themselves as such.[2]

By beginning with the workers of the First Republic and ending with those of the Second, Henisch's remarks exemplify the kind of historical comparison and reasoning that he finds so lacking in his fellow citizens. Henisch's historical perspective allows him to see more clearly the concrete improvements that have occurred from the 1920s to the late 1980s in the lives and working conditions of the majority of Austrians.[3] While rightfully celebrating these material advances, Henisch simultaneously decries the socio-economic apparatus that has helped to bring them about. In its unceasing efforts to advance the production and consumption of goods—of whatever type, of whatever use or uselessness—the apparatus of advanced capitalism has transformed the individual citizen into the mass consumer, who not only consumes the individual products of advanced capitalism but also serves to reinforce its underlying logic.

The pervasive power of the apparatus proves particularly insidious in its ability to negate resistance to it. "What is decisive today," Max Horkheimer and Theodor Adorno have argued in *Dialectic of Enlightenment*, "is no longer puritanism . . . but the necessity inherent in the system not to leave the customer alone, not for a moment to allow him any suspicion that resistance is possible."[4] Indeed, in the passage from Henisch's essay cited above, it is not only the fact that the apparatus conceives of the working individual first and foremost as consumer that so concerns Henisch, but also the fact that the individual, over the course of time, has come to internalize this conception and adopt it as his or her own. The freedom to consume thus presupposes the unfreedom upon which the affluent society has been built and according to which it functions. As Herbert Marcuse has observed in this regard:

> Contemporary civilization has developed social wealth to a point where the renunciations and burdens placed on individuals seem more and more unnecessary and irrational. The irrationality of unfreedom is most crassly expressed in the intensified subjection of individuals to the enormous apparatus of production and distribution, . . . in the almost indistinguishable fusion of constructive and destructive social labor. And it is precisely this fusion that is the condition of the constantly increasing productivity and domination of nature which keeps individuals—or at least the majority of them in the advanced countries—living in increased comfort. Thus irrationality becomes the form of social reason, becomes the rational universal. . . . The individual reproduces on the deepest level, in his instinctual structure, the values and behavior patterns that serve to maintain domination, while domination becomes increasingly less autonomous, less "personal," more objective and universal.[5]

The destructive interplay between culture and consumption, between distribution and domination which plays a part in Henisch's 1988 essay assumes an even more prominent role in *Kommt eh der Komet* (The Comet's Coming For Sure), a fictional text published in 1995. *Kommt eh der Komet*

Intertextual Satire and the Affluent Society 213

derives its title as well as its point of departure from Johann Nestroy's *Der böse Geist Lumpazivagabundus oder Das liederliche Kleeblatt* (1833, The Evil Spirit Lumpazivagabundus or The Slovenly Threesome), a "Volksstück" (popular comedy) in which the impending comet serves as a harbinger of the coming revolution and thus as a potential corrective for the social, political, and economic inequities of the Metternich era.

Nestroy's drama premiered at the Theater an der Wien, one of Vienna's three "Vorstadt-" (suburban) or "Volkstheater" (popular theaters) which emerged in the late eighteenth century as a broad-based alternative to the theatrical offerings and cultural politics of the Viennese Hofburgtheater, the institutionalized theater of the feudal aristocracy. More than a century and a half after the premiere of *Lumpazivagabundus*, and in keeping with his own aesthetic program of producing accessible and usable texts, Henisch self-consciously recasts Nestroy's immensely popular nineteenth-century satire into a contemporary satirical narrative.[6] But why, we may well ask, might Henisch, an author acutely aware of the dynamics of intertextuality, choose precisely this nineteenth-century drama as a foil for exploring socio-economic realities at the end of the twentieth century? Why might Henisch, a self-consciously *Austrian* author, one who writes both within and against the Austrian literary tradition, be drawn to Nestroy's text as a vehicle for thematizing contemporary Austrian (consumer) culture? After all, economic life, particularly among Nestroy's cast of wandering craftsmen and artisans, was particularly harsh. The very real struggle for food and shelter in the mid-nineteenth century stands in sharp contrast to the affluence that has come to characterize post-World War II Austria. The very real struggle for political freedoms in the Habsburg Empire seems to have little in common with what has become the broad-based and stable democracy of the Second Republic. Furthermore, the Viennese "Volksstück" and its attending theatrical institution, the "Volkstheater," constituted a significant cultural challenge to the prevailing aesthetic practice of the mid-nineteenth century; Henisch, however, is producing literature at a time in which the culture of protest that emerged in the 1960s has been transformed into the dominant (and commercially successful) aesthetic paradigm of a globalized culture industry. How then, if indeed at all, might a reading of *Kommt eh der Komet* against the horizon of *Lumpazivagabundus*—and vice versa—enable us to better understand the dynamics of consumption and resistance? It is the task of this essay to explore the ways in which the specifics underlying Henisch's consumption and reproduction of Nestroy's text can, in fact, potentiate acts of resistance—even in an age in which resistance appears increasingly difficult.

As if to ward off any potential anxiety of influence, and in order to make his act of narrative reconstruction apparent from the beginning, Henisch takes a quote from *Lumpazivagabundus* as his epigraph for *Kommt eh der Komet*. In Act I, Scene 6 of *Lumpazivagabundus* as well as at the outset of *Kommt eh der Komet*, Nestroy's journeyman cobbler Knieriem (whose name means "shoemaker's stirrup" in German) laconically remarks: "My story's not very long, but extremely tragic."[7] In order to extend the story of Knieriem and his fellow journeymen Zwirn (a tailor whose name is the German word for "thread") and Leim (a joiner whose name means "glue" in German) into the present, Henisch retains important elements of Nestroy's basic plot. He includes, for example, a trio of socially marginalized protagonists who proceed to strike it rich in the lottery, and he chronicles the divergent paths their lives take subsequent to their sudden and unexpected wealth. In addition, Henisch directly quotes from Nestroy's dialogue and incorporates some of the songs from *Lumpazivagabundus* into his reworking of the drama. While reproducing these central features of Nestroy's text, Henisch, at the same time, significantly and necessarily reconfigures the characters and their conflicts in order to depict what he considers to be the tragic poverty of contemporary Austrian affluence, in which the promise of the "cultural nation" has given way to the pestilence of the "consuming nation." By mediating between Nestroy's drama, on the one hand, and the social, cultural, and economic contexts of late twentieth-century Austria, on the other, Henisch's text functions, in part, to historicize the unfreedom underlying the affluent society. *Kommt eh der Komet* thus serves to thematize the difficulties in resisting contemporary consumer culture while simultaneously providing a structural model for subverting the dynamics of internalized domination characteristic of it.

Satire, it has been argued, "is culture's way of exposing the violence that civilization conceals."[8] If this is the case, then Henisch's intertextual satire serves to expose the social and economic violence that has been concealed in civilization's march from the advancing capitalism of the early nineteenth century to its advanced state in the late twentieth. In order to explore and expose this violence, Henisch's narrative focuses on the fortunes and misfortunes of Scheck, Glasl, and Kuli, the postmodern descendants of Nestroy's journeymen who appear to meet by chance on a bench near the Autobahn interchange Ulm-East. In addition to sharing a seat and some conversation amidst the noise and exhaust of the seemingly endless flow of traffic, Scheck, Glasl, and Kuli are united in their position as ostensible social outcasts. Their coming together at the outset of the text—especially when seen in light of their Nestruvian precursors—represents the potential for considerable solidarity and social opposition, a potential that is literally shot down in the final image of the text.[9]

As was the case with Nestroy's protagonists, the names of Henisch's characters tell us much about them. Scheck ("check") is a disaffected bank employee who, at the beginning of the text, attempts to overcome his growing alienation at work and his emotional distress over his apparent inability to win the affection of his beloved Peppi by quitting his job, withdrawing his savings, and traveling through India for as long as his money holds out. Glasl ("small glass"), a member of the functional underclass[10] who has served time in various "correctional" facilities as the result of petty crimes, is a cobbler by training, a manual laborer by necessity, an amateur astronomer by passion, and an alcoholic by conviction. Finally, Kuli ("pen") was until very recently a doctoral student in his thirty-fifth semester, attempting to complete a dissertation entitled "Faustian and Don Juanian Elements in Eighteenth-, Nineteenth-, and Twentieth-Century Philosophy, Literature, and Art" (63). However, as a result of his increasing frustration over what he considered to be a preponderance of theory and a paucity of praxis, Kuli decided to leave the university and devote the majority of his energies to amassing experiential—and, in particular, carnal—knowledge. At the time of his arrival in Ulm, he aspires to be a writer, one who seeks to harmonize theory and practice as well as physical and spiritual knowledge by transforming the topic of his dissertation into the act of the "Faustian fuck" (64). The development of Henisch's narrative is framed by Nestroy's drama. Nestroy's drama, in turn, like many nineteenth-century "Volksstücke," is framed by the activities and authorities of the supernatural realm. Act I of *Lumpazivagabundus* begins in the "Cloud Palace of the Fairy King Stellaris," where various magicians have gathered with their children to decry the subversion of order within their realm. The evil spirit Lumpazivagabundus has infiltrated the supernatural sphere and insinuated himself into the hearts and lives of the magicians' children. "He's seized hold of our son's hearts and lured them from the orderly path," Mystifax laments to Stellaris. "Now they abhor work. They're gambling, drinking, throwing themselves into wanton liaisons. In short, they're lost if you don't banish the evil spirit" (137). As a result of their abandoning all forms of socially productive work and giving themselves over to the pleasures of alcohol and the flesh, the children have squandered their material assets and now risk accumulating considerable debt. To their parents' chagrin, they profess to prefer the prospect of physical incarceration to any form of self-discipline or self-improvement. Moreover, even the promise of a reinfusion of capital cannot guarantee that all of the children will return to the orderly existence they once led. While Fludribus assures Stellaris, "if we were to get rich again, then we'd become well-behaved again as well" (138), Hilaris immediately counters his claim: "I'll be frank: wealth will never make me mend my ways" (139).

In order to determine the relative power of order and anarchy, of capital and conformity, and of productivity and passion within the supernatural world, Fortuna, the "Mistress of Good Fortune," proposes a test to be carried out among the mortals. She will choose three human beings who have long suffered the privations of poverty and shower them with riches. Should they respond, as Lumpazivagabundus predicts they will, by squandering the money, she will then provide them with a second influx of capital. If they once again refuse to react to their newfound wealth with sufficient gratitude and moderation, Fortuna will consider herself defeated and allow the incorrigible Hilaris to marry her daughter. However, neither Fortuna, the love-struck children, nor the majority of supernatural beings expect that such a wedding will occur. With complete faith in the supreme rationality and ultimate power of the bourgeois order, the "Mistress of Good Fortune" emphatically adds: "But—and there can be little doubt about this—if they receive their good fortune with gratitude and prudent restraint and, for fear of future indigence, keep it their whole life long, then I'm the victor, and Hilaris will forever be separated from my daughter" (140).

It is under these conditions that Fortuna reappears in Act I, Scene 6 and provides the sleeping journeymen with the winning lottery number. The trio's sudden wealth provides them with the means to enter and attain happiness within bourgeois society, a society that had previously excluded them on account of their poverty and illiteracy. The fictional Zwirn, Knieriem, and Leim are thus able to enact the very real nineteenth-century scenario in which sound investments in the expanding Austrian economy of the 1830s and 1840s could result in substantial financial gains. Of the three lumpen, however, only Leim actively pursues the promise of capitalist enrichment. Upon receiving his lottery winnings, he immediately returns to Vienna and marries his beloved Peppi, daughter of the oppressive "Master Joiner" Hobelmann. By the end of the drama, Leim himself has become a master of his trade, and his increased education and capital have resulted in the establishment of a productive joinery, a financially secure household, and a growing family.

While Leim embodies such middle-class values as productivity, stability, moderation, and renunciation, Zwirn and Knieriem actively oppose them. Subverting Fortuna's claims regarding the invincibility of the bourgeois order, the cobbler and tailor proceed to squander their money on alcohol and women. Rather than engage in any form of renunciation, they prefer to satisfy their immediate physical needs; they insist on challenging institutionalized codes of social and economic behavior instead of submitting to them. As a result, a year after winning the lottery, Zwirn and Knieriem are just as economically destitute as they were at the outset of the drama. Confronted with his fellow journeymen's sloth and excesses, a distressed Leim offers to provide them with the financial means to integrate themselves into the established socio-economic order. However, upon learning that the precondition for such capital is the necessity to become "industrious, upright, and orderly" (182), a horrified Zwirn responds with an unequivocal "I couldn't stand that" (182). He thereby echoes Knieriem's reaction to Peppi's earlier insistence that Knieriem "has to become respectable. He has to mend his ways" (178).

As a result of Zwirn and Knieriem's adamant refusal to submit to the dictates of bourgeois society, Nestroy's drama functions to subvert the conventions of the "Besserungsstück" (Drama of Improvement), an institutionalized staple of Vienna's Volkstheater. In a typical "Besserungsstück," such as Ferdinand Raimund's *Der Alpenkönig und der Menschenfeind* (1837, The Alpine King and the Misanthrope, translated in 1852 as *The King of the Alps*), the dramatic conflict arises from an individual character flaw—such as greed, envy, or mistrust—which must be remedied. Mere human intervention, however, typically proves incapable of correcting the exaggerated and seemingly incurable characteristic. Accordingly, supernatural beings descend to Earth and manipulate the mortals at will, always to positive ends. The supernatural beings prove totally superior to the human characters in the play, and their absolute authority remains unquestioned. Indeed, social harmony returns to the "Besserungsstück" only through the intervention of an omnipotent spirit who succeeds in "improving" the individual, thereby assuring his or her reintegration into the unchanged and unchallenged social order. In *Lumpazivagabundus*, however, the supernatural realm is sub-

Intertextual Satire and the Affluent Society 219

ject to the same subversions as the human one, and the absolute power of benevolent authorities to impose—or reimpose—a harmonious social order is undone. The act of transformation is thus presented as a collective, social necessity rather than an individual, psychological one—a significant shift that did not go unnoticed by either Nestroy's audiences or the imperial censors.

In light of Nestroy's radicalization of the "Volksstück" into a vehicle for social and political change, and in light of his repeated arrests by state authorities, the final tableau of *Lumpazivagabundus* appears particularly satirical. The play ends with a *deus ex machina* image of Leim, Knieriem, and Zwirn, along with their respective families, living and working together "industriously, uprightly, and orderly." Having undercut the conventions of the "Besserungsstück" and its underlying ideology throughout *Lumpazivagabundus*, Nestroy mockingly resurrects them at the conclusion of the play. As if to throw a self-consciously provocative bone to both the censors and popular expectations, the curtain falls as the chorus sings the praises of productivity, domesticity, and their attending contentments: "Domesticated and hard-working —and only in this way / Can a person be happy every single day" (187). In the context of the entire drama, such praises can best be understood as a final and ironic subversion of these very values as well as of those forms of literature that serve to affirm them.

The concluding chorus of *Lumpazivagabundus* strategically appears in Part II of Henisch's narrative. Yet whereas Henisch knowingly quotes from Nestroy's drama throughout *Kommt eh der Komet*, he purposely and playfully fails to attribute these particular words explicitly to Nestroy. Subsequent to learning of Scheck, Glasl, and Kuli's respective dissatisfactions following their lottery winnings, we read:

> So what are all the busy little people supposed to say, those who spend their whole lives doing nothing but earning & spending money so that the rat race continues apace for all of us?
> *Domesticated and hard-working*

*and only in this way
can a person be happy
every single day,
like the poet says,
was it Schiller (?),
well, it's not that important, anyway.* (106-7)

Taken out of context, the concluding chorus of *Lumpazivagabundus* could well appear to promote the very social and economic conformity that Nestroy's drama indicts. Henisch's conscious (mis)reading of the passage serves to disassociate it from Nestroy's text, thus subverting any attempt at a socially affirmative reading of the drama upon which *Kommt eh der Komet* is based. Henisch's act of authorial negation echoes the multiple thematic and formal negations so central to Nestroy's play. Moreover, Henisch's negation serves to underscore the tradition of the Austrian "Volksstück" in particular, and certain tendencies in Austrian literature in general, as both popular and socially critical. At the same time, by evoking Schiller (1759-1805) as the possible author of the passage, Henisch provides yet another context within and against which his narrative unfolds.[11] For if Nestroy's text represents and promotes the active resistance to the constraints of the established order, Schiller's aesthetic essays call for a very different response to them. In "Über das Erhabene" (1801; "On the Sublime," 1966) for instance, Schiller argues for the necessity of overcoming such forces by exercising one's physical or moral faculties. If one cannot negate force with force, Schiller argues, then one must strive to negate its concept. "To destroy the very concept of a force," Schiller explains, "means simply to submit to it voluntarily."[12]

Having thus evoked the possibilities of either actively opposing the social order in order to transform it or willfully submitting to social force in order to transcend it, Henisch ironically depicts characters who are ultimately incapable of realizing either option. As a result of their lottery winnings, Scheck, Glasl, and Kuli possess the financial means to purchase the physical and emotional comforts with which the affluent society seduces and allegedly rewards its members. It soon becomes apparent, however, that such comforts presuppose burdens and constraints that serve to undermine the very pleasures they supposedly provide. Upon winning the lottery, Scheck immediately returns to Vienna to be with his beloved Peppi; Kuli quickly departs to immerse himself in the sensual pleasures of Paris; and Glasl initially remains in Ulm, content to continue to explore the local bar scene there with his newfound friends Johannes Kepler and Albert Einstein. The two scientists function as contemporary equivalents to the supernatural beings of the nineteenth-century "Volksstück," and their presence in *Kommt eh der Komet* attests to the ways in which advanced industrial society uses "the scientific conquest of nature for the scientific conquest of man."[13]

Although Glasl may be content to continue to carouse in Ulm and sleep off his drunken binges in the city's parks, the municipal authorities think differently, and they respond quickly and forcefully to what they consider to be his social and economic transgressions. Glasl's spirited and physically harmless revelries land him in jail once again, and his incarceration serves as a reminder of the frequently painful institutionalized response to the individual pursuit of "unproductive" pleasure: "Now Glasl's sitting in the clink. And feeling a little smashed in his head and joints. And that's not just on account of the alcohol. He allegedly put up resistance; they allegedly had to bring him to reason" (105). While external authorities are required to put an end to Glasl's apparent resistance and to discipline this member of the underclass to "reason," external force proves unnecessary in bringing both Kuli and Scheck in line with the principles of the affluent society. On account of their more elevated socio-economic positions, the dynamics of internalized domination characteristic of consumer society are far more evident and effective in them.

Having traveled to Paris first-class and having bought his privacy as well as various indiscretions along the way by means of excessive tips, Kuli proceeds to engage in an orgy of urban consumption. Lavish hotel rooms, extravagant meals, and enticing women are the primary objects of his attention and money. While such consumption does in fact bring him temporary sensual pleasures, he finds himself unable to attain the transcendent form of sexual and spiritual intercourse that he has so long desired. Indeed, it is his very ability to possess, as it were, so many women, so many "goods" that leads to his ultimate dissatisfaction with any particular one: "Whenever he's sleeping with a woman he always regrets the fact that, in the meantime, he's missed an opportunity with not just two, but with millions of others. Every decision in favor of *one* negates—at least for the moment—all the others. And he sees Laura & Camilla in his mind's eye, how they're sitting in the PALETTE waiting for him, feeding their pugs brioches" (102). Kuli's dilemma points to a central dynamic informing the affluent society. As both Kuli and Scheck painfully experience—the former primarily in regard to sensual desires, the latter largely in terms of emotional needs—the ceaseless production and consumption of goods does not culminate in the ultimate satisfaction of wants. Instead, such unbridled production and consumption only serves to create even more ultimately unfulfillable desires. As John Kenneth Galbraith explains in his analysis of the affluent society:

> As a society becomes increasingly affluent, wants are increasingly created by the process by which they are satisfied. This may operate passively. Increases in consumption, the counterpart of increases in production, act by suggestion or emulation to create wants. Expectation rises with attainment. Or producers may proceed actively to create wants through advertising and salesmanship. Wants thus come to depend on output. In technical terms, it can no longer be assumed that welfare is greater at an all-round higher level of production than at a lower one. It may be the same. The higher level of production has, merely, a higher level of want creation necessitating a higher level of want satisfaction.[14]

The ultimately deadening consequences of the spiraling increase in the production of goods and their attending wants appear throughout *Kommt eh der Komet*, but they are particularly evident in the fate of Scheck subsequent to his winning the lottery. At the beginning of the text, Scheck arrived in Ulm with the intention of leaving the comforts and constraints of Western society behind. Upon winning the lottery, however, he unhesitatingly reverses his direction, returning at once to Vienna and his Peppi. With his newfound wealth, which Peppi and her security-obsessed parents[15] unquestioningly interpret as an admission and submission to the prevailing socio-economic order, Scheck's dream of pursuing an alternative existence on the margins of society is quickly undone—ironically enough at precisely that point in time in which it would have been more economically feasible. Scheck's return to his job at the bank and his marriage to Peppi signal his reintegration into the capitalist fold, a reintegration marked by an increased consumption of goods, an increased need to secure them, and an increased need to produce more income so that even more goods can be consumed. At the same time, this process also produces a growing sense of alienation of which Scheck becomes increasingly aware and which he is increasingly unable to overcome.

Having submitted himself to the demands of consumer society, Scheck can neither resist nor transcend it. At most, he merely finds more opportunities to buy, more opportunities to lose himself temporarily in a seemingly endless and stultifying morass of goods:

> And on Saturday it's off to SHOPPING CITY.
> The urban planners set that one up wisely.
> Out, where it used to be green, in the Southern part of the city.
> So that consumption may stay tied to production—: In this case, the production of exhaust fumes.
> It used to be rural here. Meadows. Hills.
> Now, grass no longer grows here. Just a Potemkin Village.
> FURNITURE COUNTRY, CARPET COUNTRY, TILE COUNTRY—look at what they call a country.
> In between, the biggest traffic jam in Central Europe.

> Nevertheless, you just have to come here on Saturday.
> For where else can you find such offers?
> Every offer a special offer, every special offer an offer for everyone. (109)

The metaphor of SHOPPING CITY gives concrete expression to the social and political transformations that have accompanied the development from the advancing capitalism of Nestroy's time to its advanced state in the present. The establishment of a so-called city whose sole purpose is to bring its inhabitants together in order to consume replaces the notion of the social contract with the terms of the purchase agreement. The proliferation of such "countries" as "Furniture Country," "Carpet Country," and "Tile Country" underscores a sense of globally-capitalist nationhood in which the realm of one's civic activities does not include the right to vote for distinct political platforms and candidates but rather consists only in the obligation to choose among the virtually indistinguishable array of available consumer goods. The calls for greater social and political democracy of the early nineteenth century have given way to the pseudodemocracy of the contemporary marketplace, where everyone—providing, of course, that they possess sufficient capital—is free to purchase the goods that others have determined they should want.

Henisch's terse and pulsating prose reproduces the wholly functionalized language of advanced industrial society, a language, according to Marcuse, "that orders and organizes, that induces people to do, to buy, and to accept. It is transmitted in . . . a syntax in which the structure of the sentence is abridged and condensed in such a way that no tension, no 'space' is left."[16] By consciously and satirically reproducing this type of language, Henisch's text functions to create the very tensions between appearance and reality, between want creation and want satisfaction, that contemporary consumer culture attempts to conceal. By foregrounding these contradictions, and by contrasting the unfreedom of the affluent society with that of the previous century, *Kommt eh der*

Intertextual Satire and the Affluent Society 225

Komet creates a degree of historical comparison that serves to subvert the closed space of one-dimensional, consumerist thought and thereby produce the possibility for critical reflection. As a result, the reader of *Kommt eh der Komet* is in a position to engage in the very type of opposition and resistance that the text's characters cannot.

Notes

1. Volker Kaukoreit, "Wider die Anpassung. Im Gespräch: Der Schriftsteller Peter Henisch," *Marabo: Magazin fürs Ruhrgebiet* Oct. 1995: 114.

2. Peter Henisch, "Warum ich nicht will, daß Österreich untergeht," *Reden an Österreich: Schriftsteller ergreifen das Wort*, ed. Jochen Jung (Salzburg and Vienna: Residenz, 1988) 84.

3. For a discussion of the changing patterns of production and consumption in post-World War II Austria, see Inge Karazman-Morawetz, "Arbeit, Konsum, Freizeit: Veränderungen im Verhältnis von Arbeit und Reproduktion," *Österreich 1945-1995: Gesellschaft, Politik, Kultur*, eds. Reinhard Sieder, Heinz Steinert and Emmerich Tálos (Vienna: Verlag für Gesellschaftskritik, 1995) 409-25. According to Karazman-Morawetz, participating in consumption and the expanding productivity became the most important form of social legitimation in postwar Austria (417).

4. Max Horkheimer and Theodor W. Adorno, *Dialectic of Enlightenment*, trans. John Cumming (New York: Continuum, 1972) 141.

5. Herbert Marcuse, "Freedom and Freud's Theory of Instincts," *Five Lectures: Psychoanalysis, Politics, and Utopia*, trans. Jeremy J. Shapiro and Shierry M. Weber (Boston: Beacon, 1970) 3.

6. The explicit intertextuality at work here in fact

encompasses more than just these two texts. *Lumpazivagabundus*, like the majority of Nestroy's dramas, is loosely based on another text, Karl Weisflog's "Das große Los" (1827, The Big Ticket), which appeared in Weisflog's anthology *Phatasiestücke und Historien* (1824-29, Imaginary Pieces and Stories). *Kommt eh der Komet*, in turn, constitutes Henisch's third reworking of Nestroy's play. In 1974, Henisch's "dramatic dialect version" *lumpazimoribundus: antiposse mit gesang* (lumpazimoribundus: anti-farce with music [Vienna and Munich: Thomas Sessler]) appeared, followed in 1980 by Henisch's initial narrative recasting of the text. The prose version "Lumpazimoribundus" comprises one of the three texts in Henisch's *Vagabundengeschichten* (Vagabond Stories [Munich and Vienna: Langen Müller]). In this essay, I will only consider *Kommt eh der Komet* in light of Nestroy's drama.

7. Johann Nestroy, *Der böse Geist Lumpazivagabundus oder Das liederliche Kleeblatt: Zauberposse mit Gesang in drei Akten*, *Sämtliche Werke: Historisch-kritische Ausgabe*, eds. Jürgen Hein, Johann Hüttner, Walter Obermaier and W. Edgar Yates, vol. 5, ed. Friedrich Walla (Vienna: Jugend und Volk, 1993) 147; Henisch, *Kommt eh der Komet: Eine Erzählung* (Salzburg and Vienna: Residenz, 1995) 5. The quote subsequently reappears on page 42 of *Kommt eh der Komet*.

8. Brian A. Connery and Kirk Combe, "Theorizing Satire: A Retrospective and Introduction," *Theorizing Satire: Essays in Literary Criticism*, eds. Brian A. Connery and Kirk Combe (New York: St. Martin's, 1995) 7.

9. The text ends when a destitute Glasl and Kuli, trying once again to strike it rich, are shot by Scheck as they attempt to rob the bank where Scheck has returned to work.

10. According to John Kenneth Galbraith, "The underclass is deeply functional; all industrial countries have one in greater or lesser measure and in one form or another. As some of its members escape from deprivation and its associated compulsions, a resupply becomes essential" (*The Culture of Contentment* [Boston/New York/London: Houghton Mifflin, 1992] 31).

11. By evoking both Schiller and Nestroy, Henisch also

evokes the institutionalized dichotomy between "high" and "low" literature, a dichotomy that Nestroy's texts challenge both thematically and formally, and a dichotomy that postmodern literature has allegedly overcome.

12. Friedrich von Schiller, "On the Sublime," *Naive and Sentimental Poetry and On the Sublime: Two Essays*, trans. and intro. Julius A. Elias (New York: Ungar, 1966) 195.

13. Marcuse, *One-Dimensional Man: Studies in the Ideology of Advanced Industrial Society* (Boston: Beacon, 1964) xiv.

14. Galbraith, *The Affluent Society*, 3rd ed. (Boston: Houghton Mifflin, 1976) 131.

15. For Henisch's observations on Austria as a nation obsessed with security, see his "Irgendwo hineinrutschen: Sicherheitsverständnis 'auf österreichisch'," *Die Furche* 12 Dec. 1996: 16.

16. Marcuse, *One-Dimensional Man* 86.

Facts and Fiction: On the Process of Development in and to *Schwarzer Peter*

EVA SCHOBEL

In 1991, Louis Begley's impressive novel *Wartime Lies*[1] was published. The author fictionalizes a part of his life story in the novel. In fact, one could even go so far as to say that the novel fictionalizes a part of its author's life story, since novels quite frequently take on a dynamic force of their own. Unlike historians who are obliged to keep to the facts, authors can only dispose of their subject matter up to a certain point. The story of *Wartime Lies* is set in Nazi-occupied Poland and focuses on the life of a Jewish child who survives the Nazi period by pretending to be a Catholic. On the one hand, Louis Begley was *that* child; but, on the other hand, he was not. He evidently made some changes in the characters of the story and did not treat the text as a document, but rather structured it according to literary and aesthetic criteria. Both in the United States and Europe Begley's novel was received with great attention and considerable enthusiasm, but there was criticism as well. In one disparaging review which appeared in the German magazine *Der Spiegel*, Leon de Winter, a Dutch-Jewish author belonging to the second generation of

Shoa survivors, insisted on authenticity as an absolute requirement for all texts centering on the murder of the Jews.[2] His criticism of *Wartime Lies* is rooted in his objection that the novel, which is written in the first person (it does have a frame story which we forget as we proceed), seems leading, creating a semblance of authenticity. He contends, however, that the text is not, in fact, authentic because the author has taken liberties with the treatment of the matter.[3] Nevertheless, I think that Begley's method is legitimate. The problems of identity arising from a denial of Jewish origins are obviously his own, and an identification with the aggressor resulting from his life-threatening position is at least understandable to the author. The fundamental historical facts are correct. In my opinion, there is nothing wrong with the authentic impression the novel creates; however, one should not confuse it with an autobiography such as Klüger's *weiter leben*.

Using Louis Begley as an example, I have briefly addressed the problematic disparity between novel and autobiography, between facts and fiction, because such disparity also appears in Peter Henisch's *Schwarzer Peter* (2000, Black Peter), albeit in a substantially more moderate manner. The terrain on which Henisch's story develops is not weighed down by the Shoa, a significant difference, indeed. Nevertheless, as an author of European origin who lends his voice to a protagonist of European and African-American origins (Black Peter tells his story babbling at the piano in a New Orleans bar), Peter Henisch has to be aware of the risks involved in such an undertaking. Is an author allowed to proceed this way? Can someone really step into the shoes of a person whose skin has a different color and be credible? And if, under certain circumstances, the author succeeds in doing so, isn't that all the more problematic because it goes beyond the particular story and suggests a general factuality that a fictional story can never have? No matter how one may choose to answer these questions, I believe that the responsibility lies not only with the author but also with the reader, who has to come to a decision about his or her reading.

The need among readers—even among those who deal with literature professionally—for so-called *true* stories seems to be very strong, indeed. Hence, a culture editor from Austrian television asked Peter Henisch whether he would be willing to talk about his African-American origins in front of the camera. But Peter Henisch, of course, is not Black Peter, definitely not. His mother was not an attractive Viennese streetcar conductress, but an attractive Viennese housewife. His father was not an American GI, but a photographer who, as a war correspondent in the German armed forces, suppressed his half-Jewish ancestry. In spite of these facts, however, the story of Black Peter has a lot to do with the author's own horizon of experience; in an interview, Henisch described himself as being the stuntman for the characters in his novel.[4] *Schwarzer Peter* thus marks the temporary climax of a literary development leading from the earlier, fundamentally autobiographical texts to works in which Henisch treats the autobiographical subject with increasing poetic license. One basic theme, however, constitutes a central thread connecting the author's entire body of work: the dynamics of conformity with or resistance to societal norms with which one cannot identify. In order to illustrate this point, I will, in summarizing fashion, delineate the position of *Schwarzer Peter* within Henisch's oeuvre.

In 1975, the autobiographical text *Die kleine Figur meines Vaters* (*Negatives of My Father*, 1990) appeared, marking the author's literary breakthrough. In this work, *Peter* Henisch comes to terms with the problematic role his father, *Walter* Henisch, played as a successful reporter during the National Socialist regime despite his Jewish origins. The son's engagement with the problem is based on the tape recordings of actual conversations he had with his then seriously ill father. The father, who hoped to reconstruct his life in his own fashion and who wanted to tell an impressive adventure story full of the tricks and joys of survival "in times of war," defends himself against the critical questions posed by his son: "How could that have happened, why did you go along with it, why didn't you do anything against it?"[5] "What should I have done? Should I have gone there and given myself up?" the father asks back (49). "What would you all have done . . . in *my* place?" (101). Walter Henisch's reply is indeed worth thinking about, and it is important to note that it can only be contradicted from a position of self-righteousness. At the end of the day, the son's criticism of his father cannot simply end in the reproach that his father failed to act heroically, that he failed to declare himself to be a Jew and thus sacrifice his life. (A sacrifice his son never could have honored, simply because then he never would have been born). The problem that emerges from reflecting upon the conversations between father and son is that the elder Henisch's understandable external survival strategy eventually tips over and turns into internal conformity. It is precisely this opportunistic attitude that causes the son to level criticism against his father. The father increasingly came to like his role as a war correspondent; he even identified with this role after the war. It was the best time of his life, a time from which he drew self-confidence right up until his death. "Dear Papa, . . . I don't want to become what you became," the son writes in a letter which he never sent. "I don't want to be the way you were, although I understand you" (101). The generational conflict set against the background of World War II recollections, portrayed here as a father-son conflict which the author himself experienced, also led the son to critical self-reflection. What is his attitude toward writing? Does Peter, the author, exploit the dubious, problematic or even murderous reality in the same brutally affirmative way as Walter Henisch, the photographer? Understanding the father without accepting his behavior is a respectable attempt at not following in his footsteps.

In Henisch's next novel, *Der Mai ist vorbei* (1978, May Is Over), the author consistently follows up on these issues by coming to grips with the story of his own, anti-father generation. *Der Mai ist vorbei* is set at the time of the 1968 student demonstrations and is characterized by a vital impulse of rebellion derived from a dissociation from the world-war generation of fathers. "*We* don't want to become what *you* have become!" It is a *collective* protest, joined halfheartedly by both the author of the novel and his schizoid protagonist, at times called *Paul* Grünzweig, at other times *Peter*. There are, however, reasons underlying the halfheartedness and schizoid split alike. To be sure, this protagonist is a Hamlet (a figure that Henisch had already dealt with in 1971, in his very first book *Hamlet bleibt* [Hamlet Remains]) ailing from the paleness of thought and hence unable to act, or at least inhibited in his actions. Still, owing to his critical sensorium he can clearly identify authoritarian tendencies, even those within the anti-authoritarian movement. Eventually, he cannot and does not want to conform, not even with other outsiders: as soon as a group of people takes shape, thus running the risk of losing their outsider status, he intuitively suspects that they will mutate, stop being the *others* and turn into the *ones* as soon as they take power. "You shouldn't be like everybody else, but sometimes you have to be many," writes the German poet Peter Rühmkorf (1929-),[6] another person unwilling to give up his individuality for the sake of agreement within a group. Henisch/Grünzweig's place was and is on the periphery, "neither outside / nor inside," "because how can you be identical / with yourself / in view of / a reality / that makes you / want to / turn away?"[7] In both *Die kleine Figur meines Vaters* and *Der Mai ist vorbei*, the author's personal experience serves as evidence for the truth; he has turned himself or his father into an example.

In subsequent books Henisch disengages himself from the corset of autobiography, giving free rein to his imagination without, however, leaving the terrain of facts, of locations and social conditions he has researched. A good opportunity to break away from his own story came in his next book *Hoffmanns Erzählungen: Aufzeichnungen eines verwirrten Germanisten* (1983, Tales of Hoffmann: Notes of a Confused Germanist), an artist's biography of and homage to the poet E.T.A. Hoffmann (1776-1822), who in Henisch's opinion was as much of a Realist as he was a Romantic. Particularly significant here is the fact that E.T.A. Hoffmann also suffered from the "deficiency disease of the time,"[8] of *his* time, a state of schizophrenia he experienced as something existential. In contrast to the popular opera *Contes d'Hoffmann* by Jacques Offenbach (1819-80), a work that has greatly influenced how we view Hoffmann today, Hoffmann's schizophrenia was not rooted in the pathological imagination of an artistic genius who, after a day of serious work in the legal profession, becomes addicted to alcohol and creative madness at night, but rather is a response to the external circumstances of the times and the exigencies of the day. "In a period of transition when the old value system is crumbling and any certainty that a generally valid new era will ever dawn has hopelessly faded—which in the age of Hoffmann was the era of reason—the old specters meet the new ones," writes Franz Fühmann in his essay "Fräulein Veronika Paulmann aus der Pirnaer Vorstadt oder Etwas über das Schauerliche bei E.T.A. Hoffmann,"[9] which Henisch read while he was working on his Hoffmann novel. Henisch was particularly interested in the correspondence of epochs. In the past, it was the French Revolution, the Napoleonic Wars, and the ensuing Reaction; what is at stake today (or rather, in the eighties, when the novel was written) are the hopes that have largely faded after the atmosphere of change that characterized the previous two decades.

It is interesting to note that Henisch was already thinking of the novel about Jim Morrison (*Morrisons Versteck*, 1991 [Morrison's Hideout]) when E.T.A. Hoffmann prevented him from starting it because Henisch chanced upon a book in a rummage sale box under the archways of Ravenna, Italy. What Henisch read as a result of this chance encounter brought him close to Hoffmann again; he had already appreciated the author in high school, especially the texts *Ritter Gluck* (1807), *Der Sandmann* (1817), and *Lebensansichten des Kater Murr* (1820). However, the foreword written by a certain Heinrich Kurz[10] provoked Henisch's protest and caused him to start writing about Hoffmann. Everything that Henisch had always liked about Hoffmann was seen by Kurz as a regrettable artistic or moral error—including the fact that the young lawyer could not help caricaturing the authoritarian Prussian state, represented by the military bureaucrats in occupied Poznán, or that some of the best Hoffmann texts are characterized by a schizoid structure.

In retrospect, the text that foreshadows *Black Peter* most clearly is the novel *Pepi Prohaska Prophet*, published in 1986. The childhood landscape of Pepi and Black Peter is also that of the author. It is situated on the banks of the Danube

Canal, "the smaller, more vulgar brother of the great Danube"[11] which, unlike the big river which is diverted around the city, flows right through Vienna. Pepi and Peter find a free area there, one ripped open by the war, by bombs, and by conflicts lying bare, conflicts that had not been covered up by concrete in the course of restoration and reconstruction. In that immediate postwar period, many things could have developed differently; at that time in Austria there was still a potential for a conscious and critical approach to one's own history.

If that approach had prevailed, if the material consolidation made possible by the Marshall Plan had not helped gloss over the issue of shared responsibility for the war and the persecution of the Jews, then Max Stein, the title character in *Steins Paranoia* (1988; *Stone's Paranoia*, 2000), might not have heard that ominous, fatal sentence in Vienna towards the end of the 1980s, that sentence that quickly spread throughout the whole city. And even if that sentence had been uttered (it is never cited in the novel, but one can assume that it is an anti-Semitic sentence), Stein would have contradicted it. And not only Stein would have contradicted that sentence, but a significant number of people would not have allowed the sentence to remain uncontradicted, and Stein would thus not have had to develop his paranoia about the sentence spreading like an epidemic because he had failed to contradict it in the first place. Max Stein, who had never been interested in his Jewish roots, who did not want to hear the stories of his Jewish father with whom he could easily have identified, is in a certain sense a counterexample to the son in *Die kleine Figur meines Vaters*, who definitely wants to hear his father's stories but does not want to identify with him.

But let us now return to Pepi and Peter, kindred spirits with a slightly oblique view of conditions that have been smoothed over, people who as a matter of course would like to feel at home, "but home," Henisch asks, writing in the first person in his cycle of poems "Heimkehr mit Heine" (Returning Home with Heine), "home, where is that?"[12] "Of all possible places in the world," said the real Joe Logsdon to the real author, "your Black Peter would most likely feel at home in

New Orleans." "Most likely"—only this relative truth simultaneously contains the whole truth. In any case, Pepi Prohaska, the prophet torn by self-doubt in spite of all his vanity, beams himself away in an ironic sleight of hand at the end of the book, disappearing from the horizon precisely on the day the Pope visits Vienna, i.e., just when he could have made himself heard. Pepi hijacks a bus far away from the spectacle on Heroes' Square in the heart of Vienna, only to stop at a gravel pit where he drives children around in circles as if they were on a carousel ride. And before he can get arrested, he transports himself to an unknown place where no one can find him. Strictly speaking, his disappearance is the only miracle he was able to perform throughout his career as a prophet. It is a miracle that releases him—in the true sense of the word, and irreversibly—from the unrewarding duty of being a prophet in his own country. In spite of his talent, he probably did not want to become a guru after all and abuse his suggestive authority.

There is a ten-year gap between the creation of *Pepi Prohaska Prophet* and *Schwarzer Peter*, ten years in which optimistic Austrians were forced to dispense with a few illusions. First and foremost, they had to say farewell to the illusion that they were living in a country where, at least to some extent, critical public opinion was working, a country where a man like Kurt Waldheim—who presumably had not been a war criminal but a nominal party member believing he had only done his duty during the Nazi regime, a man who accepted that he was campaigning for votes with the help of reemerging anti-Semitic resentments—would not have succeeded in being elected President. The immediate literary response to this political situation was *Steins Paranoia*. Owing to this, the Morrison novel, long planned and not subject to any particular timing, appeared precisely twenty years after the death of the rock star.

Subsequently, Henisch started to write a novel which was supposed to be entitled "Nachwort zum Nachsommer," an epilogue to Adalbert Stifter's *Nachsommer* (1857), in which a descendant of Paul Grünzweig (the character from *Der Mai ist vorbei*) chooses passive resistance in contemporary Austria.

Having written about forty pages of the epilogue and published an early draft,[13] he interrupted that work because Black Peter had appeared, and this is how it came about: In 1995, Peter Henisch was invited to join a journalist friend for a walk in the neighborhood of his childhood days along the Danube Canal. It was not supposed to be a straight interview, but rather an associative conversation inspired by the locality.[14] After all, the journalist was no longer a straight journalist, either. He had given up his secure job with a newspaper and was in the process of writing a novel, one in which he could express the conflict between his biological existence as a man and his psychological feelings as a woman.

The journalist was not Black Peter, either, although he, too, feels uncertain about his sexual identity. However, that conversation triggered something. It was the desire to retell the story of the Second Republic from a totally different angle, from the angle of a person who is not only different because he likes being different and because it is possible for him to be different—like the author, or his protagonist Pepi Prohaska for that matter—but also from the angle of a person who is forced to start from a different point of departure, who has no other choice. Before Black Peter, Henisch's protagonists chose difference from positions of relative luxury and privilege. Even Max Stein would not have been forced to profess his Jewish origins had they not mentally caught up with him. Black Peter, however, who is not jet-black but nevertheless still too black to blend into an all-white environment, does not stand a similar chance. The impetus for Henisch to invent a black protagonist was not a "politically correct" idea emerging from the worsening political situation in Austria, as has been assumed by some.[15] Nor did the idea have anything to do with the death of Marcus Omofuma, a Nigerian refugee who in 1999 was bound and gagged for deportation from Vienna to Bucharest and died of asphyxia aboard the plane. The idea emerged in the early stage of the novel and is connected with a childhood recollection Henisch had previously turned into a poem:

My childhood

> a wooden toy boat
>
> fastened
> to pulp yarn
> that gets soggy[16]

Black Peter's wooden boat is also carried away, and the protagonist, running up and down the banks of the Danube Canal, can no longer find it. "Blow your nose," his mother says when he finally comes home with a tear-stained face and burs on his pants and shirt. "If your ship got into the Danube where the canal joins the river at the Praterspitz, then now it's on its way to the Black Sea" (8). This is precisely the moment when the author knew that his protagonist would be black.

Black Peter's story is not a true story, but one that might really have happened between Austria in the years of the Second Republic and New Orleans in the past two decades, between the Danube Canal and the Mississippi River, between the boat ride across the Danube Canal and the ferry to Algiers. To ensure these possibilities, research had to be done into many details, research that in New Orleans was possible due to the open-minded and competent assistance of Joe and Mary Logsdon, Günther Bischof, and Melanie Bischof Boulet, as well as some of their friends and acquaintances.

To cite one example: Henisch had a conversation with Leon C. Standifer. Even though Standifer had been stationed in Bavaria, and not in Austria, in the years 1945-46, he drew on his personal experiences and expressed doubts as to whether the U.S. Army High Command in Vienna would really have assigned an African-American soldier to the legendary "Four in the Jeep." This prompted the author to change his original idea in a productive way. The story of Peter's father waving at the pretty conductress in her streetcar from precisely that jeep is not presented as a real incident, as had originally been planned. Rather, it is a romantic fantasy dreamed up by his mother, one that Peter believes throughout his childhood but then sees from a more realistic angle as he starts to get interested in his roots in more specific terms. Joe Logsdon drew Peter Henisch's attention to the marvelous detail that people in New Orleans do not so much use directions such as north, south, east, and west to find their bearings, but the course of the Mississippi—which is not that easy to grasp in the beginning. The author also gained in-depth information about the history of New Orleans, the way in which people live together in the city, and the wonderful idea of Creolization from Joe Logsdon.

Significant research was also required in Austria, even though the author is, of course, more familiar with the local conditions. For example, clarification was needed as to whether those soldiers of the German Army who were allowed to return from Soviet prisoner-of-war camps only after the Austrian State Treaty had been ratified were specially incriminated by the function of their former units or by personal involvement. According to the historian Ernst Hanisch, Professor of History at the University of Salzburg, it is impossible to make a general statement in this regard. In any event, once Ferdinand, the first husband of Black Peter's mother, returns from the war after long captivity, he becomes a very positive figure for Black Peter, which would not have been the case had he been a war criminal.

Another essential aspect of the novel was the author's research on how asylum-seekers are dealt with in Austria today. Curiously enough, when visiting his old home country, Black Peter finds himself in custody awaiting deportation because he has lost his documents and is thus unable to prove his identity. Sources from Amnesty International doubted whether a person who is black and claims to be a US citizen would be detained for days on end. They would certainly try to check the data provided as quickly as possible. On the occasion of a half-day visit to the police prison at Rossauerlände in Vienna, Major Z., the prison's Commander-in-Chief, provided Henisch insight into the closed department after the author had obtained permission from the public relations division of Vienna's police force. The major's opinion differed from that of Amnesty International. He thought that it was quite probable that the so-called Identification Division of the Aliens' Police Office would take a few days before they clarified the identity of any potential deportee. Major Z. also gave the author the yellow form which is used to collect schematized data with bureaucratic objectivity about each subject in an equally outrageous and ridiculously depersonalizing way. In the novel, Henisch transforms that bureaucratic instrument into a text approaching concrete poetry. It was only a few days after Henisch's visit to the police prison that deportee Marcus Omofuma died. It is rather improbable that the author would have been given access to the prison all that easily subsequent to Omofuma's death.

By way of conclusion, I would like to point out that, within the context of Peter Henisch's complete works, *Schwarzer Peter* is the author's first book dealing with the theme of the mother. The novel pays homage to a simple and courageous woman in an exceptional situation who gives her son enough emotional support to enable him to survive the disasters in his life. Still, the search for the father—inevitable in Henisch's work—forms a major thread throughout the novel. Black Peter does not find his biological father, the enigmatic Mr. Meredith, and that's good. (Ironically, the man whom he finally meets after a few thwarted attempts is white.) The bottom line is that the biological roots are not so important to the author and the protagonist. Psychological affinities, congeniality, an oblique view of the established order, and a fundamental humanitarian attitude—these are the traits that all of the father figures in *Schwarzer Peter* have in common: the ferryman who takes the child across the Danube Canal; Ferdinand, who returns from the prisoner-of-war camp a broken man and later commits suicide by drowning himself; Mr. Jericha, the Jewish bookseller who introduces Black Peter to the world of literature; and last, but not least, Joe, who helps him settle down in New Orleans. All of these father figures—and this is the confidence-building basic frequency of the vibrations that emanate from them—are outsiders, each in his own distinct way.

Translated by Elisabeth Frank-Großebner

Notes

1. Louis Begley, *Wartime Lies* (New York: Knopf, 1991).
2. Leon de Winter, "Shoa für die Couch," *Der Spiegel* 2 Jan. 1995: 135-36.
3. I have encountered similar reactions on the part of my university students, as they initially and naively tend to identify the author, Begley, with his protagonist, Maciek. Part of our educational task lies in raising awareness about the differences between a biographical record like Ruth Klüger's *weiter leben: Eine Jugend* (1992, surviving: A Youth) and a novel like Begley's.
4. Hannes Dobelhofer, "Der Schwarze Peter: Erkundungen zu Peter Henischs neuem Roman," *Tonspuren, Hörbilder zur Literatur*, Österreichischer Rundfunk, Österreich 1, 5 March 2000.
5. Peter Henisch, *Negatives of My Father*, trans. Anne Close Ulmer (Riverside, CA: Ariadne, 1990) 139.
6. Peter Rühmkorf, "Allein ist nicht genug," *Gedichte, Werke I*, ed. Bernd Rauschenbach (Reinbek bei Hamburg: Rowohlt, 2000) 310.
7. These lines appear in the poem "Oh wie schön schizophren ich doch bin" (Oh, how beautifully schizophrenic I really am) contained in Henisch's *Der Mai ist vorbei* (Frankfurt/M: Fischer, 1978) 235-36.
8. Henisch refers to schizophrenia as the "deficiency disease of the time" in *Der Mai ist vorbei* (235).
9. Franz Fühmann, "Fräulein Veronika Paulmann aus der Pirnaer Vorstadt oder Etwas über das Schauerliche bei E.T.A. Hoffmann," *Fräulein Veronika Paulmann aus der Pirnaer Vorstadt oder Etwas über das Schauerliche bei E.T.A. Hoffmann* (Hamburg: Hoffmann und Campe, 1980) 102.
10. Heinrich Kurz, "Einleitung," *Hoffmanns Werke*, ed. Heinrich Kurz, vol. 1 (Leipzig and Vienna: Verlag des Bibliographischen Instituts, n.d.) 5-10.
11. Henisch, *Schwarzer Peter* (Salzburg and Vienna: Residenz, 2000) 7.
12. Henisch, *Hamlet, Hiob, Heine* (Salzburg and Vienna: Residenz, 1989) 149.

13. Henisch, "Nachwort zum Nachsommer, Beginn eines Romans," *Literatur und Kritik* April 1997: 21-28.
14. See Klaus Khittl, "Wo die Gespenster wohnen," *Elisabethbühne* Nov./Dec. 1995: 26-31.
15. For instance, Hans Christian Kosler, "Spiel dein Spiel, Negerl! Peter Henisch schreibt den Roman der Zweiten Republik," *Neue Zürcher Zeitung* 14 June 2000: 67.
16. Henisch, *Hamlet, Hiob, Heine* 26.

The Jambalaya Principle: Otherness and Multiculturalism in *Schwarzer Peter*

JENNIFER E. MICHAELS

Since its publication Peter Henisch's multifaceted novel *Schwarzer Peter* (2000, Black Peter) has enjoyed success in Austria where it has aroused lively debate. The novel tells the story of Peter Jarosch, the "Black Peter" of the title, the son of a Viennese tram conductor and an African-American soldier who was part of the postwar occupation. Henisch examines in the novel the protagonist's struggle to find his identity and a sense of belonging in an Austria where because of his skin color he is immediately perceived as being different. Through Peter's struggle with his otherness Henisch sheds light on Austria's treatment of its minorities during the postwar years and questions the myths that for many years underpinned Austrian identity in the Second Republic. The novel has been popular, not only due to its literary qualities but also because it addresses such urgent social problems as the treatment of those seeking asylum. In the following, I will first position the novel within sociopolitical and literary developments in the Second Republic as well as within Henisch's own previous work. I will then examine how in *Schwarzer Peter*

Henisch explores otherness and Austria's treatment of minorities and how he skillfully structures his novel not only to reinforce themes of otherness and separation but also to offer a different cultural paradigm that recognizes cultural difference but also suggests possibilities for integration and connection. By presenting a model of how different cultures can enrich one another *Schwarzer Peter* makes an important contribution to the current discourse on multiculturalism in Austria.

Schwarzer Peter is informed by postmodern discourses on identity, diversity, and cultural difference that have preoccupied literary and cultural critics for the past decades. Edward Said's *Orientalism* (1978), which was "a watershed in the recent thinking about cultural difference,"[1] and the work of such postmodern philosophers as Gilles Deleuze and Félix Guattari stimulated thinking about identity and otherness and promoted a respect for and interest in the cultures of groups other than one's own. Their thinking encouraged writers and critics to view the majority discourse critically and to give voice to those groups who are either absent or marginalized. The work of Charles Taylor in Canada gave an influential philosophical justification for multiculturalism.[2] By positioning multiculturalism within the liberal tradition of political thought Taylor provides "a needed situating of and perspective on the often ill-informed and overheated current debates on multiculturalism."[3] These postmodern discourses have shaped debates in Austria about identity and multiculturalism and have encouraged Austrian writers and critics to challenge concepts of national identity and cultural homogeneity and to insist that multicultural and marginal voices be heard in Austria. Like their counterparts in other countries, Austrian writers encourage "the celebration of difference and heterogeneity and the assertion of plurality as opposed to reductive unities."[4]

Peter Jarosch's life (he was born in 1946) spans the years of the Second Republic, a setting designed to allow Henisch to depict developments in postwar Austria and to address questions about how postwar Austrian identity was formed. Like many contemporary Austrian writers such as Elisabeth Reichart (1953-), Felix Mitterer (1948-), and Doron Rabinovici (1961-), to mention but a few, Henisch has long been concerned that present-day Austrian identity has been shaped by his country's unconfronted Nazi past. As Alexander and Margarete Mitscherlich argued in their pioneering work *Die Unfähigkeit zu trauern* (1967; *The Inability to Mourn*, 1975), if people refuse to come to grips with this past it continues to live on, deform present identity, and poison not only the present but also the future. With his novel *Die kleine Figur meines Vaters* (first published in 1975; *Negatives of My Father*, 1990) Henisch was in fact one of the early voices in Austrian literature to insist on the importance of confronting the fascist past. *Schwarzer Peter*, in turn, continues and furthers the debate among contemporary Austrian writers about the role of the past in shaping current Austrian identity. Like many other Austrians, Henisch has criticized Austria's reluctance to address its responsibility for the Nazi period. The Moscow Declaration of 1943 referred to Austria as the first victim of Nazi aggression, and this enabled Austrians after the war to propagate the myth that they were victims rather than perpetrators, "that the Nazi bacillus had been a foreign germ."[5] They avoided remembering that Nazism originated in Austria, that Austrian Nazis were involved in running "some of the most notorious concentration camps,"[6] and that even though Austrians comprised only about eight percent of the population of the Greater German Reich they nevertheless made up thirteen to fourteen percent of the SS.[7] For many years after the war they thus minimized their role in the Nazi regime.

Doron Rabinovici expresses the concerns of many of his fellow writers when he criticizes the politics of silence that in his view have characterized the Second Republic. He argues that from the very beginning the Second Republic was built on denial and the silencing of basic ideological controversies. Neither the Austro-fascist period nor Austria's involvement in National Socialism were discussed. Instead, Austria was absolved from guilt and declared the victim of Hitler. In his view, Austrian identity after 1945 was based on a flight from responsibility and accountability.[8] Unlike their counterparts in

Germany such as Heinrich Böll (1917-85) and Günter Grass (1927-), most Austrian writers in the early postwar period did not deal extensively with their country's Nazi past, and those who did, such as Ilse Aichinger (1921-) in *Die größere Hoffnung* (1948; *The Great Hope*, 1974), were not able through their works to promote widespread debate. In the sixties, however, some began to confront the Nazi past more systematically and critically in their literary works.[9]

Several events in the Second Republic accelerated an active confrontation with the past and a consideration of how postwar Austrian identity had been formed. A major catalyst was Kurt Waldheim's campaign and subsequent election to the presidency of Austria in 1986. The questions raised during the campaign about Waldheim's involvement in the Nazi past demonstrated to writers like Henisch, historians like Erika Weinzierl, and political scientists like Anton Pelinka the necessity of reexamining their country's recent history. Echoing the views of many at the time, Pelinka and Weinzierl observe that Austria was still seen as a country that had learned little, if anything, from its past, even though it was the breeding ground for National Socialism.[10] For many in Austria the presidential election was shocking since it became painfully clear that the Second Republic had refused to accept any responsibility for the past. The campaign was also troubling because it brought latent anti-Semitic prejudices to the surface, an issue that Henisch addresses in his novel *Steins Paranoia* (1988; *Stone's Paranoia,* 2000). The social scientist Bernd Marin points out how widespread anti-Semitic beliefs and attitudes and traditional stereotypes of Jews are in Austria. In his view, this mass prejudice "has become embedded in the 'collective unconsiousness' through a process of cultural sedimentation, and is frequently reproduced unintentionally and unconsciously in everyday language."[11] Rather than confronting their own past, some Austrians instead blamed the Jews for raising questions about Waldheim's past.

For many Austrians the anti-Semitism and xenophobia that became increasingly evident during the Waldheim campaign was particularly shocking since such views were not confined to the older generation that had fought under Hitler but were also shared by young people. Incidents of hostility toward immigrants and guest-workers, anti-Semitism, and authoritarian behavior were seen as proof that the past continued to live on. Franz Danimann, a survivor of Auschwitz, remarks that many had thought that the Nazi problem would solve itself as the old generation died out:

> We assumed that in a democratic Austria, with healthy economic and social policies, and the lessons of the past at hand, there would be no place for neo-Nazis, anti-Semitism, and similar poisonous ideas. For this reason the young did not get proper instruction. . . . We are seeing again the old xenophobia and clichés about foreigners, and unfortunately there is now a whole generation that has not been taught the lessons of the past.[12]

Such recurring anti-Semitism and xenophobia seemed to suggest other troubling aspects of Austrian identity. For example, Anton Pelinka notes that studies of the authoritarian personality have shown time and again that anti-Semites also hold other antidemocratic and antirational views.[13] By asking uncomfortable questions in their literary texts about how present Austrian identity was shaped, contemporary Austrian writers like Henisch wish to encourage their readers to question and examine not only their society but also themselves.

Other recent events in Austria, such as the fiftieth anniversary of the Anschluss in 1988, the fortieth anniversary of the signing of the Austrian State Treaty in 1995, and the celebrations for Austria's millennium in 1996, gave even more momentum to the debate about Austria's identity and its role in the New Europe. In recent works, many writers express their fears that remnants of the unconfronted Nazi past still influence Austrian identity and lead to racism, xenophobia, anti-Semitism, and attacks on refugees, foreigners, and Roma. They continue to question the myth of Austria as the innocent victim of Nazi aggression as well as the idyllic postwar identity that Austria constructed for itself. Inge Merkel (1922-) observes, for example, that "with talent, skill and charm the stage setting of a small but beautiful Austria, pregnant with culture, was fashioned. A country of music, of magnificent baroque buildings and landscapes. A country one visits like a museum to look at and admire."[14] Like many recent writers, Merkel finds this identity dishonest.

With the growing strength of right-wing extremism, represented by Jörg Haider and the new populists, the debate about what kind of society Austria should become became urgent. Many contemporary writers, Henisch among them, are dismayed by the success of Haider's FPÖ (Austrian Freedom Party).[15] Although in the most recent campaigns Haider and the new populists have toned down their anti-foreigner rhetoric, many Austrians regard them as racists and fear that by promoting a homogenous Austrian society Haider and his followers create an atmosphere in Austria that is hostile to foreigners and minorities. In their creative works and in numerous essays and newspaper articles, contemporary writers criticize how minorities are treated in Austria. They feel a strong sense of responsibility for helping to shape this debate about how Austrians should define themselves and their society. They reject the exclusive and homogenous society they believe that Haider promotes and argue instead for an inclusive and heterogeneous one. Through their works they attempt to make their fellow citizens more tolerant and accepting of minorities and able to appreciate their different cultures. They conceive of a society in which not only Austria's traditional minorities such as Jews, Roma and Sinti, and other groups from the former Austro-Hungarian Empire, but also more recently arrived immigrants and refugees can live together and mutually enrich one another's lives. For some like Barbara Frischmuth (1941-), the pluralist Austro-Hungarian Empire provides a possible model for their vision of a multicultural and multiethnic Austria. Frischmuth observes: "If I'm not mistaken, Austria was never a completely German-speaking country. Instead, Austria was the first model—and not such a bad model, as one recognizes now—for the coexistence of different peoples."[16] Although she regrets that this model of a multinational state failed, she notes that it worked for a long time and that overall "one tried very many things then in a serious attempt at doing everyone justice" (148). She acknowledges that not everyone viewed this state positively, but at least at that time "one had to come to terms with one another" (148). In contrast to Frischmuth, Henisch offers in *Schwarzer Peter* the multiethnic city of New Orleans as a possible model for the future.[17]

Schwarzer Peter contributes to and furthers this debate about identity, tolerance, and an open multicultural society. Like Henisch, many contemporary writers are concerned with what they see as their fellow citizens' lack of tolerance for any person they perceive as an outsider, and these authors speak out against the intolerance they observe. Ilse Krüger (1939-) remarks, for example, that some Austrians have again found a common scapegoat, namely, foreigners, whom they blame for any injustice they experience in their lives.[18] Reinhold Brandl (1960-) points to widespread prejudices and racism, manifested, for example, in the behavior of those who insist that Slovenian children should be separated from Austrian children (as if the former had a communicable disease) and those who try to avoid contact when a Yugoslav sits next to them in the tram.[19]

As the historian Harry Ritter has pointed out: "There has never been a single *Austrian* identity, despite popular stereotypes which conflate Viennese *Heimatgefühl* and 'Austrianism.'"[20] Many recent writers try to remind their fellow citizens of their multicultural heritage and criticize what they see as the development of a homogenous Austrian society in the postwar years. Marie-Thérèse Kerschbaumer (1936-) believes that it is difficult for ethnic groups in Austria because beginning in early childhood the majority opposes the whole notion of minority. The postwar concept of an ethnically homogenous national state, she writes, hinders the development of democratic structures and creates a climate in which ethnic groups are rejected. She fears that in such a climate potential crimes against weaker national groups already slumber.[21] In a short article in *Profil* in 1995, Ruth Beckermann (1952-) blames the postwar focus on "We Austrians" for creating a climate hostile to minorities.[22] Beckermann does not only hold Haider and the new populism responsible for what

The Jumbalaya Principle 249

she sees as the marginalization of minorities in Austria. A major reason for this marginalization, she believes, is that the "frantic search for a homogenous Austrian identity"[23] has created in the post-World War II years a climate that makes it difficult for Austrians to accept cultural, religious, and ethnic difference. In her opinion, Jews, for example, were never left in any doubt that they were undesirable strangers.

Several writers criticize in their works their fellow citizens' intolerance of Roma. The four Roma killed in Oberwart in the Burgenland in February 1995 by a booby-trapped bomb when they tried to remove a racist sign bearing the words "Roma back to India" that had been put up outside their settlement was shocking proof that, as Kerschbaumer had observed, prejudice against minorities can lead to violence. Elisabeth Reichart believes that schools foster such prejudice. She recalls that students in her school ostracized a gypsy girl. Rather than trying to prevent such behavior, the teachers and the priest actually encouraged it.[24] Karin Ivancsics (1962-) investigates prejudices against Roma in her native Burgenland. As she was growing up she experienced prejudice herself because her father was Croatian and thus in the minority in the Burgenland. She had hoped, she writes, that such prejudices were in the past, but she realizes that new minorities have been cast as scapegoats. As she talks to ordinary people in the Burgenland about the murders, deep-seated prejudices and stereotypes about Roma emerge. One man regrets, for example, that only four Roma were murdered. Another declares that the victims dealt drugs, that one already had illegitimate children and a criminal record, and his wife had loose morals. Although some claim they are not prejudiced against Roma in general, they nevertheless stereotype those in Oberwart as lazy, dishonest good-for-nothings.[25] Ruth Beckermann describes the funeral service held for the four Roma and is dismayed by what she sees as its hypocrisy. The three thousand or so people who attended, all of whom were important figures in Austrian society, were, in her opinion, using the occasion not to express outrage or mourn the victims but rather to demonstrate Austria's maturity for integration into the European community. The murders led well-meaning people to organize lectures about Roma history and culture. Beckermann believes, however, that these four men were not murdered because people did not know enough about them and their culture but because people hated them. She is pessimistic that such irrational racism can be changed through education.[26]

Contemporary Jewish writers in Austria also perceive the political and cultural climate in Austria to be hostile to them and other minorities. In his essay "Warum ich nicht will, daß Österreich untergeht"[27] (1988, Why I Don't Want Austria to Sink) and in *Steins Paranoia*, for example, Henisch contributes to this debate by exploring his own identity as an Austrian writer with some Jewish heritage. Like the title character in *Steins Paranoia*, Henisch asks how he can fit into a society in which anti-Semitic stereotypes and prejudices are still widespread. Doron Rabinovici also examines the extent to which it is possible for a Jew to fit into Austrian society. Rabinovici describes his reactions to a question posed by an Austrian journalist about whether he, as a Jew, would emigrate if Jörg Haider were to become federal chancellor. He remarks that this question contains both sensitivity and obscenity. It is sensitive because it recognizes that a gulf of emotions and the recent past separate Austrian Jews from their non-Jewish fellow citizens. But he also finds the question obscene because it demonstrates that his society views him as an outsider. Instead of being asked his views as an Austrian he is asked for his views as a Jew.[28] Another Jewish writer who senses a feeling of not belonging in Austria is Ruth Beckermann. In her writing and in her films she makes her readers and her audience aware of Jewish contributions to Austrian culture and of the difficulties she and other Jews encounter in living as a minority in Austria, difficulties that she shows are made worse because many Austrians are still prejudiced against their Jewish fellow citizens.

Contemporary Austrian writers are concerned not only with deeply rooted prejudices, such as those against Jews and Roma, but also with how newer immigrants are treated. Some, like Barbara Frischmuth, attempt "to initiate a dialogue about the new circumstances, to urge the majority to promote the acculturation and assimilation of the minority, to practice tolerance toward the culturally different, the stranger."[29] As Frischmuth observes, Austria's many Moslems have raised families in their new country and some have been granted citizenship. Their children have gone to local schools and speak a German colored by the areas where they now live. Although they are no longer "foreigners" they are nevertheless still treated as outsiders.[30] In her literary works such as the novels *Das Verschwinden des Schattens in der Sonne* (1973; *The Shadow Disappears in the Sun*, 1998) and *Die Schrift des Freundes* (1998, The Writing of the Friend), her translations from Turkish, and her essays, Frischmuth hopes to foster cross-cultural understanding and tolerance and nurture "a genuine interest and a readiness to become spiritually and emotionally involved with the other."[31] The ten "Ex Oriente" articles that she published in *Die Presse* in 1996 are examples of her goal of making her readers appreciate the richness and diversity of contemporary Turkish and Moslem cultures as well as their contributions to the culture of their new countries. Since the writers she discusses are "border-crossers" they have a unique perspective on their own and on European culture. Frischmuth believes strongly that if people are prepared to try to understand each other and develop respect for other cultures, they can coexist peacefully, and through her works she hopes to nurture such mutual understanding and respect.

Another issue of concern to many contemporary Austrian writers is the injustice of Austria's asylum laws. Human rights groups have criticized Austria's asylum policies for being too restrictive.[32] In *Die Schrift des Freundes* Frischmuth criticizes the arbitrariness (and the strained bureaucratic reasoning) with which petitions for asylum are routinely rejected. In this novel she mentions the case of a woman from Afghanistan whose mother had died because of mistreatment by the mujaheddin and whose five-year-old daughter had been kidnapped and then killed. Her request for asylum in Austria was rejected because it was her family members—and not she herself—who had suffered abuse.[33] Like Frischmuth, Josef Haslinger (1955-) takes issue with Austria's restrictive asylum policies.[34] He reminds his readers that Austria has traditionally been a land of immigration for people from eastern and south-eastern Europe. He argues that the restrictiveness of asylum policies is a conscious destruction of the principle of the universality of human rights. According to international laws and treaties, he observes, refugees are defined as people needing protection. Throughout Europe, however, those seeking asylum are not treated in this way and, he points out, 95% of petitions for asylum are denied. Instead of being willing to grant asylum, European countries (of which, he notes, Austria has the dubious fame of being in the avant-garde) have talked behind closed doors about how to rid themselves of refugees without seeming to violate the various treaties intended to protect them. The solution they devised was to make them criminals. If one wants to get rid of a refugee, one does not see him or her as a refugee but rather as a foreigner who is in the country illegally. Haslinger urges writers and intellectuals in Austria and throughout Europe to speak out against such policies because he thinks they can play an important role in shaping public perception about whether a society views refugees as people needing protection or as parasites and criminals. *Schwarzer Peter* contributes also to this widespread debate in Austria.

Schwarzer Peter also takes up and further develops themes that inform Henisch's earlier works. He emphasizes that in many respects his previous works have been steps on the way to this novel.[35] As in his earlier works, Henisch sets the protagonist's quest for identity in *Schwarzer Peter* into the broad context of the history and social concerns of the time and draws extensively on his own experiences. Common to all his works is the focus on the outsider, one who stands on the periphery and looks in. In the novel Peter Jarosch reflects upon the fact that many literary works originate from difference, or at least from the feeling of being different.[36] In his speech accepting the Anton Wildgans Prize in 1977, Henisch remarked that he is an outsider out of passion,[37] and he recently observed that all his books deal with difference.[38] Outsiders such as Paul Grünzweig in *Der Mai ist vorbei* (1978, May Is Over) populate his works and prefigure "Black Peter." In novels such as *Die kleine Figur meines Vaters* and *Steins Paranoia* Henisch explores otherness, racism, and anti-Semitism in Austria. According to Henisch, Peter Jarosch resembles his earlier protagonists, but because of his skin color he is unable to deny his difference.[39] As in his previous works, Henisch in *Schwarzer Peter* casts a critical eye on Austria and its postwar problems. Although he is convinced that literature must address such problems, he is not sure that it can help solve them or that they can indeed be solved. To be silent about them, however, would be dishonest.[40] Because he explores many of his previous concerns in his most recent novel, Henisch sees *Schwarzer Peter* as the sum of his previous writing.[41]

Henisch emphasizes the theme of otherness from the beginning of the novel. "Black Peter," who throughout the novel shows himself to be a perceptive observer of his times, begins the story of his life that he is telling to an anonymous audience in a piano bar in New Orleans with the words: "You will laugh, but I come from Vienna. Even if I possibly don't quite look as if I do" (7). From early childhood, Peter senses he is an outsider because his fellow citizens are unwilling to see him as one of them. They make him feel like a stranger and a foreigner because his appearance does not conform to the norm. When he is growing up, he is subjected to several incidents of overt racism. At school his classmates attack him because he is different. An anonymous enemy, representative of many of his fellow citizens, dogs his footsteps and treats him with contempt. Peter reflects upon how hard it is to accept that there is someone who appears to hate you, even though he or she doesn't know you, just because you are different (44). Henisch also points out how parents communicate their racist feelings to their children. Some parents, for example, refuse to let their children play with Peter, and other children in the park in his new neighborhood call out, "Go away, Moor" (88). Instead of becoming more tolerant, new generations echo the racist sentiments of the past. After the first performance of his blues band, Peter and the other musicians want to celebrate. When they go to eat, the waiter refuses to seat them, saying that there are no tables for people like them—and then adding: "Twenty-five years ago we would have gassed people like you" (345), an indication of Henisch's concern that Nazi thinking still pervades and shapes present behavior.

Such overt acts of racism are, however, relatively rare when Peter is growing up. The problem lies more in the insensitivity with which people treat him and the stereotypical roles into which they force him. Instead of treating him like everyone else, people constantly remind him that he is different and draw attention to his difference. The local shoemaker, for example, always jokes that he should wipe the shoe polish off his face. He does not say this to be mean and is unaware that it is offensive (15). Peter's grandmother reads him the story of "The Ten Little Niggers" until his mother throws the book away. He is forced to postpone entering school because the director, influenced by stereotypes that blacks do not do well at school, thinks that his command of the language is not good enough, even though it is his native tongue. When with a year's delay Peter enters school, the well-meaning teacher attempts to integrate him into the class, but instead draws attention to his otherness. He tells the other children that even though Peter is black he is just like them and stresses that they must all be especially nice to him because Peter does not have an easy time among them (25). In the Christmas play, Peter is cast as the Moorish king because of his skin color. He reflects that it was distressing to have his skin color used as part of a disguise (30). Peter avoids going skiing because he is made uncomfortable by the comments of his fellow citizens about the contrast between the color of the snow and his skin (133).

Henisch also emphasizes how deeply racist thinking pervades culture, from songs set to music by Mozart to the popular children's book *Struwwelpeter* (89). Such racist notions are reflected in everyday language. For example, black is associated with ugliness and white with beauty. Even more disturbing, black is equated with sin and evil. When Peter is preparing for confirmation the chaplain refers to a sinful soul as a black soul, thereby implying that a black body is also a sinful body. Another such example occurs when Peter's mother-in-law visits Peter and Natascha's apartment. She reacts to their living arrangements with refugees from Czechoslovakia and the mess she sees there by likening the apartment to a gypsy camp (340).

Against this background of intolerance and insensitivity, Peter struggles to shape a coherent identity from his Austrian and his African-American roots. He emphasizes, however, that he feels comfortable with himself and, even if he could, he would not want to get out of his black skin. Using the genre of the *Entwicklungsroman*,[42] Henisch examines Peter's various unsuccessful attempts to integrate himself into Austrian society. One such attempt is through his soccer. To get accepted into the soccer club, Peter's friend lies that Peter comes from Brazil. The club managers, excited at the prospect of having another Pelé (they attribute the success of the Brazilian soccer team to a soccer gene), are nonplussed when they hear Peter's Viennese dialect. Peter becomes a successful soccer player, whose fans call him "Negerl" (little nigger). While the diminutive "l" suggests that he is partly accepted, the rest of the word emphasizes his difference (164). Upon returning from hitchhiking through Europe (a trip that provides him with a breath of fresh air from the claustrophobia in Austria), Peter realizes that he does not feel that he is among his fellow citizens and that they do not see him as one of them. He also explores his African-American roots to which he feels attached. For example, he prefers the black notes on the piano and he reads about Martin Luther King and the Civil Rights movement. But he does not feel any close identity with Africa. He attempts twice to visit this continent; the first time when he is in Gibraltar he loses his passport and the second time the ferries from Palermo are not running because of a strike. Even when he moves to New Orleans he still senses that he is a rootless outsider. He makes rather half-hearted attempts there to find the father who does not know he exists. Even though in New Orleans his skin color does not make him stand out, he still feels like a stranger because he speaks with an Austrian accent and does not like to have ice in his Coke or to sit in air-conditioned rooms. His sense of not belonging anywhere carries over to his private life. He does not feel at home in his marriage to Natascha or even in his sexual identity, as his several homosexual encounters suggest. Even as the successful Austrian pop star Paul White, whose first record is called *Paul White: Not Quite Black*, he feels alienated since this commercially packaged Paul White has little to do with the real Peter Jarosch. His music has been rearranged to the extent that he hardly recognizes it and even his biography, according to which he was born in New Orleans where he spent his childhood, has been falsified. Like many of Henisch's characters, Peter feels he is living a life of schizophrenia (461),[43] an indication of his awareness of his split, inauthentic identity. Henisch views schizophrenia, a key concept in his works, not as a clinical but as an existential and political phenomenon.[44] In his opinion this disease is prevalent today because the present age causes individuals to become divorced from themselves.

Schwarzer Peter not only portrays Peter's but also Austria's development during the postwar years. According to Henisch, it is also an *Entwicklungsroman* of prejudice in Austria.[45] Although the novel focuses on Vienna, Henisch makes it clear that the problems he depicts are not unique to Vienna and Austria but are common throughout Europe. Vienna is thus used here like Grass's Danzig and Fellini's Rimini.[46] Because the novel shows few, if any, positive developments in Austria's attitudes to minorities, Henisch uses the term *Entwicklungsroman* ironically. Although Henisch notes that Austrians treated political refugees from Hungary and Czechoslovakia well, he makes it clear that this was an exception. Peter's own experiences demonstrate the continuing lack of tolerance of those perceived to be outsiders.

Unlike some of his other works in which the Nazi legacy plays a central role, this novel touches more briefly on this period, enough only for Henisch to develop a repeated pattern of racism. When the Austrian State Treaty was signed in 1955, a teacher tells the children that for ten years their homeland was occupied by foreign soldiers and talks about the terrible war that befell our poor small country like a devastating storm (53). Now, he comments, Austria will be free. He does not express gratitude that these "foreign soldiers" liberated Austria from the Nazis, and his reference to the storm underscores the victim stance taken after the war. The coach of Peter's first soccer team was rumored to have been in the SS: "He was only a cook, to be sure, so he probably had little opportunity to kill someone himself, but still" (135). Peter's employer, Mr. Jericha, a Jewish second-hand bookseller who fled to London after the *Kristallnacht*, tells him that before the Nazi period he felt different from the others but thought that this was a normal feeling for any half-way sensitive person. Once the Nazis came to power, he tried not to notice that people treated him with contempt or avoided him. When his store was vandalized during the *Kristallnacht*, his wife forced him to leave, which for him was difficult because, as he notes, this was his house, his district, his town, and his country in which he had grown up. He remarks that it is strange that there are obviously people who tend to feel themselves as "the ones" as opposed to "the others." They feel that "we are we." When given a chance to develop, this feeling becomes aggressive (377).

Henisch shows in his novel that not only Jews but all who, in some way, however small, do not conform to the norm or who are perceived as different, are singled out for callous treatment. Before Peter is persecuted at school, two other boys are the targets of aggression, one because unlike the other boys he comes from the middle class and speaks High German, the other because he comes from another part of Austria and therefore does not speak the "correct" dialect. Another such example occurs when Peter is doing his military service. At the training camp the hapless Freislinger is tormented because he is different. Peter is grateful to Freislinger, whose otherness deflects aggression for a while away from Peter himself.

Such intolerance and racism lead to the insensitive and harsh treatment of those seeking asylum in Austria. Through his novel Henisch protests forcefully against the way Austria and other European countries treat such refugees. When Peter returns to visit Vienna after twenty-two years in New Orleans he loses his passport and his money and is arrested for playing music without a permit. The police, who treat him brutally, suspect him of being a drug dealer just because he is black, and he is imprisoned with other asylum seekers. Peter tries unsuccessfully to persuade them that he is "an African-American of audible Austrian origin" (403), but they remain convinced that he comes from Africa. Henisch, who carefully researched how asylum seekers are treated and reproduces in the novel an authentic form used by the police to describe the appearance of those imprisoned (408), sheds light on Austrian attitudes toward asylum seekers. One official thinks that it is strange that people from Africa still view Austria as the goal of their dreams, since as soon as they reach Austrian soil they are there illegally and just do not belong there (407). Henisch notes that the average time asylum seekers spend in prison before they are deported is 13.7 days. He describes the humiliating and demeaning treatment they endure, from being arrested, to having their fingerprints taken, to being forced to submit to body searches. They are not treated as human beings but as criminals. Henisch observes that those waiting to be deported don't realize how important they are to the "real" Austrians since they represent those from whom the Austrians differentiate themselves (440). Henisch shows that the thinking "we are we and the others are the others" (440) that Mr. Jericha experienced during the Nazi period is still prevalent.

Henisch skillfully structures his novel to reinforce the themes of alienation and otherness and to underscore Peter's inability to find a coherent, unified self. Henisch's characteristic use of humor and irony creates the critical distance that he values.[47] He considers irony important because it encourages complexity of thought.[48] The humor in this often very funny novel is in the tradition of the Jewish joke, which Henisch defines as the ability to see the tragic from a comic perspective without minimizing it.[49] In an interview, Henisch observes that irony and humor are a means of survival and he adds that he hopes he has the humor to cope with the world as God had not intended it.[50] Peter's separation in time and in geography (the piano bar in New Orleans) from most of the events he is relating provides the ironical distance for Henisch to cast a critical eye on developments in postwar Austria.

Henisch's characteristic irony is particularly evident in his use of the *Entwicklungsroman*. Instead of the positive development this genre traditionally suggests, Henisch shows repeated patterns of hostility toward minorities and depicts Peter's life in Austria as a downward spiral. In the first five sections of the novel, which Peter tells from the perspective of the piano bar in New Orleans, his tone is more distanced as he looks back at his childhood years, his marriage to Natascha, and the birth of their two children. He seems to have come to terms, at least to some extent, with his former life in Austria. His companion Jenny tells him to forget Austria: "You're born in Vienna, so what" (392). In part six, however, the tone changes to become bitter. In this last part Peter tells about his life while he is imprisoned in Vienna. When he sees what is happening to asylum seekers he reflects that he is happy that he left Austria (440). In prison Peter looks back at events that finally led to his flight to New Orleans: the break-up of his marriage, his betrayal by his former friend Robert, and his inability to feel part of Austrian society. In this part, examples of racism proliferate. When he is in prison, Peter reflects on several occasions that his skin color is too black for Austrians. Peter remembers that after a separation from Natascha he slept for a while in Mr. Jericha's store until the landlady told him to leave because the old people would get a heart attack if they saw such a black ghost in the hallway (421). He recalls the difficulties he had finding an apartment. When he appeared in person, the apartment was suddenly no longer available, even though landlords were supposedly not permitted to discriminate in this way. He faced similar difficulties finding a job. After his failure as a pop star he worked for a few weeks in a store. The customers kept asking the owner why he did not employ native Austrians, and Peter was fired. When Peter protested that he was Austrian, the owner, who was aware of the fact, responded that Peter did not look Austrian (482).

In addition to his ironic use of the *Entwicklungsroman*, another important structural principle in the novel is Henisch's use of contrasts. Henisch builds his novel on a series of seemingly unbridgeable contrasts that appear to underscore separation. One such contrast is Vienna and New Orleans, and as a border-crosser Peter perceptively depicts both cultures. Henisch does not idealize New Orleans. In discussions with Joe and other friends, Peter learns about the Civil Rights struggle and past discrimination in New Orleans. Whites have fled to the suburbs and black children still get killed in the black ghettoes. But the city has a black mayor and, in sharp contrast to Vienna, it has integrated many different groups. Peter's friend Joe suggests that Peter should feel at home in New Orleans since it is a city settled by many different strangers who became at home there (81). Other contrasts include the Danube Canal that plays an important role in Peter's childhood and the tamed Mississippi that nevertheless still has elemental force, and the many images of black and white that pervade the novel.

Henisch uses these contrasts, however, to also suggest the possibility of integration and by so doing undermines what appear to be sharp differences that separate people. Although Vienna has not become an inclusive society like New Orleans, it too has been shaped by people from many different ethnic groups. As Henisch observes, the Viennese are made up of Czechs, Slovaks, Hungarians, Croatians, Slovenians, and Ruthenians, to mention just a few groups, who came from all parts of the former monarchy to settle in the capital. However, within two or three generations this multiethnic heritage has been forgotten (323). Because of its heritage, Vienna nevertheless has the potential to become more like New Orleans. Peter, in fact, stresses similarities between the two cities and even refers to a lost arm of the Danube as a bayou and draws parallels between the Danube Canal and the Mississippi. Through his stress on the ferries that go back and forth across the Danube Canal and the Mississippi, Henisch suggests that perceived separations can be overcome and connections can be built between different places, cultures, and people. Henisch also undermines the sharp difference between black and white, thereby pointing out the absurdity of differences based on skin color. Like many in New Orleans, Peter's complexion is neither black nor white, but rather a *café au lait* color (82). Peter is also fascinated with negatives, because on them black people become white and white people become black.

Similarly, Henisch uses music in the novel not only to express alienation and separation but also integration and con-

The Jumbalaya Principle 261

nection. Peter's father could play both boogie and Schubert (9), thus linking New Orleans, the cradle of blues and jazz, and Vienna, the capital of classical music. Through music Peter struggles to find his own identity. His African-American roots draw him to blues and jazz and he becomes, like the novel's author, an accomplished blues and jazz musician who is well-versed in the history of this music. At first, Peter uses his improvised blues pieces to separate himself from the Viennese songs and waltzes which, he stresses, are not his music and whose sentimentality he satirizes (196). His playing of the blues is a defiant assertion of his difference. In the tradition of blues music, Peter's compositions express loneliness and sorrow but also humor and defiance. He uses his music as a weapon, as for example when he succeeds through his playing in driving one of his mother's lovers away. But because blues and jazz integrate aspects of other musical traditions into their compositions, they serve to connect different cultures. Peter even mentions a Viennese song that with its stress on fatalism provides a bridge to the blues, or at least to a parody of the blues (236). Jazz can blend religious music and harmony from European classical music with gospel songs, spirituals, and rhythms from West African music. Henisch points out how such music that originated in a particular culture goes beyond its roots to become a part of universal human culture. Such music becomes a model because it not only combines but also further develops traditions from various cultures. It also becomes a model for society because with its mixture of individual improvisation and group playing it allows people the freedom to express their creativity and individuality within the context of a supporting group. Joe remarks that in jazz everyone plays his or her own thing but all play together (245).

Henisch argues in his novel for a diverse and multiple identity and for an Austria in which such identities are not threatened, singled out, and deported.[51] Henisch stresses that he has always identified with those perceived as different. He notes that yesterday it was the Jews, today it is blacks or homosexuals. He says that one has to accept different coloring of the soul if one wants to live together peacefully, and he stresses that his novel contains an appeal to discover the other.[52] The novel not only contains a powerful plea for acceptance of those perceived to be different but also presents a model for the fruitful and dynamic cross-fertilization of cultures. In New Orleans, Peter's friend Joe introduces him to jambalaya, a dish that always contains certain ingredients but which, like the city of New Orleans, is multicultural because a variety of ingredients can be added to the mix at will. This is what Joe calls "Creolization," and he defines it as interaction—between white and black, old and new, above and below. He also calls this the jambalaya principle since all add their own different ingredients (245). Henisch uses this jambalaya principle to suggest a model for how different cultures can live together and mutually enrich one another while simultaneously maintaining a firm sense of their own identities.

Notes

1. Joel S. Kahn, *Culture, Multiculture, Postculture* (London/Thousand Oaks/New Delhi: Sage, 1995) 5.
2. See, for example, Charles Taylor, "The Politics of Recognition," Amy Gutmann, Charles Taylor, Susan Wolf, Steven Rockefeller and Michael Walzer, *Multiculturalism and "The Politics of Recognition"* (Princeton: Princeton UP, 1992; reissued as *Multiculturalism: Examining the Politics of Recognition* [Princeton: Princeton UP, 1994]) 25-73.
3. Lawrence Blum, "Multiculturalism, Racial Justice, and Community: Reflections on Charles Taylor's 'Politics of Recognition,'" *Defending Diversity: Contemporary Philosophical Perspectives on Pluralism and Multiculturalism,* eds. Lawrence Foster and Patricia Herzog (Amherst: U of Massachusetts P, 1994) 182.

4. Satya P. Mohanty, *Literary Theory and the Claims of History: Postmodernism, Objectivity, Multicultural Politics* (Ithaca and London: Cornell UP, 1997) 120.

5. Robert Edwin Herzstein, *Waldheim: The Missing Years* (New York: Arbor House/William Morrow, 1988) 240.

6. Bruce F. Pauley, *Hitler and the Forgotten Nazis: A History of Austrian National Socialism* (Chapel Hill: U of North Carolina P, 1981) xiii.

7. Pauley, *From Prejudice to Persecution: A History of Austrian Anti-Semitism* (Chapel Hill and London: U of North Carolina P, 1992) 297.

8. See Doron Rabinovici, "Literatur und Republik oder Ganz Baden liest die Krone," *Was wird das Ausland dazu sagen? Literatur und Republik in Österreich nach 1945*, ed. Gerald Leitner (Vienna: Picus, 1995) 127-39.

9. Joseph McVeigh, *Kontinuität und Vergangenheitsbewältigung in der österreichischen Literatur nach 1945* (Vienna: Braumüller, 1988) 135. See also Elke Atzler, "Beharren, Adaptieren, Neuorientieren? Aspekte zur literarischen Entwicklung der 70er Jahre in Österreich," *Illusionen—Desillusionen? Zur neueren realistischen Prosa und Dramatik in Österreich*, ed. Walter Buchebner Gesellschaft (Vienna and Cologne: Böhlau, 1989) 56-65.

10. Anton Pelinka and Erika Weinzierl, eds., *Das grosse Tabu: Österreichs Umgang mit seiner Vergangenheit* (Vienna: Verlag der Österreichischen Staatsdruckerei, 1987) 7.

11. Bernd Marin, "Antisemitism before and after the Holocaust: The Austrian Case," *Jews, Antisemitism and Culture in Vienna*, eds. Ivar Oxaal, Michael Pollak and Gerhard Botz (London and New York: Routledge and Kegan Paul, 1987) 219.

12. Elfriede Schmidt, *1938 . . . and the Consequences: Questions and Responses*, trans. Peter J. Lyth (Riverside: Ariadne, 1992) 48.

13. Cited in Klaus Zeyringer, *Innerlichkeit und Öffentlichkeit: Österreichische Literatur der achtziger Jahre* (Tübingen: Francke, 1992) 228.

14. Inge Merkel, "An jene Österreicher, die es ablehnen, zur 'Mehrheit' zu gehören," *Reden an Österreich: Schriftstel-*

ler ergreifen das Wort, ed. Jochen Jung (Salzburg and Vienna: Residenz, 1988) 110.

15. See, for example, Doron Rabinovici in his essay mentioned above, "Literatur und Republik oder Ganz Baden liest die Krone."

16. Gerlinde Ulm Sanford, "From a Meeting with Barbara Frischmuth," *Barbara Frischmuth in Contemporary Context,* ed. Renate S. Posthofen (Riverside: Ariadne, 1999) 147.

17. As Paul Michael Lützeler observes: "If one looks for models of multicultural identity, one is more likely to find them in Australia, Canada, and the United States than in Europe." In Europe, he notes, multicultural thinking and behavior are less developed than in these other countries. Paul Michael Lützeler, "Introduction," *Multiculturalism in Contemporary German Literature,* special issue of *World Literature Today* 69. 3 (Summer 1995): 453-54.

18. Ilse Krüger, "Heimat Österreich," *Schriftstellerinnen sehen ihr Land: Österreich aus dem Blick seiner Autorinnen,* ed. Barbara Neuwirth (Vienna: Wiener Frauenverlag, 1995) 124.

19. Reinhold Brandl, "Anwesende!" *Reden an Österreich* 8, 12.

20. Harry Ritter, "Austria and the Struggle for German Identity," *German Studies Review,* special issue on German Identity (Winter 1992): 111.

21. Marie-Thérèse Kerschbaumer, "An gewissen Zeichen," *Was wird das Ausland dazu sagen?* 72, 76.

22. Ruth Beckermann, "Die Wegbereiter," *Profil* 27 Feb. 1995: 83-84.

23. Beckermann, *Unzugehörig: Österreicher und Juden nach 1945* (Vienna: Loecker, 1989) 21.

24. Elisabeth Reichart, "Die vielen Ichs der Republik und ich," *Was wird das Ausland dazu sagen?* 119.

25. Karin Ivancsics, "Hrvat Mi Je Otac" (Mein Vater ist Kroate), *Schrifstellerinnen sehen ihr Land* 16-29.

26. Beckermann, "Die Wegbereiter" 83-84.

27. Peter Henisch, "Warum ich nicht will, daß Österreich untergeht," *Reden an Österreich* 81-94.

28. Rabinovici, "Literatur und Republik oder Ganz Baden

liest die Krone" *Was wird das Ausland dazu sagen?* 127-39.
   29. Lützeler, "Introduction," *Multiculturalism in Contemporary German Literature* 453.
   30. Barbara Frischmuth, "Ex Oriente 1: Zur Literatur von Einwanderern, Auswanderern und Gratwanderern." The series "Ex Oriente 1" to "Ex Oriente 10" appeared weekly in *Die Presse* from 1 February to 4 April 1996.
   31. Frischmuth, "Looking over the Fence," trans. Lisabeth Hock, *Multiculturalism in Contemporary German Literature* 459.
   32. See, for example, "Human Rights Group Attacks Austrian Asylum Policy," Vienna (RNC Agency), 19 June 1997, http://www.romnews.com/news.html.
   33. Frischmuth, *Die Schrift des Freundes* (Salzburg and Vienna: Residenz, 1998) 256.
   34. Josef Haslinger, "Aux armes citoyens!" *Was wird das Ausland dazu sagen?* 140-51.
   35. Julia Kospach, "Ein Schwarzer wie du und ich," rev. of *Schwarzer Peter*, *Profil* 6 March 2000: 148.
   36. Henisch, *Schwarzer Peter* (Salzburg and Vienna: Residenz, 2000) 144.
   37. Henisch, "Kurze Denkadresse des Autors (Trotz Entgegennahme des Anton Wildgans-Preises)," *Zwischen allen Sesseln: Geschichten, Gedichte, Entwürfe, Notizen, Statements 1965-1982* (Vienna: Hannibal, 1982) 187.
   38. Cited in Elisabeth Hirschmann, "Alltäglicher Rassismus," rev. of *Schwarzer Peter*, *Format* Aug. 2000: 143.
   39. Cited in Hirschmann 143.
   40. Henisch, "Kurze Denkadresse des Autors" 187.
   41. Cited in Kospach 148.
   42. The term "Entwicklungsroman" refers to a novel of inner or spiritual development.
   43. See also, for example, Henisch's use of schizophrenia in *Der Mai ist vorbei*.
   44. Eva Schobel, *Peter Henisch: Eine Monographie*, diss., U. Vienna, 1987 (Vienna: Verband der wissenschaftlichen Gesellschaften Österreichs, 1988) 28.
   45. Henisch, "Der Entwicklungsroman des Vorurteils," interview with Michael Cerha, *Der Standard* 11 April

2000: 15.
46. Henisch, "Der Entwicklungsroman des Vorurteils" 15.
47. Henisch, "Kurze Denkadresse des Autors" 187.
48. Henisch, "1. Teil des endlosen Interviews," *Zwischen allen Sesseln* 8.
49. Henisch, "1. Teil des endlosen Interviews" 9.
50. Henisch, "Das Gefühl, etwas anders zu sein," *Tiroler Tageszeitung* 3 May 2000: 15.
51. Cornelius Hell, "Nicht ganz schwarz," rev. of *Schwarzer Peter*, *Spectrum* 4 March 2000: V.
52. Henisch, "Das Gefühl, etwas anders zu sein" 15.

"A Person Who Is Normal... Doesn't Write": A Conversation with Peter Henisch

ANNE CLOSE ULMER

Since I have translated two of Peter Henisch's books, *Die kleine Figur meines Vaters* (1987; *Negatives of My Father*, 1990) and *Morrisons Versteck* (1991, Morrison's Hideout, as yet unpublished), I was initially invited to write something for this volume about literary translations in general and translating Henisch in particular. Upon consideration, however, it seemed to me more worthwhile to let the author speak for himself. The following conversation with Peter Henisch took place on November 21, 1997 in Henisch's apartment in Vienna. I began by alluding to the differences between the "German" and "Austrian" languages and to the challenges of distinguishing between the two for an American reading public that barely differentiates between the two countries. I asked Henisch to what extent he considers himself to be an Austrian—rather than a German—writer.

PH: I am certainly an Austrian author, someone who attempts not to take the joy out of my own language. This language of mine is certainly a kind of German, but a German that is spoken in Austria. In relation to Germany, Austria has a different history, a different tradition, a different mentality, and these are expressed in language. To give you a simple example: in Austrian colloquial speech the imperfect tense is virtually nonexistent. So if I write dialogues that are supposed to be realistic, that are set in Vienna or Graz or somewhere else in Austria, and I have people speaking with one another in the imperfect tense, it's totally unbelievable, and would seem so to everybody here. Of course, in the meantime people have been so miseducated by television that they believe that's the way it should be. When people [on television] speak, they speak in this strange West-German language. I don't mean to say that one language is more correct and the other one deviates from High German, that's not true. It isn't "German" that people speak in Kassel or in Berlin, but a dialect. The Austrian dialect is not only a dialect, but also a habit of speech.

Even if someone is trying to speak "High German," a person in Austria would speak differently than someone in northern Germany or in central Germany. The Austrian colloquial language certainly has a definite relationship to Bavarian, and vice versa, but it's still different, right? It's connected to the history of this country, and to the mentality, which is still more influenced by eastern and southern Europe. In addition, it's more multilingual than German, because Austria was a multicultural state, and the German principalities never were, right? That means that when I write, I attempt to write Austrian German. I can't write colloquial German, that wouldn't work, but at least in the passages that contain direct speech or indirect speech I try to have the people speak the way they actually do speak around me. It's clear that there is still a discrepancy between my writing and reality, because literature and reality are different, but I've always avoided "northing up" the language (as people say in Austria, for geographical reasons), and then pretending that the results were somehow more correct, better, prettier, or something. When I was publishing in Frankfurt, with Fischer Verlag, and a reader attempted to replace my Austrian turns of phrase with German ones—from Frankfurt or Berlin or somewhere—I put them back again.

AU: And they let you do that.

PH: The greatest difference, or the clearest difference, is really that between the imperfect and perfect in colloquial speech. Or even the past perfect tense. It's completely idiotic to our ears, but Germans will say things like this: "Yesterday I had met Jürgen." Nobody here would ever say that. We'd say, "yesterday I met Jürgen."[1] And besides, "yesterday I had met Jürgen" is wrong, it's really wrong.

AU: Yes, because there is one past event being alluded to.

PH: But it's common there, just as it's common here to use the dative instead of the genitive, that's wrong too, although with time it's become so common that it almost sounds right. But such linguistic habits exist. Then, of course, there are entirely different vocabulary words. It's all flattening out; unfortunately, it's being flattened out by this TV-culture, right? Because almost everything is dubbed in Germany. That is to say, you see and hear TV series, etc., that are set in San Francisco or Los Angeles. But the people speak like people in Dortmund or Kassel or someplace . . .

Yes, there are a lot of differences in linguistic usage, but above all, in Austrian there is a vocabulary that comes from the monarchy, and that is steadily on the decline. But my Grandmother, for instance, or my parents, and you know this yourself from your relatives, they still spoke that way: they said the "Trottoir," the "Portemonnaie," the "Tramway," the "Kondukteur"[2]—things like that.

AU: "Tramway" being the streetcar itself, and not the tracks.

PH: Yes.

AU: And those are all influences.

PH: Most of that comes from the French. Well, "Tramway"

[German pronunciation] is somehow distorted, it comes from "Tramway" [English pronunciation]. It's true, it doesn't relate to the object itself because, as you say, it refers to the moving car, and of course not to the tracks, as you might expect if you just heard the word and had not grown up in Austria. Well, there are a lot of expressions like that. And especially in dialect. And besides, in Austria people are constantly speaking in a dialect. By that, I mean that Austrian writers, when they write, are already writing in a foreign language, because the language here is not a written language, or at least it cannot be presented as a written language. Of course a person can try unsuccessfully to write dialect poems, or even novels in dialect, but that wouldn't work. It wouldn't be accurate, people don't think that way. But when people speak with one another, there's naturally always a difference between the way people would represent it and the way they really speak. One can get pretty close. [Ödön von] Horváth captured it very well, [Johann] Nestroy captured it very well, [Helmut] Qualtinger of course—and that is also a tradition I consider important.

AU: And does Qualtinger write like Nestroy? Does he try to capture the sound phonetically?

PH: Well, Nestroy didn't write phonetically, it's always an approximation, one tries to get the word down approximately as it sounds. But the great thing about Horváth, for instance, is that he accomplishes it with something close to High German. And still the sound is there, as people actually could have spoken with one another. . . .The Austrian mentality— of course one has to be careful when speaking about an Austrian mentality, because it's very different between East and West, and Vienna and its surroundings certainly have a different mentality than Tyrol, Vorarlberg or Carinthia, but Vienna has a certain effect upon all of Austria. But this mentality creates, if one wants to express it musically, a different time, a different groove, right? That is, it's a totally different tempo of speech, it's another rhythm, another timing, right? And you can hear that. There is naturally a clear difference for non-Austrians as well as for Austrians. If someone has lived for a long time in Germany, has become assimilated, and then comes back here, his language sounds funny to our ears. On the other hand, the Austrian language in Germany is either rejected or considered charming or something, right?

AU: Yes. In America too.

PH: An extreme example: we heard that today would have been Oskar Werner's seventieth birthday.

AU: Seventy-fifth. [Actor Oskar Werner was born in 1922 and died in 1984.]

PH: Oskar Werner, a great speaker, who really lived above all from his voice.

AU: And where did he come from?

PH: Oskar Werner was Viennese. His name was originally Oskar Bschliessmayer. Anyway—Oskar Werner was a great master of the spoken word who really lived, first and foremost, from his musical voice, who really emphasized his vowels much more than a lot of present-day actors, who speak more like machine guns. Well, Oskar Werner, at the height of his career, made several marvelous international films, including one with François Truffaut, *Jules and Jim*. In the original, of course, he spoke his own part. The German film studio dubbed Oskar Werner's voice with the voice of a German actor, because they said nobody could understand him. So—there you see what sort of misunderstandings there are between German and Austrian!

AU: But the actor in that film had an Oskar Werner voice!

PH: If we didn't see it in French, then we heard the voice of a German dubber. That was not Oskar Werner. And that was idiotic! That's as if I were to synchronize Callas's voice and then would say: "She screams so much! We can make her softer." Be that as it may, there are simply differences in mentality here, of a very clear nature. Two years ago, or whenever it was, there was an Austrian Book Fair in Frankfurt. I read there in a bookstore, at an event organized by the Residenz publishing house, and afterwards there was a newspaper review. There they wrote, "Peter Henisch reads like Peppi Meinrath." Josef Meinrath came to mind because of his intonation—everything gets lumped together. OK, for me it was an honor, Meinrath was a good speaker, but it was this Austrian intonation, this Austrian idiom, that they heard. And vice versa, the same would be true [of Austrians reacting to German speakers].

You ask how you can make [the Austrian idiom] comprehensible to Americans—there are certainly great differences between English and American.

AU: And inside America as well.

PH: Yes, of course, that too, but English and American. One thinks that England and America are far apart, but basically it's similar. It's a language that developed differently under specific circumstances, and then there is a certain parameter where one can say, "that's clearly English, and that's clearly American."

AU: I admit one can hear that, but one can't necessarily produce it. For instance, I could not produce British English. I know certain expressions—"lift" instead of "elevator," and "lorry" for "truck"—but I couldn't speak in a way that would sound like British English. If you wanted to, could you write something that would sound North German, or not?

PH: Hmm—that's not so easy either. I could try, but it's not simple.

AU: For example, in a translation, when one is trying to make it fluent and beautiful, so that the reader won't stumble over it when reading, then I wouldn't attempt to sound British.

PH: In any case, I believe many Austrian writers try to write so that people in Germany won't recognize that they are Austrian writers, and I find that totally wrong. Oddly enough, [H.C.] Artmann was really angry back then at that reading in the Frankfurt bookstore, because I said I felt I was an Austrian writer.

AU: Artmann was angry?

PH: Artmann says, "I'm a German poet," which is supposed to signal his membership in this great cultural realm. But he is clearly an Austrian writer.

AU: He writes in German, but that's something different.

PH: Yes, but I merely said I'm an Austrian writer.

AU: . . . one writes in this or that idiom, and therefore . . .

PH: Yes, but it's not entirely the same, because there's also a great difference in expression between Baden-Württemberg and Berlin-Brandenburg, or between Saxony and the Rhineland or something, right? But for centuries Austria has developed on its own. The German principalities were also different from one another, but still they didn't develop in such divergent directions. Austria was subjected to different influences than Germany, to particular influences of foreign languages. One can hear them, of course. For instance, in Viennese dialect, this flattening of the diphthongs, right? That comes from the Slavic, the fact that no long "aı" can be pronounced. There is a Viennese dialect that is downright ugly, that I don't like at all, but one has to admit that it's different . . . There are certain things—misunderstandings that are never cleared up, for example—between Germans and Austrians. For traditional reasons, the Germans, at least since 1918 or thereabouts, have a certain feeling of superiority and imagine that they know better, that they're right or something, and that Austrians are just a little odd. The word "Schmäh," nobody understands that.[3]

[Germans] think "Schmäh," "that's blarney," that's a situation in which someone is lying, but that's not right. "Schmäh" is something totally different. How can I translate it? It's . . .

AU: There's a little exaggeration associated with it?

PH: Well, above all, when you say someone has a good "Schmäh," then it means he's funny, he's somehow ironic, communicative, relating well to other people, cheerful, something like that. But it absolutely doesn't have anything to do with pretending or deceit, or with "schmähen" [to speak ill of, defame], although the word stem is similar.

AU: But "Schmäh" has something subversive about it, doesn't it?

PH: If I say, "go on, don't give me any 'Schmäh,'" then it means "don't tell me any lies." That's something different. If you say, "someone has a good 'Schmäh,'" then it's actually something positive, right? And the Germans, they never have a good "Schmäh," that's out of the question, it just doesn't happen. You couldn't say that of someone from Germany, it wouldn't fit. Not really.

AU: Why no "Schmäh"?

PH: He has something else.

AU: Maybe the Germans tend to be less playful? I mean, if one writes in a really great style, that's playful. And Germans also use Austrian expressions . . .

PH: Yes, yes, yes, yes . . .

AU: . . . and they don't ask, for instance, what the word "stad" means. The expression is "sei stad,"[4] "hush!"

PH: Yes, "be quiet," right?

AU: But a German author used it assuming that it meant something like that, and then it somehow got printed incorrectly, "the state" ["der Staat"] or something like that, and he got very annoyed. And then he asked an Austrian whether that was correct usage, with "stad," what that means, "sei stad," and then she did a real translation into German and said, "shut your trap!"[5]

PH: No, no, that's not it either! "Sei stad" isn't the same thing as "shut your trap." It's not so indelicate. "Shut your trap," that's really . . . "sei stad," you can say to a child, "Hush, the Christchild is coming." You wouldn't say, "Shut your trap, the Christchild is coming!"

AU: Here's a question that perhaps doesn't quite fit into this conversation, but . . . There are a number of characters in your work who are situated on the edge of society, of Austrian society—peripheral figures. And that's deliberate, I think, and consistent. Now it's reached the point where the characters in your current novel [*Schwarzer Peter* (Black Peter), in progress at the time of this conversation and published in 2000] are over in America—but still with a connection to Austria. I assume the fact that you regard yourself as an Austrian writer, and that you consciously use the Austrian language, is an entirely different matter. You don't somehow look on Germany in some sense as a center, and on Austria as linguistically peripheral?

PH: No, I don't see it that way. These peripheral figures, as you call them, they simply come from the fact that I see authors, and intellectuals, as peripheral figures. I mean, a person who is normal or who belongs to the mainstream doesn't write. The identification with such figures comes from that. But I think I would feel that identification even if I lived in France or Italy or America.

AU: Although your father always tended so towards the center. Your father (in *Die kleine Figur meines Vaters*) always wanted to belong to the group, and you preferred to stay on the edge.

PH: That may be so, but that may also be the reason why I'm especially allergic to this "wanting to be in the middle." And of course that also has historical reasons, because this wanting to take part—in the Nazi era that led to terrible consequences. But it simply isn't my way of doing things. So I can't say to what extent these terrible events, which occurred before I was alive but which I became aware of little by little, starting at a very young age—how much that may have affected my own development. For instance, I have never visited the Danube Island [a popular man-made island in Vienna with bike paths, hiking trails, and other amusements]. We have friends who say, "This weekend we're going to the Danube Island." There are forty thousand Viennese on the Danube Island. That's precisely the reason why I don't go there. I imagine it must be terrible. I don't want to be where there are forty thousand people, whether they are Viennese or anyone else. These shopping centers, the Shopping City South or whatever, they drive me crazy. I don't like that. Who knows, maybe I'm elitist or something, but I just can't stand that. And I simply think that authors are people who would not be authors if they did what everyone else does. Because—who writes, pray tell? That's where it comes from. This identification with peripheral figures, and the way in which I am now writing about "Black Peter," that is precisely the representation of Otherness. To be black would be especially Other. And not exactly black either, but half-black, half-white. That is, he actually doesn't belong there either. He is an ideal identification figure.

AU: (Laughs) Especially for you! Getting back to language: I don't see in your work any sign of two linguistic areas at war with each other—Austrian/German—you simply write in the language that is comfortable for you. I believe the best a translator can do is to translate into her own language. The reader does not need to be aware that Austrian German is different from German.

PH: Well, one can't do that in any case. One has no direct comparison in the book, so I believe it would be natural to translate into one's own language, and to find a language that is relatively close to colloquial speech, that is simple and unpretentious. The language is very musical, of course that plays a great role—it's important to me to hear the sentences, how they sound. And one can analyze it if one wants to, but it sounds so simple. Basically, I write in a strophic form, right? Paragraphs with generally four sentences, sometimes five, and basically each of them is oriented to iambic pentameter, with five stresses, de *da* de *da* de *da* de *da* de *da*. But of course that's often deliberately interrupted by long open phrases, otherwise it becomes rigid. But that is the basic pattern, so to speak, that I've found for my own language. For that reason I polish every sentence and every phrase for a very long time, and try over and over again to make them work as well as possible. That is my inner rhythm; it's the rhythm of my heart, my pulse, that it corresponds to.

AU: I think I'm glad that I didn't know that earlier, otherwise I still wouldn't be finished with the first book.

PH: It would certainly be very, very difficult to translate that into a foreign language, and one can't really try—or rather, I don't think that the attempt would promise much success, managing that in another language in quite the same way. It would be the likeliest in English though, which is the closest related language in terms of form. You couldn't translate it into French, not into Italian, and, of course, not at all into Chinese or something like that, you'd just have to capture the feeling of it. I've tried to translate myself, now and then, never professionally, but . . .

AU: What did you try to translate?

PH: Well, very early, when I was twenty, a somewhat eccentric actor got in touch with me. He wanted to become [Klaus] Kinsky's successor. He went on stage alone and declaimed poems, and back then he made a program out of Oscar Wilde and Baudelaire. And so I translated from Oscar Wilde's "The Ballad of Reading Gaol" and selections from Baudelaire's *Les Fleurs du mal*. Especially with Oscar Wilde I tried to capture the rhythm pretty exactly, but of course it didn't come easily. You do it at some cost to the meaning.

AU: Exactly!

PH: Somewhere you have to compromise—you end up coming up with really funny and cramped figures of speech.

AU: Yes, it's very hard.

PH: With Baudelaire, of course, it was even harder, because French is even harder to force into this Procrustean bed of the German language. And German is a cumbersome language. Then, in connection with the Morrison book [*Morrisons Versteck*] I got involved with Rimbaud texts. One can't quite capture Rimbaud. I have five or six translations into German here, there are certainly more in existence, but I have that many here. A poem like "Le Bateau ivre," "Das trunkene Schiff" in German ("The Drunken Ship"), in these five or six translations it sounds as different as if you, as a teacher, went into an elementary school class and said, "OK, there's a ship going down the river, and all around there is jungle, and there are some natives there, and people on the ship. Now, each of you write a poem." That's what it looks like. They are totally different poems. And there's barely a single one that gives you any idea of the original. Well, OK, so that's the way it is. But, as I said, French and German are . . . they have a different sound, from the beginning. English and German are closer . . . But there is really a totally different tempo if we have an Austrian speaking and a German. They normally—not the Saxons, and not the Alemans either, but what is now habitual in [much of] Germany is that people speak at least twice as fast as people here in Austria. Maybe that's why they are so successful.

AU: (laughs) Could be—if the other folks can listen and absorb meaning that quickly! My students and I just saw [Carl] Sternheim's *Bürger Schippel* (1913; *Burger Schippel*, 1969) in Graz. Three of the main characters spoke as though they were from Berlin. And the play was all very clipped and without pronouns, that Expressionist language that Sternheim writes. And the students had problems understanding the play, although they had read it, because it was coming at us so fast. Only Schippel, who is still not a member of the middle class, spoke at an Austrian speed (but not in Graz dialect)—a little slower, and much, *much* easier to understand.

PH: The movement is different, the movement, the manner of expression is different. Those aren't the same people, they are different people—and please, this has nothing to do with any value judgment.

AU: The music is different too.

PH: Before I used to identify more strongly with the Austrians. Meanwhile, I think, for heaven's sake, most of them really get on my nerves, but nevertheless I can't deny that I am an Austrian, and the language can also have something very lovely about it, right? Beauty, above all in the vowels. Basically the Germans are inclined—let's say the mainstream Germans, they are inclined to shove the consonants so much together, in haste and out of aggression or being on the offensive, that no vowels are possible any more. Whereas Austrian has also changed a lot over time. The Viennese dialect that was spoken in my childhood has almost disappeared, things have gotten worse. But the vowels are still there. And that links Austria more with Italy, or even—in the Slavic countries the consonants also hop together, but there's a different linguistic melody than in German, right?

AU: That's the reason why the Austrian language is so pleasant to my ears. Still—I don't know—not everything German is Prussian! And there are also Germans who speak very beautifully and have interesting things to say. And above all, I find, most Germans are so verbal. I mean, for instance, if one compares how Austrian politicians speak, or how German politicians speak, then I have the impression that German politicians can express themselves, and it is not fifty percent embarrassing. They don't just stutter, right?

PH: Yes, but that's partly because the Austrians, as soon as they have a microphone in front of them, are speaking a foreign language. They try to speak in a way that isn't natural to them. The soccer players are especially embarrassing. When an Austrian soccer player attempts to explain in the imperfect tense how he shot a goal, that's really idiotic, right? But left to his own devices, he would never explain that in the imperfect.

AU: He has the feeling that there's a TV audience listening?
. . .
I like the way your books employ Austrian German. Most Americans have no real concept of Austria in the context of the German language, but rather think only of Germany.

PH: Well, in a text there is naturally only one language, and one doesn't hear another, but I believe that especially in America there are attempts to approach colloquial language in literature. Maybe people did that totally unself-consciously, in a less cramped way, than over here, hmm? Because America, after all, is a larger and more victorious country. One can't say that doesn't play a role.

AU: Because of the book market?

PH: Well, they don't give a hoot whether other people understand or not, they simply *have* to. That's like with the Romans, right? Back then they spoke their silly Latin all over the place, and the others had to learn Latin, and so it stayed around . . . But the fact that an Austrian literature exists, I wouldn't doubt that for a moment. There are a lot of examples, right? You say, OK, that isn't simply a part of German literature, OK, but it is a German-language literature that's simply a kind of German, but that's the point! From [Adalbert] Stifter to [Franz] Grillparzer or the other way around, to [Hugo von] Hofmannsthal and [Arthur] Schnitzler and [Robert] Musil, [Karl] Kraus, Horváth, not to forget Kuh. Anton Kuh, he was a competitor, so to speak, of Karl Kraus. Kraus was, so to speak, the strict and, how shall I put it, in psychological terms somewhat anal-retentive type, and he got under Kuh's skin, so they argued, had public disputes.

AU: Because Kraus idolized the language?

PH: Horváth, and then Qualtinger too, Artmann. Certainly, one can look at them. There you see what Austrian literature is, although Artmann claims he's a German poet. [Thomas] Bernhard, no question, right? [Heimito von] Doderer, [Peter] Handke.

AU: Doderer, for sure—the playfulness of his language. What about Handke?

PH: Well, Handke belongs to those who really tried like prize pupils to shape their language so nobody would notice that they come from Austria or, in Handke's case, from Griffen [in Carinthia].

AU: That annoys me about Handke. Whereas [Günter] Grass, for example, whose idiom is fairly difficult for me, is speaking the language of the place where he grew up. That's what makes him challenging for me to read, because my entire sense of German is different from his.

PH: Yes, you can get the impression from their language that many authors of the Austrian—what shall I call them—*avant-garde*? modern movement? whatever . . . After 1965 a lot of them put on a language mask, and they can't take it off again. They can't get rid of it . . .

AU: Hans Weigel, in "Sprache als Schicksal: Vorläufige Bemerkungen über 'Das Österreichische' in der österreichischen Literatur" (1964, Language as Fate: Preliminary

Remarks about the 'Austrian' in Austrian Literature),[6] speaks of the playfulness in the Austrian language, and I think you find that everywhere here.

PH: Well, I don't know whether the word playful catches it precisely, it has something to do with it, it's part of it, but that's all connected to this other mentality and with this musicality, but also with—there may be more dimensions there. It's not so focused on efficiency. Yes, and it's often ambiguous, right? But not because someone artfully brings in another layer in order to make some sort of a carnival show of things, but because reality really is ambiguous. It has at least two layers! And because people here are somewhat more aware than those in other countries, where such total efficiency covers it up, that there is another layer beneath the top one . . .

AU: They're misled by all those consonants . . .

PH: No, seriously, it's not only in Austria that it would be this way. It might be the case in Portugal or someplace. Those are countries which somehow—basically they are "losers," right? They aren't so blinded by political success. And thereby, perhaps this sounds contradictory, their reflective mentality is stronger; people take more time for things like that. And, for all I know, perhaps they're forced to by circumstances, right? And people don't take everything so seriously. That's the terrible thing for us about this German mentality sometimes—people there take everything seriously, especially themselves. They don't understand any "blarney." It's terrible if people like that can only take themselves seriously. And the fact that Austrian authors, many of them, don't take themselves entirely seriously is not to say that they don't consider it important and right to do what they are doing. It just means that one sees the relativity of all that, and that really comes right down to a not too successful, but otherwise very famous, play such as *Jedermann* (1911; *The Salzburg Everyman*, 1911) by Hofmannsthal, where the floor is very thin upon which the protagonist's success takes place. And the great Mr.

Everyman can fall at any moment. We know that, we can sense it. I don't know how it happens that in Germany, in spite of the catastrophe of the Nazi period, the word still hasn't gotten out about that.

AU: Well, the catastrophe of the Nazi period doesn't necessarily lead to irony, does it?

PH: Well, in Austria the catastrophe was probably too big. But there are different mentalities which react differently to different things. Maybe Ireland would be comparable to Austria in many respects. It too is a rather peripheral area, right? It's also a country that hasn't always had it so easy, or that never really had a real success . . . After all, Portugal was once a large successful country, and then it wasn't anymore, and people are somehow thrown back upon culture, right? And related things. But they are naturally always different after that, right? Well—one can't really exactly compare it, but I think that this history naturally has something to do with the way mentality is formed.

AU: Nevertheless, I have a problem with these sorts of generalizations, because one can't say that the Germans are all deadly serious and lack wit, or lack humor, or anything. That's simply not true! Naturally there are exceptions.

PH: It's a different sort of humor.

AU: The Germans I know all have a sense of humor, no Austrian "Schmäh," but they have humor. Peter, thank you very much for this conversation!

Notes

1. The difference is that between "gestern hatte ich Jürgen getroffen" and "gestern habe ich Jürgen getroffen." The German present perfect translates into English as imperfect, "yesterday I met Jürgen."
2. Das Trottoir = sidewalk; das Portmonnaie = wallet, change purse; die Tramway (pronounced Trommwye) = the streetcar; der Kondukteur = conductor (of the streetcar, train, etc.).
3. "Schmäh" is a complicated word to translate, as the ensuing conversation will reveal. Perhaps the closest English approximation to the Austrian usage of the noun would be something like "blarney," which can be used both admiringly and pejoratively. The Irish, with their "Blarney Stone," view blarney as a positive attribute, whereas it is perhaps unlikely that an Englishman would view it as a compliment when applied to himself. The contrast in German is even more pronounced: the German verb "schmähen" means "to revile, abuse, or speak ill of" someone, and a German dictionary gives only pejorative meanings of the word. Peter Wehle's helpful volume of Austrian expressions, *Sprechen Sie Wienerisch? von Adaxl bis Zwutschkerl* (Vienna: Ueberreuter, 1980), defines "Schmäh" as "Gag, punch line, cutting up, entertainment; derives from street slang verb *schmaien* = to hear, from Yiddish *schemá*, (spoken) tale" (251). It seems clear how misunderstandings could arise!
4. "Sei stad" is a typically Viennese expression. Depending upon the context, it can be translated as "hush," "be quiet," "pipe down" or "take it easy."
5. The German expression—a very rude one—is "halt's Maul!"
6. Hans Weigel, "Sprache als Schicksal: Vorläufige Bemerkungen über 'Das Österreichische' in der österreichischen Literatur," *Wort in der Zeit* 10.4 (1964): 1-5.

A Bibliography of Peter Henisch's Works

Prose

Bali oder Swoboda steigt aus. Munich and Vienna: Langen Müller, 1981.
Baronkarl: alte und neue Peripheriegeschichten. Weitra: Bibliothek der Provinz, 1993.
Das Wiener Kochbuch. Munich: Hahn, 1982.
Der Mai ist vorbei. Frankfurt/M: Fischer, 1978.
Die kleine Figur meines Vaters. Frankfurt/M: Fischer, 1975.
Die kleine Figur meines Vaters. rev. ed. Munich and Vienna: Langen Müller, 1980.
Die kleine Figur meines Vaters. 2nd rev. ed. Salzburg and Vienna: Residenz, 1987.
Hamlet bleibt. Frankfurt/M: Fischer, 1971.
Hoffmanns Erzählungen: Aufzeichnungen eines verwirrten Germanisten. Munich: Nymphenburger, 1983.
Kommt eh der Komet. Salzburg and Vienna: Residenz, 1995.
Morrisons Versteck. Salzburg and Vienna: Residenz, 1991.
Morrisons Versteck. rev. ed. Munich: Deutscher Taschenbuch Verlag, 2001.
Pepi Prohaska Prophet. Salzburg and Vienna: Residenz, 1986.
Schwarzer Peter. Salzburg and Vienna: Residenz, 2000.
Steins Paranoia. Salzburg and Vienna: Residenz, 1988.
Vagabundengeschichten. Munich and Vienna: Langen Müller, 1980.

Vom Baronkarl: Peripheriegeschichten und andere Prosa. Frankfurt/M: Fischer, 1972.
Vom Wunsch, Indianer zu werden: Wie Franz Kafka Karl May traf und trotzdem nicht in Amerika landete. Salzburg and Vienna: Residenz, 1994.
Zwischen allen Sesseln: Geschichten, Gedichte, Entwürfe, Notizen, Statements 1965-1982. Vienna: Hannibal, 1982.

Poetry

Black Peter's Songbook. Salzburg/Vienna/Frankfurt/M: Residenz, 2001.
Hamlet, Hiob, Heine. Salzburg and Vienna: Residenz, 1989.
mir selbst auf der spur / hiob. Baden bei Wien: Grasl, 1977.
wiener fleisch & blut. Vienna and Munich: Jugend und Volk, 1975.
Zwischeneiszeit. Vienna: David-Presse, 1979.

Plays

Hoffmann oder die Renitenz. Vienna and Munich: Sessler, 1984.
lumpazimoribundus: antiposse mit gesang. Vienna and Munich: Sessler, 1974.

Selected Essays

"Black Peter was here: Notizen zur Lage des Schwarzen Peter in New Orleans (1)." *wespennest* 109 (1997): 6-14.
"Drunt in Afrika: Notizen zur Lage des Schwarzen Peter in New Orleans (2)." *wespennest* 111 (1998): 32-37.
"Frei. Schwebend." *O Österreich!* Ed. Heinz Ludwig Arnold. Göttingen: Wallstein, 1995. 41-50.

"Für Eliten schreiben?" *Solidarität* 3 (1987): 22-23.
"Hand aufs Hirn." *Die Wochenpresse* 9 April 1985: 50-51.
"Herz in Randlage." *Österreich, Europa, die Zeit und die Welt: beobachtet von Schriftstellerinnen und Schriftstellern aus Österreich*. Eds. Angelika Klammer and Jochen Jung. Salzburg and Vienna: Residenz, 1998. 43-52.
"Hier geht es nicht um die sogenannte Soldatengeneration. Sondern um jene, die aus der Geschichte nichts gelernt haben." *Die Wochenpresse* 3 July 1987: 62.
"instant city: Der Schriftsteller Peter Henisch über New York." *Arbeiter Zeitung* 24 March 1990: 37-39.
"Ironie und was daraus wird: Drei Vorlesungen." *manuskripte* 35.128 (1995): 62-85.
"Kein 'Deutscher Dichter.'" *heute* 4 (1983): 20.
"marginalien zur produktion von texten." *Wiener Kunsthefte* 2 (1972): 27.
"Warum ich nicht will, daß Österreich untergeht." *Reden an Österreich: Schriftsteller ergreifen das Wort*. Ed. Jochen Jung. Salzburg and Vienna: Residenz, 1988. 81-94.

Interviews

"Ist der Mai ganz vorbei?" *Arbeiter Zeitung* 21 Feb. 1981: 17.
Künstlergespräch: Alois Riedl—Peter Henisch. Braunau: AMAG Art, n.d.
"Peter Henisch im Gespräch." *Neue deutsche Literatur* 35 (1987): 73-77.
"Schreiben bringt Konsumverzicht." *Wiener Zeitung* 22 March 1988, *Lesezirkel*: 7-9.
"Sympathie quer durch die Zeiten." *Arbeiter Zeitung* 21 March 1989: 26.
"Wider die Anpassung. Im Gespräch: Der Schriftsteller Peter Henisch." *Marabo: Magazin fürs Ruhrgebiet* Oct. 1995: 114-15.

English Translations

Hamlet, Fables and Other Poems. Trans. Herman Salinger. Washington, D.C.: Charioteer, 1980.
Negatives of My Father. Trans. and afterword Anne Close Ulmer. Riverside, CA: Ariadne, 1990.
Stone's Paranoia. Trans. and intro. Craig Decker. Riverside, CA: Ariadne, 2000.

Contributors

BOHDAN BOCHAN received his Ph.D. in German and Italian at the University of Minnesota and is currently Associate Professor of German at Indiana University Southeast. He studied philosophy at Urbana University in Rome and at the Catholic University of Louvain. He has published on Heinrich von Kleist, J.R.M. Lenz, and Franz Kafka and Peter Turrini.

ARND BOHM is finishing a study of Goethe's *Faust* and European epic, tentatively entitled "Forgetting the Future." His research interests include German literary history, 1750 to the present, Anglo-German literary relations, and theory. Among his recent articles are studies of Kleist's "Die Heilige Cäcilia" and Goethe's "Es war ein König in Thule."

KATHY BRZOVIĆ is Lecturer in the Department of Marketing, International Business, and Business Writing at California State University, Fullerton. She is the author of *Bonaventura's* Nachtwachen: *A Satirical Novel*, and has also published on turn-of-the-century Viennese literature and on literary representations of Austrian fascism.

CRAIG DECKER is Professor of German at Bates College. He has published on the history and theory of the "Volksstück" (Nestroy, Horváth, Turrini, and Kroetz) and on literary representations of Austria's Nazi past. He recently translated Peter Henisch's *Steins Paranoia* into English.

Contributors

ANTJE HARNISCH has published on nineteenth-century German Realism and also on contemporary German literature. She is particularly interested in issues surrounding gender and ethnicity as well as the relationship between text and context.

JENNIFER E. MICHAELS is Professor of German and Samuel R. and Marie-Louise Rosenthal Professor of Humanities at Grinnell College. She has published four books and numerous articles about twentieth-century German and Austrian literature and culture, her main teaching and research interest.

JEFFREY SCHNEIDER received his Ph.D. from Cornell University and is currently Assistant Professor of German Studies at Vassar College. He is presently completing a book on militarism and masculinity in German culture around 1900.

EVA SCHOBEL specializes in contemporary German-language literature and exile literature and teaches at the University of Vienna. She is the author of *Peter Henisch: Eine Monographie*. Since the publication of that volume in 1988, she has been in constant conversation with the author. She is currently working on a biography of Albert Drach.

HELGA SCHRECKENBERGER is Professor of German and Director of Women's Studies at the University of Vermont. Her research focuses on exile literature and contemporary Austrian literature, with particular emphasis on women writers. She has published on Gerhard Roth, Lilian Faschinger, Elisabeth Reichart, and Marlene Streeruwitz.

ANNE CLOSE ULMER, Professor of Geman at Carleton College, is particularly interested in Austrian literature and culture from turn-of-the-century Vienna to the present. In addition to articles on Heimito von Doderer, Gert Hoffmann, Peter Henisch, Felix Mitterer, and Lilian Faschinger, she has translated two novels by Peter Henisch into English, *Die kleine Figur meines Vaters* and *Morrisons Versteck*.

JENIFER K. WARD is Associate Professor of German at Gustavus Adolphus College. She has published on films by Margarethe von Trotta, on the novelist Jurek Becker, and on novel to film adaptation. Currently she is collaborating on a monograph exploring discourses of authority in several novel-film adaptations in postwar Germany.

FRIEDEMANN WEIDAUER teaches German language, literature, and culture at the University of Connecticut. His research focuses on post-World War II German culture, including such topics as contemporary German-Jewish literature, H.M. Enzensberger's essays on post-colonialism, and the image of the United States in recent German poetry and film.

Index

Acker, Kathy, 188
The Act of Reading (Iser), 44
Adorno, Theodor, 211
Aichinger, Ilse, 245
Der Alpenkönig und der Menschenfeind (*The King of the Alps;* Raimund), 218
Amerika (*Amerika*; Kafka), 172, 175
Amnesty International, 238
Anschluss, 139, 209n33, 246
anti-Semitism: Henisch's exploration of, 132–33, 234, 250, 252–53; and Nazism, 9; and paranoia, 132–33, 135, 142, 234; reemergence of, 138–41, 143, 235, 245, 246; rhetorical success of, 136, 141–42; and transcendence, 137
Anton Wildgans Prize, 252
Arbeiterzeitung (Workers' Gazette), 12, 17, 25, 28
Arbeitsdienst (Labor Service), 16

art: consumers of, 54–56, 57; and fascism, 51; and museums, 57–58; and owners of capital, 57; and social class, 70; useful, 57
Artaud, Antonin, 63
Artmann, H.C., 273, 281
Auschwitz, 246
Aussenminister (secretaries of state), 55
ausserparlamentarische Opposition (extra-parliamentary opposition), 55
Austin, J.L., 141
Austria: "alternative," 210–11; asylum seekers in, 251–52, 257, 258, 259; attacks on, 131; *avantgarde* in, 281; First Republic of, 136, 145n14, 211; and foreign languages, 190; foreigners in, 246, 247, 248, 251, 252; freedom from history of, 50; and

294 Index

Germany, 23, 136; Grand Coalition and, 46; Henisch on, 145n11, 210–11, 250; and Holocaust, 134; and identification, 139, 141; identity in, 134–35, 138–39, 242, 244, 245, 246, 248, 249; immigrants in, 246, 247, 250, 251–52, 256; lack of political activism in, 152; language of, 267–75, 276, 279–82; literary scene in, 181; literature of, 3, 280, 281–82; "Mahnwache" (Memorial Watch) in, 143; minorities in, 242, 243, 247, 248, 249, 250, 256, 259; Moslems in, 251; Nazi period in, 4, 12, 13, 23, 33, 41, 44, 134, 153, 244, 246, 256, 283; and Nazism, 244, 245, 253–54; new populism in, 247, 248; past and future of, 173; persecution complex of, 133; political rhetoric in, 142; post-World War II, 4, 213; president of, 143, 245; racism in, 246–50, 252–57, 259; research in, 238; rhetorical situation in, 133, 136; rightwing extremism in, 158, 247; Second Republic of, 2, 20, 24, 46, 134, 136–37, 139, 141, 211, 213, 236, 237, 242, 243, 244, 245; student movement (late 1960s) in, 19, 148, 151–59, 196, 231; tradition of, 43; *Vormärz* (pre-March) struggles in, 196; xenophobia in, 245, 246. See also Vienna

Austrian Freedom Party (FPÖ), 247
Austrian People's Party (ÖVP), 132, 133
Austrian State Treaty, 246, 256
Austro-Hungarian Empire, 247
Austro-Israeli Society, 132

Bachmann, Ingeborg, 49, 188
Bachofen, Johann, 63
Bakhtin, Mikhail, 169; analysis of Dostoevsky, 183nn21&28; on authors and characters, 170, 175, 183n21; on laughter, 129n18; as model, 173, 181
The Ballad of Reading Gaol (Wilde), 278
Barthes, Roland, 174, 175
"Le Bateau ivre" ("Das trunkene Schiff"; "The Drunken Ship"; Rimbaud), 278
Baudelaire, Charles-Pierre, 113, 278
Baudrillard, Jean, 63
Bayern, Ludwig von, 169

the Beatles, 204
Beckermann, Ruth, 248, 249, 250
Beckett, Samuel, 50
"Bedenkjahr" (Year of Remembrance and Reflection), 135, 143
Befreiung der Phantasie (liberation of one's fantasy from externally imposed influences), 78
Beginnings: Intention and Method (Said), 50
Begley, Louis, 228–29, 240n3
Benjamin, Walter, 41–42
Berlin, postwar, 104, 109–10
Bernhard, Thomas, 49, 50, 281
Besserungsstück (Drama of Improvement), 218, 219
Bible, 89, 96, 97, 98, 194–95, 200, 207n22, 208n23
Bildersprache (picture language), 90
Bildungsbürgertum (educated middle class), 63
Bildungsroman, 61, 63, 66, 67, 68, 70
biography: conventional, 182n3; fictional, 167; new form of, 70; pop, 63, 66, 67
Bischof, Günther, 237
Black Peter's Songbook (Henisch), 185
Blake, William, 63

Bleier, E.F., 127n8
Bloom, Harold, 42, 48, 173
Bochan, Bohdan, 101–30
Bohm, Arnd, 185–209
Böll, Heinrich, 245
Der böse Geist Lumpazivagabundus oder Das liederliche Kleeblatt (The Evil Spirit Lumpazivagabundus or The Slovenly Threesome; Nestroy), 213, 214, 216–19, 220, 226n6
Boulet, Melanie Bischof, 237
Bourdieu, Pierre, 54, 57, 70
Brandl, Reinhold, 248
Branigan, Edward, 76
Brecht, Bertolt, 188, 193, 194, 207n22
Brinkmann, Rolf Dieter, 62, 63
Brod, Max, 169, 170, 172, 176, 178
Brzović, Kathy, 40–53, 131–45
Bürger Schippel (*Burger Schippel*; Sternheim), 279
Burke, Kenneth, 49, 131, 134, 135, 142

Callas, Maria, 271–72
capitalism: and alternative economy, 187; apparatus of advanced, 211–12, 215, 224; and art, 57; and language, 186–87
Celan, Paul, 186, 188, 197, 198

Chopin, Frédéric, 169
Christ, 90, 96
Civil Rights movement, 255
Cocteau, Jean, 63
Cold War, 200
commercialism, cultural, 69–70
communes, 154–55, 160
consumerism, 179, 211–12, 214, 221–24, 225
consumption: and culture, 211–12, 213, 214, 215, 221–23; and production, 211, 222–23, 225n3; and resistance, 214, 215, 225
Contes d'Hoffmann (Offenbach), 232
copyright, 187, 206n8
counter-culture, 58, 59, 65–66, 191–92
culture: American pop, 69; bourgeois, 71; commercial, 69–70; conservative, 165n18; consumer, 211–12, 213, 214, 215, 221–23; globalized industry of, 4, 56–57, 70, 214, 224; high *vs.* popular, 179, 181; and identity, 71; minority and majority, 4, 248; new view of, 71; and politics, 200, 210; pop mass, 64; popular, and cultural elitism, 62, 63, 66, 89; of protest, 54–55, 213–14; revolution in, 64, 65; Western, 69, 74, 75

Danimann, Franz, 246
Decker, Craig, 1–6, 22, 78, 131–45, 210–27
Delacroix, Eugene, 122
Deleuze, Gilles, 243
Deutscher Turnerbund (German Gymnasts' Association), 17
Deutschland: Ein Wintermärchen (*Germany, A Winter Tale*; Heine), 195, 196
Dialectic of Enlightenment (Horkheimer & Adorno), 212
Dionysus, cult of, 66
Doderer, Heimito von, 281
The Doors, 75, 88, 163n5; and Henisch, 56, 60; text from album of, 92; video on history of, 94. *See also* Morrison, Jim
The Doors (film), 59
Dostoevsky, Fyodor, 109
Dutschke, Rudi, 151
Dylan, Bob, 62

Eagleton, Terry, 71
Eckermann, Johann, 169
Eco, Umberto, 180
Eich, Günter, 197
Einstein, Albert, 109, 221
Eisemann (tightrope walker), 28, 30
Eisenstein, Sergei, 76
"Endless Interview" in *Zwischen allen Sesseln* (*Between All the Stools*; Henisch), 156

Index 297

Entwicklungsroman, 255, 256, 258, 259, 265n42
eschaton (end time), 90, 97
Eulenspiegel, Till, 118
Die Fackel (The Torch; Kraus), 201
fantasy: absence of, 122, 162; and freedom, 106, 107–8; and Hoffmann, 75, 105–6, 121–23; liberation of, 78; and magic of slogans, 203–4, 208n24; subversive nature of, 127n11
fascism, 50, 51; and masculinity, 9, 11. *See also* National Socialism
Fellini, Federico, 256
fiction, 169–70, 177; biographical, 167; and facts, 228–41; in Henisch, 229, 237; postmodern, 76
film: conventions of, 85; crosscutting in, 75, 77, 85; and Henisch, 74–88; language of, 85, 88, 89, 94, 98; and novels, 74, 79, 87, 89; and postmodern fiction, 76; storyboard directions in, 85–86; time in, 77. *See also Hoffmann's Erzählungen*
Les Fleurs du mal (Baudelaire), 278
Foucault, Michel, 123
The Four Seasons (Vivaldi), 160, 165n19
FPÖ. *See* Austrian Freedom Party
Frank, Niklas, 49
"Fräulein Veronika Paulmann aus der Pirnaer Vorstadt oder Etwas über das Schauerliche bei E.T.A. Hoffmann" (Fühmann), 233
Free Corps, 9
French Revolution, 233
Freud, Sigmund, 47, 63; on the uncanny, 137, 138
Frischmuth, Barbara, 247–48, 250–51
Fühmann, Franz, 233

Galbraith, John Kenneth, 222, 226n10
Gates, Bill, 187
Gaullism, 151–52
geistige Väter (spiritual fathers), 78, 94, 96, 98, 99
gender, 68, 69, 70, 71
Generation X, 56
Gentz, Friedrich von, 196
German Army, 17, 238
Germany, 10, 23, 136, 271, 282, 283; Third Reich in, 18, 74, 134, 139. *See also* National Socialism
Gestapo, 138, 209n34
globalization: and culture, 4, 56–57, 70, 214, 224; and localization, 57
Gnam, Peter, 132
Goebbels, Joseph, 9, 21, 26,

298 Index

28
Goethe, Johann Wolfgang von, 48, 64, 112
Gogh, Vincent van, 57
Der goldene Topf (Hoffmann), 110, 111
"GOLGOTHA/IVENTARAUFNAHME" (GOLGOTHA/INVENTORY; Henisch), 200–201
A Grammar of Motives (Burke), 142
Grass, Günter, 245, 256, 281
Grillparzer, Franz, 281
Grimm, brothers, 169
"Das grosse Los" (The Big Ticket; Weisflog), 226n6
Die grössere Hoffnung (*The Great Hope*; Aichinger), 245
Guattari, Félix, 243
Günderrode, Caroline von, 168

"Haben Sie Mut für die Bahamas" (Take a Dare on the Bahamas; Henisch), 190
Haider, Jörg, 2, 247, 248, 250
Hamlet (Shakespeare), 193, 194
Hamlet bleibt (Hamlet Remains; Henisch), 232
Hamlet, Hiob, Heine: Gedichte (Hamlet, Job, Heine: Poems; Henisch): accessibility of poems in, 185–86; American trademarks in, 191; counterculture in, 191–92; and Heine, 196; intertexts in, 193–95, 197, 198–99, 201, 203
Handke, Peter, 49, 62, 281
Hanisch, Ernst, 238
Harnisch, Antje, 166–84
Härtling, Peter, 167
Haslinger, Josef, 40, 251–52
Hausbesetzer (squatters), 55
Hegel, Georg Wilhelm Friedrich, 65, 111, 112, 113, 120
Heidegger, Martin, 127n10
"Heimkehr mit Heine" (Returning Home with Heine; Henisch), 234
Heine, Heinrich, 173, 195, 196
Hendrix, Jimi, 62
Henisch, Peter: and anxiety of influence, 46–51; archaic spellings and, 85; on authors, 175; and automatic writing, 175; balancing acts in work of, 1–4; and character of Lizard-King, 59; and father, 2–3, 7–33, 79, 99, 230–31, 237, 239; film in novels of, 74, 79, 87, 89; as free-lance writer, 28; historical perspective of, 211; humor of, 113–14, 258; on imagination, 178; imitation of father's "brutal

curiosity" by, 22, 29; and "inner movie screen," 74–99; interdependence of voyeur and exhibitionist in, 68; and intertextuality, 4, 187, 192–204, 213, 215; interview with, 4, 267–83; kenosis as narrative strategy of, 42–43, 46; on language and literature as dialogue, 181; language of, 224, 267–75, 276–77; literary identification figures of, 167; literary journal of, 186; on literary realism, 164n11, 178; narrative style of, 74–75, 84, 88, 90–94; as photographer, 25, 26–27; and plurilingualism, 190; poetry of, 185–209; on popular literature, 179; protagonists of, 131–32, 145n11, 147, 214, 236, 237, 242, 252; punctuation and, 83, 85; on schizophrenia, 146, 204, 256; and shame, 9, 23, 27; and student movement of 1960s, 148; on thinking colorfully, 128n12; and translation, 277; use of allusions by, 187, 192–204; use of capital letters by, 189–90; use of irony by, 130n21, 133–34, 258; use of quotations by, 187–89, 190, 192, 194, 200, 201, 204, 214; and the visual, 79, 85, 94, 99; and Waldheim, 245; and writer's block, 25; writing style of, 67

Henisch, Sonja (wife), 43

Henisch, Walter (father), 2–3; alcoholism of, 25; "brutal curiosity" of, 20, 26, 30, 33, 49; death of, 46; and escape, 24, 25, 33; freedom from anxiety of influence, 46; iron crosses of, 12, 42; as Nazi war correspondent, 3, 9, 12, 13, 15, 21, 41, 230–31; and Nazism, 3, 9–11, 13, 17, 23, 74; need for self-dissolution of, 17, 20; as Papa Henisch, 30–31; and parable of the telescope, 40–41; as photographer, 12, 15, 19, 20–22, 24, 25, 27, 30–31, 74, 99; and photographic daredevilry, 10, 28, 42; postwar activities of, 20, 23–33; and Prinz, 15; and shame, 10–12, 14–17, 23, 32; small size of, 15–16; transformation of, 32; and uniforms, 13, 15, 16–17, 152; as victim of fate, 44; war stories of, 19; as writer, 25–26, 29–30

Hildesheimer, Wolfgang, 167

hippie movement, 65–66
Hitler, Adolf, 18, 46, 153, 209n33, 244, 245
Hitler Youth, 17, 46
Hoffmann, E.T.A.: biography of, 106, 108; diary of, 110, 128n15; fantasy and, 105–6; and the fragment, 111–13, 114, 127n8; and Henisch, 78, 79, 82, 86, 102, 105, 167, 168, 232, 233; and Morrison, 88, 99, 233; motifs in stories of, 127n8; narrative style of, 80, 81, 85, 87, 90, 104, 127n9; reincarnation of, 75, 84; retelling life of, 101–2; schizophrenia of, 232–33; and the visual, 85
Hoffmanns Erzählungen: Aufzeichnungen eines verwirrten Germanisten (Tales of Hoffmann: Notes of a Confused Germanist; Henisch), 80–88; ambiguity in, 102, 103, 105, 108, 125n3; compared with biographical novels, 167; compared with *Morrisons Versteck*, 91, 95, 98, 99; crisis in chronology in, 81; deconstruction in, 105, 122; epistolary form of, 80, 87, 98, 122; fantasy in, 75, 106, 121–23; as filmic novel, 79, 87, 89; the fragment in, 108–10, 117, 118, 121, 123, 124, 128n14; humor in, 109, 115–17, 123; identity and, 103–4; insertion of screenplay in, 86; irony in, 108–9, 117–18, 123, 124; Janus as symbol of, 98; narrative of, 101, 103, 105, 164n10; narrator of, 102–3, 106, 108, 118; schizophrenia in, 75, 81, 85, 86, 89, 103, 126nn6&7; and *Steins Paranoia*, 130n24; stream of consciousness in, 109; structure of, 101, 164n10, 232; style of, 90
Hofmannsthal, Hugo von, 174, 281, 282
Hölderlin (Härtling), 167
Holocaust (Shoa), 198, 229
homosexuality, 68, 255
Horkheimer, Max, 211
Horváth, Ödön von, 270, 281
Hutcheon, Linda, 181, 182n7
Huyssen, Andreas, 55, 57

Ich Wolkenstein (I Wolkenstein; Kühn), 167
identity: Austrian, 134–35, 138–39, 242, 244, 245, 246, 248, 249; crisis of, 80, 82, 84, 87, 98, 149, 150, 160; cultural, 71; and *Hoffmanns Erzäh-*

lungen, 103–4; individual, 4; mirror stage in development of, 87; multiple, 261; projection of, 78–79; and schizophrenia, 127n8, 141, 146, 256; in *Schwarzer Peter*, 252, 255; through music, 261; and voyeurism, 87
images: photographic vs. filmed, 78–79; and text, 74; of tightrope walker, 2, 3, 28, 30; visual, 88, 98, 99
innere Leinwand (inner movie screen), 74–99
intertextuality: and Bible, 89, 96, 97, 98, 194–95, 200, 207n22, 208n23; and Henisch, 4, 187, 192–204, 213, 215; and satire, 214–25
"Inventur" ("Stocktaking"; Eich), 197
Iser, Wolfgang, 44
Ivancsics, Karin, 249

Janus, 90, 98
Jedermann (*The Salzburg Everyman*; Hofmannsthal), 282
Jews, 133, 134, 137, 247, 249, 250, 257
Joplin, Janis, 62
jüdischer Mitbürger (Jewish fellow-citizen), 135, 136
Jules and Jim (film), 271

Kafka, Franz: and Brod, 169, 170, 172, 176, 178; on fictional characters, 170; and Henisch, 179; and May, 166–80; parody of, 172; readers of, 180; writing of, 176
Kant, Immanuel, 119, 120
"Kater Murr" (Tomcat Murr; Hoffmann), 126n6
Kein Ort: Nirgends (*No Place on Earth*; Wolf), 167, 168
Kepler, Johannes, 221
Kerschbaumer, Marie-Thérèse, 248, 249
Kierkegaard, Søren, 118, 130n21
King, Martin Luther, Jr., 155
Kinsky, Klaus, 277
Die kleine Figur meines Vaters (*Negatives of My Father*; Henisch): anxiety of influence in, 43–44, 46, 50; confrontation of Nazi past in, 41, 74, 244; as father-son narrative, 2–3, 8–9, 11, 13, 40–51, 168, 173, 232, 234, 275–76; narrative structure of, 164n10; otherness in, 252; photograph of Peter and father in, 7–8; publication of, 230; shame in, 9, 23; translation of, 267; two balloon stories in, 29–31, 45, 49; and the visual, 79

Kleist, Heinrich von, 168
Klüger, Ruth, 229, 240n3
Kommt eh der Komet (The Comet's Coming For Sure; Henisch), 212–15, 219–25; dramatic dialect version, 226n6
Kraus, Karl, 201, 202, 281
Kreisky, Bruno, 141
Kristallnacht, 257
Krüger, Ilse, 248
Kuh, Anton, 281
Kühn, Dieter, 167
Kurz, Heinrich, 233

Lacan, Jacques, 87, 95
language: Austrian, 267–75, 276, 279–82; and capitalism, 186–87; Expressionist, 279; German, 267–70, 273, 276, 278, 279–80, 283, 284, 284n1; High German, 268, 270; sound of, 278
Lebensansichten des Kater Murr (Hoffmann), 233
Led Zeppelin, 204
leftists, 157–58
Lenz, J.R.M., 64
Lessing, Gotthold, 176
"Letzte Nachlese zum Buch der Lieder" (Final Gleanings from the *Book of Songs*; Heine), 196
literature: Austrian, 3, 280, 281–82; father, 48, 49; German, 280; Henisch on, 179, 181; high *vs.* low, 227n11; of possibilities, 4; postmodern, 3, 4, 227n11; pure, 186
Logsdon, Joe, 234, 237, 238
Logsdon, Mary, 237
Lumumba, Patrice, 201
Luxemburg, Rosa, 201

McHale, Brian, 76
Der Mai ist vorbei (May Is Over; Henisch): and 1960s, 147, 231; Austrian reviewers of, 164n8; characters in, 235; double narrative in, 148–49; individual and collective interests in, 2, 147, 148, 153; outsiders in, 252; schizophrenia in, 147, 148, 149, 157, 162, 231–32, 240n8, 265n43
Male Fantasies (Theweleit), 9
Mao Zedong, 63
Marbot (*Marbot*; Hildesheimer), 167
Marcuse, Herbert, 63, 212, 224
"marginalien zur produktion von texten" (marginalia on the production of texts), 4
Marin, Bernd, 245
Marshall Plan, 234
Marx, Karl, 63, 200
masculinity: and fascism, 9, 11; and "magical hats," 20; proof of, 18; and size, 15; social and psy-

chological dimensions of, 18; and war, 18–19, 21
Mateotti, Giacomo, 201
The Matrix (film), 77
May, Karl: as educator of audiences, 176; fiction and reality in, 177; and fictional characters, 169–70; and Henisch, 166–81; and Kafka, 166–80; parody of, 170–71, 172; popular appeal of, 177; readers of, 180
Mayröcker, Friederike, 186
Meckel, Christoph, 49
Meinrath, Josef, 272
Menasse, Robert, 181
Mephisto, 48, 49
Merkel, Inge, 246–47
Metternich, Clemens von, 196, 213
Michaels, Jennifer E., 242–66
Milton, John, 48
Ministry for Public Enlightenment and Propaganda (Nazi Germany), 9, 21
mir selbst auf der spur/hiob: gedichte (on my own track/job: poems; Henisch), 185, 191, 198, 200, 201–2, 204
Mitläufer (fellow traveler), 9, 32
Mitscherlich, Alexander, 244
Mitscherlich, Margarete, 244
Mitten, Richard, 23
Mitterer, Felix, 244
modernism, 179, 186; American, 199
"möglichkeitsliteratur" (literature of possibilities), 4
Morrison, Jim, 58–69; biography of, 92, 96; as Christ, 90, 96; as cult figure, 78; death of, 62, 96; deification of, 90; as film student, 88, 94; and Henisch, 62, 88, 163n5, 167, 168, 170; and Hoffmann, 88, 99, 233; images of, 95; parable of, 91; and publisher, 67, 68; and the visual, 89
Morrisons Versteck (Morrison's Hideout; Henisch), 59–71, 88–98, 166; as Bildungsroman, 61, 67, 68; characters in, 68; compared with *Hoffmanns Erzählungen*, 91, 95, 98, 99; epistolary form of, 98; as filmic novel, 89; hybridity in, 59, 61, 63, 69, 70, 88–90, 92–94, 98, 99; irony in, 58, 59, 60, 61; marketing of, 71; narrative in, 69, 92, 164n10; and the New World, 167; publication of, 59, 88, 163n5, 235; and realism, 178, 179; and Rimbaud, 278; style of, 90; translation of, 267; visual in, 75, 99
Moscow Declaration (1943), 244

304 *Index*

Mosse, George, 9
Mozart, Wolfgang Amadeus, 254
multiculturalism, 243, 248, 260–62, 264n17, 268
Mulvey, Laura, 95
Münichreiter, Karl, 201
Musil, Robert, 281

Nachsommer (Stifter), 235
The Name of the Rose (Eco), 180
Napoleon, 111, 112
Napoleonic Wars, 109, 110, 158, 233
National Socialism (Nazism): and anti-Semitism, 9; Austria's involvement in, 244, 245, 253–54; catastrophe of, 283; implications of, 23; insignia of, 13; and masculinity, 9; public discourse on, 12; and Walter Henisch, 3, 9–11, 13, 17, 23, 74
Neruda, Pablo, 200
Nestroy, Johann, 201, 224; dramas of, 213–20, 226n6; and Henisch, 210, 213, 214, 215, 216, 219, 220, 226n11, 270
New Criticism, 200
New Orleans: Creolization in, 238, 262; jambalaya principle in, 262; research in, 237–38, 255; and Vienna, 253, 257–60

Novalis, 101, 112, 126n4
novels: biographical, 167; and film, 74, 79, 87, 89; as narrative alibis, 66–67; *vs.* autobiographies, 229

Oedipus the King (Sophocles), 47–48
Offenbach, Jacques, 232
Omofuma, Marcus, 236, 239
Orientalism (Said), 243

parables, 40–41, 89, 90–91, 96, 98
Paradise Lost (Milton), 48
Das Parfum (*Perfume*; Süskind), 180
Paris, 61, 151
Parry, Christoph, 185
Pearce, Roy Harvey, 199
Pelinka, Anton, 245, 246
Pepi Prohaska Prophet (Henisch), 233–35, 236
Peymann, Claus, 70
Pfadfinder (Pathfinders), 16, 17
plays: avant-garde productions of classic, 70; of Nestroy, 213–20, 226n6; *Volksstück* (popular comedy), 213, 216, 219, 220, 221
poetry: accessibility of, 185–86; and American trademarks, 191; continuity and tradition and, 43; and damnation, 48–49; of Henisch, 185–209;

Index 305

politics of quotation in, 185–209; and rock music, 65
politics: in Austria, 142, 152; and culture, 200, 210; and private sphere, 148, 151, 153, 154; of quotation, 185–209
Die Presse, 251
Prinz, Albert, 15, 46
private sphere, as political, 148, 151, 153, 154
Profil (magazine), 248
Protestgeneration (the generation of protest), 63
protest movements (late 1960s), 3, 63, 65, 66; in Austria, 19, 148, 151–59, 196, 231
Publikumsbeschimpfungen (tirades against the audience), 62
Pullmannkappe (woolen cap), 20

Qualtinger, Helmut, 270, 281

Rabinovici, Doron, 244, 250
Raimund, Ferdinand, 218
realism: literary, 164n11, 178, 232; populist, 179
Reichart, Elisabeth, 243–44, 249
revolution, 61, 66, 69; cultural, 64, 65
Rimbaud, Arthur, 63, 278
Ritter, Harry, 248
Ritter Gluck (Hoffmann), 233
rock music, 58, 64, 65, 68
Rodari, Gianni, 127
Roma minority, 246, 247, 249, 250
Romanticism, 3, 103, 104, 106, 173, 174, 196, 232
Rühmkorf, Peter, 232
Ryan, Judith, 57

Sachs, Nelly, 198
Said, Edward, 50, 243
Sand, George, 169
Der Sandmann (Hoffmann), 233
Satan, 48
satire, intertextual, 214–25
Schiller, Friedrich, 64, 169, 176, 220, 226n11
Schlegel, Friedrich, 111
Schneider, Jeffrey, 7–39
Schnitzler, Arthur, 281
Schobel, Eva, 78, 79, 205n1, 228–41
Schreckenberger, Helga, 146–65
Die Schrift des Freundes (The Writing of the Friend; Frischmuth), 251
Schwaiger, Brigitte, 49
Schwarzer Peter (Black Peter; Henisch), 1–2, 3, 4, 228–62; alienation in, 258, 260; and Austria, 242, 244, 252; characters in, 1, 275; fact and fiction in, 229, 237; father figures in, 239; homosexuality in, 255;

humor in, 258; multiculturalism in, 243, 248; music in, 260–61; New Orleans in, 248; otherness in, 242, 243, 253, 254, 257, 258, 276; quest for identity in, 252, 255; research for, 237–39; use of contrasts in, 259–60; Vienna in, 256
Schwimmer, Walter, 132, 133
Seeger, Pete, 207n18
Shakespeare, William, 193–94, 207n21
shame, 9–12, 14–18, 19, 23, 27, 32
Shoa (Holocaust), 198, 229
Sinti minority, 247
Social Democrats, 17, 25, 165n17
socialism, 156, 200, 211
Socialist Party, 151, 165n13
Soviet Union, 24, 46
Sozialpartnerschaft (social partnership), 152, 181
Der Spiegel (magazine), 228
"Sprache als Schicksal: Vorläufige Bemerkungen über 'Das Österreichische' in der österreichischen Literatur" (Language as Fate: Preliminary Remarks about the "Austrian" in Austrian Literature; Weigel), 281–82
Springer Press, 151

SS (*Schutzstaffel*), 46, 244, 257
Standifer, Leon C., 237
Steins Paranoia (*Stone's Paranoia*; Henisch), 124, 130n24; ambiguity in, 142, 143; anti-Semitism in, 132–33, 234, 250; and biographical novels, 167; irony in, 134; protagonist of, 131–32; and Waldheim, 235, 245
Sterne, Laurence, 114, 125n2
Sternheim, Carl, 279
Stifter, Adalbert, 235, 281
Stone, Oliver, 59, 90
Strelka, Joseph, 165n13
Struwwelpeter (children's book), 254
Süddeutsche Zeitung, 180
suicide, 62
Surrealists, 175
Süskind, Patrick, 180

Tate, Allen, 133
Taylor, Charles, 243
television, 76
Tendenzwende (return of more conservative climate), 148, 157, 164n9
Theweleit, Klaus, 9
Third Reich, 18, 74, 134, 139
Tomkins, Silvan, 10, 14
Tristram Shandy (Sterne), 119, 125n2
Truffaut, François, 271

Index 307

"Über das Erhabene" ("On the Sublime"; Schiller), 220
Ulmer, Anne Close, 267–84
Die Unfähigkeit zu trauern (*The Inability to Mourn*; Alexander and Margarete Mitscherlich), 244
Der Untergeher (*The Loser*; Bernhard), 51

Varnhagen, Rahel, 196
Vater-Literatur (father literature), 48, 49
Vergangenheitsbewältigung (coming to terms with the past), 23
Das Verschwinden des Schattens in der Sonne (*The Shadow Disappears in the Sun*; Frischmuth), 251
Vienna: anti-Semitism in, 138, 139, 140; Danube Canal in, 233–34, 236, 237, 260; Hofburgtheater in, 213; mentality of, 270; multiethnic heritage in, 260; and Nazi regime, 153; and New Orleans, 253, 257–60; police prison (Rossauerlände) in, 238; post-World War II, 1, 2, 12; Theater an der Wien in, 213; *Volkstheater* in, 213, 218
Viennese Opera Ball, 151
Vietnam War, 151
Volksstück (popular comedy), 213, 216, 219, 220, 221
Vom Nutzen und Nachteil der Historie für das Leben (*On the Use and Abuse of History*; Nietzsche), 124
Vom Wunsch, Indianer zu werden: Wie Franz Kafka Karl May traf und trotzdem nicht in Amerika landete (Wishing to Be an Indian: How Franz Kafka Met Karl May But Still Didn't End Up in America; Henisch), 166–67; dialogue in, 168–69, 170, 175, 179–80; and father-son relationship, 167–68, 173; and Kafka, 176; lack of annotations in, 178; and May, 177, 178; modernism and popular realism in, 179; parody in, 181; passages from *Amerika* in, 172; and quotations from author, 174, 180–81; séance scene in, 169
Vorhofer, Kurt, 131

Waldheim, Kurt, 2, 23, 47; and anti-Semitism, 141, 235; attacks on, 131, 133; election of, 245
Waldheim Affair, 12, 23, 210
Ward, Jenifer K., 74–100
Wartime Lies (Begley), 228–29

"Warum ich nicht will, dass Österreich untergeht" (Why I Don't Want Austria to Sink; Henisch), 145n11, 210, 250
"Was tun kann uns Lenin helfen" (What to Do, Can Lenin Help Us; Henisch), 200
Weidauer, Friedemann, 54–73, 88, 89, 90
Weigel, Hans, 281–82
Weinzierl, Erika, 245
Weisflog, Karl, 226n6
weiter leben: Eine Jugend (surviving: A Youth; Klüger), 229, 240n3
Werner, Oskar, 271
wespennest (wasp's nest; literary journal), 186
What Is To Be Done? (Lenin), 200, 209n30
wiener fleisch & blut (viennese flesh & blood; Henisch), 185, 191, 202, 203
Wilde, Oscar, 277, 278
Williams, William Carlos, 198, 199, 200
Winnetou IV (*Winnetous Erben*; Winnetou's Heirs; May), 171, 175, 176–77
Winter, Leon de, 228
Wittgensteins Neffe (*Wittgenstein's Nephew*; Bernhard), 50
Wolf, Christa, 167
World Jewish Congress, 133
World War II, 15, 231; end of, 2, 10, 197; post-, 1, 2, 4, 249

Young, Neil, 62
yuppies, 54–56

Zaungäste (those watching from the fence), 56, 73n5
Zenker, Helmut, 186
"Zürich, Zum Storchen" (Zurich, At the Sign of the Stork; Celan), 198
Zwischen allen Sesseln: Geschichten, Gedichte, Entwürfe, Notizen, Statements 1965-1982 (Between All the Stools: Stories, Poems, Drafts, Notes, Declarations 1965-1982; Henisch), 185, 191, 202
Zwischeneiszeit (Interim Ice Age; Henisch), 185

Ariadne Press
Studies

*Major Figures of
Modern Austrian Literature*
Edited by Donald G. Daviau

*Major Figures of Austrian Literature
The Interwar Years 1918-1938*
Edited by Donald G. Daviau

*Major Figures of Turn-of-the-Century
Austrian Literature*
Edited by Donald G. Daviau

*Austrian Writers and the Anschluss
Understanding the Past –
Overcoming the Past*
Edited by Donald G. Daviau

*Austria in the Thirties
Culture and Politics*
Edited by K. Segar and J. Warren

Jura Soyfer and His Time
Edited by Donald G. Daviau

Austria in Literature
Edited by Donald G. Daviau

*Stefan Zweig
An International Bibliography*
By Randolph A. Klawiter

*Franz Karka
A Writer's Life*
By Joachim Unseld

*Kafka and Language: In the
Stream of Thoughts and Life*
By G. von Natzmer Cooper

*Of Reason and Love
The Life and Works of Marie
von Ebner-Eschenbach*
By Carl Steiner

*Marie von Ebner-Eschenbach
The Victory of a Tenacious Will*
By Doris M. Klostermaier

*"What People Call Pessimism"
Freud, Schnitzler and the 19th-Century
Controversy at the University of
Vienna Medical School*
By Mark Luprecht

Arthur Schnitzler and Politics
By Adrian Clive Roberts

*Structures of Disintegration
Narrative Strategies in Elias Canetti's
Die Blendung*
By David Darby

*Blind Reflections
Gender in Canetti's Die Blendung*
By Kristie A. Foell

*Robert Musil and the Tradition
of the German Novelle*
By Kathleen O'Connor